The River Batteries
at Fort Donelson

The River Batteries at Fort Donelson

Construction, Armament and Battles, 1861–1862

M. Todd Cathey *and*
Ricky W. Robnett

McFarland & Company, Inc., Publishers
Jefferson, North Carolina

LIBRARY OF CONGRESS CATALOGUING-IN-PUBLICATION DATA

Names: Cathey, M. Todd, author. | Robnett, Ricky W., 1953– author.
Title: The river batteries at Fort Donelson : construction, armament and
battles, 1861-1862 / M. Todd Cathey, and Ricky W. Robnett.
Other titles: Construction, armament and battles, 1861-1862
Description: Jefferson, North Carolina : McFarland & Company, Inc.,
Publishers, 2021 | Includes bibliographical references and index.
Identifiers: LCCN 2021027786 | ISBN 9781476685908 (paperback : acid free paper) ∞
ISBN 9781476643380 (ebook)
Subjects: LCSH: Fort Donelson (Tenn.)—History. | Fort Donelson,
Battle of, Tenn., 1862. | BISAC: HISTORY / Military / United States
Classification: LCC E472.97 .C38 2021 | DDC 973.7/31—dc23
LC record available at https://lccn.loc.gov/2021027786

BRITISH LIBRARY CATALOGUING DATA ARE AVAILABLE

ISBN (print) 978-1-4766-8590-8
ISBN (ebook) 978-1-4766-4338-0

On the cover: Location of the death of Captain Joseph Dixon. On February 13, as the batteries were engaging the *Carondelet*, Dixon was stooped over passing from Gun #5 to Gun #6 when a parting shot from the gunboat struck and dismounted Gun #6. A large bolt from the gun carriage broke loose and struck Dixon in the forehead, causing instant death. Image courtesy of the authors.

Printed in the United States of America

*McFarland & Company, Inc., Publishers
Box 611, Jefferson, North Carolina 28640
www.mcfarlandpub.com*

To our grandfathers who bravely defended Fort Donelson

Private R.M. Crumpler
Company A, 50th Tennessee
(in the Lower Battery)

Sergeant Josiah Forrester
Company F, 42nd Tennessee
(in the Outer Works)

Acknowledgments

Many people made significant contributions to the research and writing of this book. The staff of the Tennessee State Library and Archives helped locate and pull microfilm and original records. DeAnne Blanton of the National Archives was instrumental in gaining access to the ordnance records, which were critical to this project. Beth Trescott and Joana Stephens provided research opportunity and permission to use materials from the archives of the Battle of Franklin Trust. Meredith McDonough from the Alabama Department of Archives and History was very helpful in the acquisition of several important images.

The staff of Fort Donelson National Battlefield Park was also accommodating. Superintendent Brian McCutchen and Chief Ranger William Fields helped approve and schedule research requests. Without the cooperation of the Fort Donelson staff, this book would have never materialized.

Former Fort Donelson employees aided greatly as well. David Nolin provided information on the construction of the carriages and mounting of the guns in the Water Battery. Jimmy Jobe, retired Fort Donelson Park Historian, shared lots of information with us, answered many questions, and put us on the trail of some vital information.

Our friend Gary Waddey, who unselfishly and continuously helps me in many ways in every research project, aided Rick and I materially in this one as well. On one occasion, Gary laid aside his research to make a trip to the Tennessee Archives to obtain a copy of the Reuben Ross Journal, which became a foundational primary source for this work.

Finally, we extend our most profound appreciation to Ranger Susan Hawkins of Fort Donelson National Battlefield Park. Susan, who has a passion for the history of Fort Donelson. She deserves a great deal of credit for this work. In fact, without Susan's encouragement and assistance, as well as connecting us with sources and knowledgeable individuals, this work would have never materialized. We met Susan several years ago when working on a separate research project on the 49th Tennessee Infantry. Since that time, we have developed a good friendship. Susan is very knowledgeable about the battle and was always helpful, usually going above and beyond any reasonable expectation of assistance.

—M. Todd Cathey

Table of Contents

Preface

"The reports of Colonel James E. Bailey, commander of the fort proper, and of Captain Jacob Culbertson, commander of the river batteries, are correct; and as official documents, I suppose, are complete, but they do not convey to the reader the disadvantages under which the batteries labored in this contest."[1]

Fort Donelson National Battlefield on the Cumberland River near Dover, Tennessee, is a beautiful park. From the river batteries, visitors observe breathtaking views of the river. Barges and smaller boats cruise past the now silent batteries. In recent years, Bald Eagles using the park as a nesting area, are frequently seen perched on limbs, seemingly disinterested in the many photographers longing for the perfect image. The cannons in the river batteries, for the most part, are original prewar and Civil War guns. A mammoth 10-inch Confederate columbiad, a veteran of the Vicksburg campaign, occupies the same position as the original which dominated the river in 1862. Markers depict the story of the battle as the Confederate batteries slugged it out with Union ironclad gunboats. While looking over the scene one has the feeling that the fort was all in a state of readiness, waiting for the day when "Iron Valentines" were exchanged, or so it appears.

When Hugh L. Bedford wrote of the battle, in which he commanded the columbiad in the lower battery, he described many of the problems the defenders faced and had to overcome in what became essentially a last-minute effort to ready the position to face the enemy. In this case the enemy were gunboats fresh from a resounding victory over Fort Henry on the Tennessee River. Bedford added, "It must be remembered however that the great fear was of the gun-boats. It was apprehended that their recent achievements at Fort Henry would be repeated at Donelson."[2]

Fort Donelson was the first line of defense on the Cumberland River that led directly to the cities of Clarksville and Nashville, and as it would turn out, the only line of defense. The troops that served the cannons were mostly farm boys, who had never seen a gun as large as the ones they were to train on, and as in the case of the Maury Light Artillery, had only a few hours training before the USS *Carondelet* appeared, firing shot and shells into their small position at the Upper Battery. Captain Reuben R. Ross, commanding the 6.4-inch rifle of the Upper Battery said afterward, "I could scarcely get my men to do their duty during this bombardment. They chattered like so many wild geese, each one having a great deal to tell others to do, but not seeming disposed to do much himself. I was compelled to use severe language."[3]

The history of the Fort Henry and Fort Donelson campaign has been covered by several very good books. At first, when this work was undertaken, it was intended to be an article about the river batteries alone, possibly for a magazine or journal. How many different ways can the battle between the river batteries and gunboats be explained? This isn't a different version of the events but an in-depth study into how the river batteries came into being, the types of armament used, the immense amount of ordnance supplies shipped from the Tredegar Foundry at Richmond, Virginia, and the Nashville Depot, and a closer look at the men who were there, taken from primary source material. The amount of material found was a bit overwhelming and the story became even more interesting than the authors imagined.

The location of Fort Donelson has drawn much criticism since 1861. Hugh L. Bedford had this to say, "If then Fort Donelson was intended to prevent the passage of gun-boats, it's [*sic*] location was an admirable one; it accomplished it's mission, and it's founder need feel no hesitation in claiming it's paternity."[4]

1

"Locate and construct defensive works"

April–July 1861

Only seventy-three years after the Constitution had been narrowly ratified, the young republic found herself on the verge of civil war. At the heart of the conflict were philosophical and political divergencies over the question of government—localism versus centralism. As the nation struggled forward, plagued by problems without solutions, the days of compromise passed as the political situation grew increasingly volatile. The disunity of the Democratic Party in 1860, leading to the election of the Republican, Abraham Lincoln, that November, was just a sign of the fractured state of the nation. Within six weeks of Lincoln's election, South Carolina made good on her threats of secession and left the Union. Mississippi, Florida, Alabama, Georgia, Louisiana, and Texas followed within the next six weeks.

The inevitable match to the powder keg came with the firing on Fort Sumter on April 12. In response, on April 15, Lincoln called for 75,000 militia from the governors of the states to forcibly subdue those states who had exercised their belief in a right to secession. Some governors eagerly complied with the order. Yet others, like Tennessee, previously loyal to the Union, were vehemently opposed to Lincoln's strong-arming those states to remain in the Union against their will. As a result, Tennessee broke ties with the United States and cast her lot with the fledgling Confederacy. Isham Harris, the fire breathing Democratic governor of Tennessee, defiantly sneered at Lincoln's call, "Tennessee will not furnish a single man for purposes of coercion but 50,000 if necessary for the defense of our rights and those of our Southern brothers."[1] Harris, true to his word, had turned over twenty-two regiments by July and in total, raised about 120,000 Tennesseans for Confederate service.[2]

Despite all the saber-rattling by politicians and local orators, Tennessee found herself in a tricky situation. Her northern neighbor, Kentucky, had declared neutrality. Neutral Kentucky provided for Tennessee a much-desired buffer between the warring states. However, if Kentucky waffled, with Tennessee's long northern border, it would be through her that the Federal armies would march to get at the deep South cotton states. Unlike Kentucky, which had the formidable Ohio River as a northern boundary, Tennessee lay wide open. To make matters worse, Tennessee had few natural barriers to impede an invading army, at least in the middle and western sections of the state. In those sectors, she had three major rivers with northern access running deep into her interior. On her western border lay the Mississippi, and further inland were the Tennessee and

3

Cumberland rivers. While good for commerce, these rivers created a defensive night-mare, and even worse, invited invasion.

In the antebellum period, the Mississippi, Tennessee, and Cumberland rivers played a crucial role in the economic development of Middle and West Tennessee. Flatboats, keelboats, and steamboats plied the waters transporting West Tennessee cotton and Middle Tennessee iron, dark-fired tobacco, corn, and other goods to New Orleans. As these rivers served as an economic lifeline in the pre-war days, their value to the war effort, for either side, was manifold. While the rivers were needed to continue the transporta-tion of resources, if utilized, they could also provide a ready highway for invasion. Once seized, they could be used to transport troops and war materiel beyond Tennessee, pen-etrating deep into the South. Benjamin Cooling described, "Of course, the twin rivers of the Tennessee and Cumberland offered the most logical avenues for invasion not only to the Tennessee capital and rich agricultural area of Middle Tennessee but far into the deeper recesses of northern Mississippi and Alabama."[3] Edwin C. Bearss writes, "No mil-itary engineer was needed to tell the officials of the Confederacy and Tennessee that the Tennessee, Cumberland and lower Mississippi rivers must be guarded by fortifications. But the question which plagued Southern authorities was: where should these fortifica-tions be located?"[4]

With a peaceful neighbor along her 440 mile-long northern border, Tennessee lead-ers put most of their focus on defending the Mississippi River on the western end of the state. Along the Mississippi, Southerners constructed several defensive positions includ-ing Island No. 10, Fort Pillow, Fort Wright, Fort Randolph, and Fort Harris.

While defending the Mississippi received the most attention, there was, however, some endeavor, albeit somewhat half-hearted, to secure Tennessee's interior twin rivers, the Tennessee and Cumberland. In this regard, Kentucky's choice of neutrality caused additional problems for Tennessee leaders. When it came to constructing suitable for-tified positions on the Tennessee and Cumberland, the best defensive ground lay in off-limits Kentucky. Tennessee leaders were therefore forced to look for adequate second-ary defensive points within their borders.

In April 1861, as Tennessee girded for war, Governor Isham G. Harris commissioned Adna Anderson, a highly respected and well-known civil engineer, then employed by the Edgefield and Kentucky Railroad, "to locate and construct defensive works on the north-ward flowing Cumberland and Tennessee rivers."[5] The Tennessee Military and Finan-cial Board, concerned about these potential avenues of invasion, stressed the urgency of Anderson's work. In an April 27 telegram, the board urged Anderson to "immediately" assess suitable defensive sites along the likely invasion routes of the twin rivers.[6]

Adna Anderson had an impressive record of accomplishments. One of his most sig-nificant endeavors was engineering the construction of the first railroad bridge over the Cumberland River in Nashville for the Edgefield and Kentucky Railroad. At the time, the bridge represented a tremendous engineering achievement as it spanned over 700 feet and had the "two longest draw spans in the nation."[7] Additionally, Anderson engineered trestle bridges over both Richland Creek and the Elk River, as well as the 1,230-foot tun-nel through Madry Hill near Pulaski.[8] At his side through each project was his trusted assistant, Wilbur Fisk Foster.

Wilbur Fisk Foster was born in Massachusetts on April 18, 1834. In 1851, Captain Childe, an old associate of Foster's father, offered the young man employment as a rod-man to help survey a rail line to be constructed in Tennessee. Foster traveled by various means, including railroad, steamboat, and stagecoach to Hamburg, Tennessee, to begin work. Adna Anderson soon noticed Foster's work, and the two began a close working relationship.[9]

When Governor Harris charged Anderson with this assignment, Anderson immediately asked for his pre-war associate, Wilbur F. Foster, to assist. Only recently, as Foster worked to accomplish his engineering assignments under Anderson near Nashville, he had enlisted as an infantry private in the Rock City Guards, Company C, of the 1st Tennessee Regiment.[10] As Foster was transferred from the 1st Tennessee to fulfill Harris's assignment, the young engineer was promoted to second lieutenant and was reassigned to the Tennessee Engineer Corps.[11]

Following orders, Foster left Camp Cheatham in nearby Robertson County, where his regiment was in training and proceeded to Nashville. On his arrival at the state capital, Anderson instructed his old associate to assemble a team that would be able to fulfill the governor's wishes.[12] This team was likely comprised of other associates who had worked with Anderson and Foster on these pre-war engineering projects.

At the beginning of May, not quite a month before Tennessee's secession, Anderson and Foster, with their team, began their surveys of the Cumberland River near the town of Dover in Stewart County, Tennessee. After completing their study, Anderson decided to locate a water battery about a mile below Dover "on the western bluffs of the Cumberland River" at the mouth of Hickman Creek.[13] By river, the position was about 60 miles south from the mouth of the Cumberland, where it dumped into the Ohio at Smithland, Kentucky. The site that would become Fort Donelson had been chosen.[14]

Strategically, this location held great importance. Eight miles up-stream, between Fort Donelson and Clarksville, was the Wood, Lewis, and Company (the Cumberland Iron Works). Thirty-seven miles up-stream was the town of Clarksville. The town was the home of the Whitfield, Bradley, and Company (the Clarksville Foundry). The Memphis, Clarksville, and Louisville railroad passed through, making it a vital production, communications, and transportation hub. The facilities of the Cheatham, Watson and Company (Sycamore Powder Mills), a significant supplier of gunpowder, were 66 miles above Dover. Beyond the powder mills, another ten miles, was Nashville, the Tennessee State capital, with its immense military manufacturing capacity. Aside from being connected to Nashville by river, Dover was connected to the capital by a road that ran through Charlotte, the seat of Dickson County. Additionally, between Dover and Nashville were scores of iron manufacturing facilities.

Despite the location chosen, some believed the better defensive position would have been at Line Port just below the Tennessee state line. W.C. Jones of Hope, Tennessee, wrote to the *Republican Banner*, "Had such a feeling prevailed at Fort Donelson and had they been fortified at Line Port, this boat [a Federal gunboat making an excursion up the Cumberland past Tobacco Port] would never have showed itself up here. It is thought that Fort Donelson was located where it is to gratify some interested parties about Dover from the fact that there is as good, or better location at the State Line."[15]

Despite opinions or politics, once their surveying on the Cumberland was complete, Anderson and Foster, with their team, headed west to the Tennessee River to continue their assessments for the river defenses. Meanwhile, Clay Stacker, with a large work party from the nearby Cumberland Iron Works, began constructing fortifications on the high ground overlooking the Cumberland River as Anderson had laid out.[16]

While work was beginning on the Cumberland River site, the surveying party

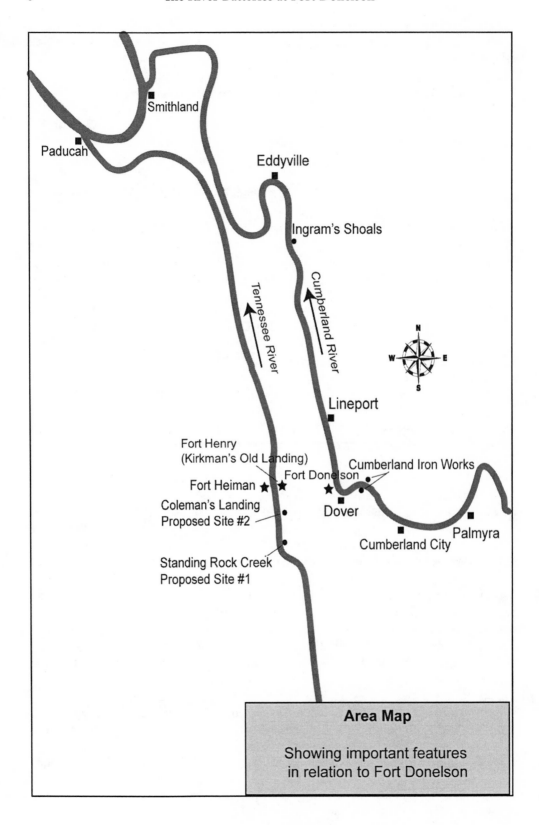

Smithland

Paducah

Eddyville

Ingram's Shoals

Tennessee River

Cumberland River

N
W   E
S

Lineport

Fort Henry
(Kirkman's Old Landing)

Cumberland Iron Works

Fort Donelson

Fort Heiman ★ ★

Coleman's Landing
Proposed Site #2

Dover

Standing Rock Creek
Proposed Site #1

Cumberland City

Palmyra

Area Map

Showing important features
in relation to Fort Donelson

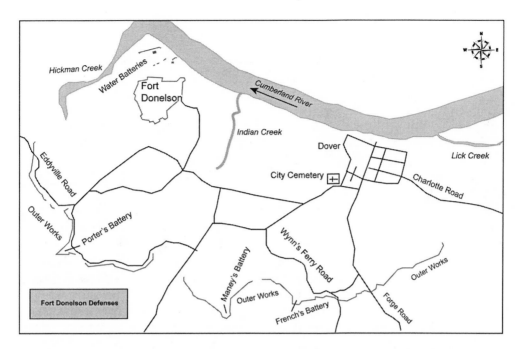

Fort Donelson Defenses

traveled across country approximately twelve miles and assessed sites along the Tennessee River for a suitable defensive position. Foster states, "The entire country between the two rivers was thoroughly examined and maps made showing the location of both forts and the country between. In all these surveys great care was taken to ascertain true high-water mark and note the conditions which would exist in time of floods."[17]

As Anderson and Foster carefully surveyed potential defensive positions, in their opinions, they located at least two possibilities suitable for defending the Tennessee River

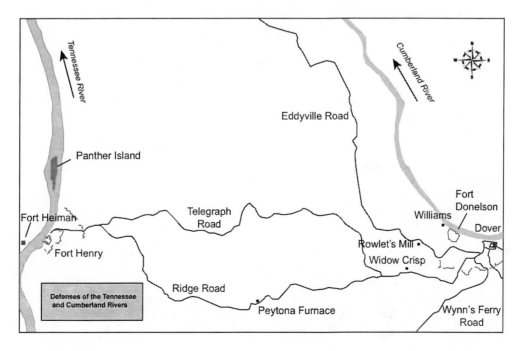

Defenses of the Tennessee and Cumberland Rivers

from Union incursion. The first was located near the mouth of Standing Rock Creek and just across from the mouth of the Big Sandy River. The second was located on the east bank of the Tennessee River at Coleman's Landing, approximately two miles north of the Standing Rock Creek site.[18]

By May 28, Colonel Bushrod Johnson, who had been appointed Chief Engineer of the Western Department, visited the sites and met with Anderson. In this meeting, Anderson explained all the work that had been done and turned over "all maps, plans, etc."[19] At this point, Anderson, Foster, and their team were relieved from their assignment, as Colonel Johnson assumed the direction of the engineering operations.

As Johnson performed his own study of the area, he rejected the suggested positions at Standing Rock Creek and Coleman's Landing. Instead, Johnson chose another site, located at Kirkman's Old Landing, some five miles downstream from Standing Rock Creek. In a letter to Governor Harris, Johnson describes, "Since my return to this place I have made a more thorough examination of the Tennessee River; and on last Sunday I selected Kirkman's old Landing, just below the mouth of Piney Creek, as the best place at which to erect defensive works."[20] Johnson continues, "I think Kirkman's landing is much superior to it [Coleman's Landing] in a military point of view. However, if the mere moral effect of a battery, with troops, is all that will be needed of cours [course] Coleman's landing will do."[21] As Johnson expressed his opinion of the matter to Harris, and even though his preferred choice rested in Tennessee, there were still potential issues with the State of Kentucky. Johnson explains, "I will add that Coleman's Landing is about one mile below the point where the line between Tennessee and Kentucky strike the west shore of the river."[22] Johnson adds, "I have examined Meigs and Cooper's Code of State of Tennessee and find pg. 82 that 'the Tennessee river is subject to the common use and concurrent jurisdiction of the two States.' So far as it forms the common boundary. I enclose herewith a drawing in pencil of the part of the river lying between and adjacent to the landings."[23] Johnson went on to state his strong opinion of the matter, "I prefer the Kirkman landing on account of the rear defenses. There are heights back of Coleman's Landing that will command any work you can construct there and which would require a large force to defend. There are no heights in the rear of Kirkman's Landing."[24] In conclusion, Johnson requested a decision from Harris regarding the Governor's preference of the location, "I presume an order from Nashville will best settle the matter."[25]

In response, Harris seemed put out with Johnson. The Governor tersely replied,

> I have only to repeat the verbal order heretofore given. That you are to determine for yourself upon examination the best point for the establishment of a battery for the protection of the Tennessee river, and when you have determined, you will proceed with such force as has been or may be sent there, to erect the same, of course the point selected must be within the jurisdiction of the State of Tennessee.
>
> In view of the fact that at Kirkman's Landing, Kentucky has concurrent jurisdiction with us, I would prefer, other things being equal, to erect the battery at some point where the jurisdiction of Tennessee is exclusive, but you must determine upon the point as the object in planting the battery is to protect the country from invasion you will of course select it with this view alone.[26]

It seems that nothing could dissuade Colonel Bushrod Johnson from his fixation of erecting the fort at Kirkman's Old Landing. To his credit in selecting this site, Cooling observes, "Notwithstanding the criticism, the position lay well forward of the railroad crossing south of Big Sandy."[27] It is interesting to see in all of Johnson's correspondence with Harris, he never mentioned the greatest peril of the Kirkman Landing site—its susceptibility to flooding.

Lieutenant Foster, of the original survey crew, wholeheartedly and adamantly disagreed with Johnson's new choice. Nevertheless, Foster was given the responsibility of laying out the lines of the fortification that would come to be known as Fort Henry. Foster must have been furious to have to lay off works in an area he knew would flood. As Foster laid out the lines, he went over Johnson's head and pointed out to Governor Harris that hills surrounded the new proposed position, and it was subject to seasonal flooding. Disregarding the young lieutenant's warnings, Harris put Foster in his place by saying that he was "too young to criticize the work of older engineers."[28] Foster replied, "that if the Governor had no confidence in his engineering abilities, he wished to return to his regiment."[29] Foster's request was partially granted as he was soon sent to Camp Buckner, Kentucky, to assist General Zollicoffer in the defenses of the Cumberland Gap.[30]

Not only did Foster have misgivings about the site, when Captain Jesse Taylor, who would command the heavy artillery at Fort Henry, arrived at Kirkman Landing, he also immediately saw problems. Taylor recounts, "Arriving at the fort, I was convinced by a glance at its surroundings that extraordinarily bad judgment, or worse, had selected the site for its erection."[31] First, Taylor noticed that the fortification was on the east bank of the Tennessee River "in a bottom commanded by high hills rising on either side of the river, and within good rifle range." Taylor's concern was "immediately reported to the proper military authorities of the State at Nashville." As in the case of Foster, the reply was that the location had been selected by "competent engineers." Taylor realized that since the site was chosen by a "West Pointer," he decided to keep his opinions to himself. Perhaps the most ominous sign—watermarks on the trees—caused him to "look carefully for this sign above, below, and in the rear of the fort."[32] Taylor concluded, "we had a more dangerous force to contend with than the Federals,—namely, the river itself."[33] Taylor explained, "Inquiry among old residents confirmed my fears that the fort was not only subject to overflow, but that the highest point within it would be—in an ordinary February rise—at least two feet under water."[34] With this observation, despite whether the site had been chosen by a "West Pointer," Taylor once again determined to make the dangerous situation known. Taylor reports,

> This alarming fact was also communicated to the State authorities, only to evoke the curt notification that the State forces had been transferred to the Confederacy, and that I should apply to General Polk, then in command at Columbus, Ky. This information was at once acted on,—not once only but with a frequency and urgency commensurate with its seeming importance,—the result being that I was once again referred, this time to General A.S. Johnston, who at once dispatched an engineer (Major Jeremy Gilmer)[35] to investigate and remedy; but it was now too late to do so effectively, though an effort was made looking to that end, by beginning to fortify the heights on the west bank (Fort Heiman).[36]

Writing later, General Tilghman who became the commander at Fort Henry wrote,

> To understand properly the difficulties of my position it is right that I should explain fully the unfortunate location of Fort Henry in reference to resistance by a small force against an attack by land co-operating with the gunboats, as well as its disadvantages in even an engagement with boats alone. The entire fort, together with the entrenched camp spoken of, is enfiladed from three or four points on the opposite shore, while three points on the eastern bank completely command them both, all at easy cannon range. At the same time the entrenched camp,

arranged as it was in the best possible manner to meet the case, was two-thirds of it completely under the control of the fire of the gunboats. The history of military engineering records no parallel to this case.[37]

It seems that neither Governor Harris's preference, nor young Lieutenant Foster's warnings, nor Captain Taylor's admonitions—and to quote the old Tennessee colloquialism, neither "hell nor high water" could deter Johnson from choosing Kirkman's Landing as the site for the Tennessee River defenses. Strangely enough, both "hell and high water" would be factors eight months later when Fort Henry fell on February 6, 1862. "Hell" came in the form of a Federal ironclad gunboat flotilla raining fiery shot and shell on the hapless defenders, and "high water" came as the river rose, flooding the fort, forcing the gunners of Taylor's Battery in their desperate defense, to serve their guns in knee-deep water. So submerged was the fort at the time of the battle that Federal authorities entered the fort by boat to accept Fort Henry's surrender. Unfortunately for the State of Tennessee and the Confederacy, the young lieutenant of engineers, Wilbur F. Foster, who was told he was too young to question the older engineers, was vindicated.[38]

Nevertheless, Kirkman's Landing, despite its misgivings, became the location of Fort Henry, Tennessee's defensive work on the Tennessee River. This ill-chosen site would play significantly in the future of the Fort Donelson river batteries.

While engineers determined the most suitable placement of defensive fortifications just south of Kentucky, Governor Harris wasted no time in calling his Tennesseans to military duty. In May 1861, companies comprised of approximately one hundred men were formed in local communities as prominent citizens, authorized by the governor, recruited and organized men for the Provisional Army of the State of Tennessee.

Within sixteen days of the completion of the surveying, General Daniel S. Donelson was using the Dover site as a recruiting center. Already by this time, this location was being referred to as "Camp Donelson," taking its name from General Donelson.[39] Here, Donelson enrolled three companies of infantry under Hiram C. Buckner, W.E. Lowe, and Nathan Brandon.[40] All of these companies, along with others raised nearby, would soon comprise the 14th Tennessee Infantry.

A whirlwind of enthusiasm ensued as Tennesseans swarmed to enlist. As their grandfathers and fathers, who in their view, had defied the unfair machinations of the English crown in preceding decades, they believed that they too would join the glorious crusade to challenge treachery—their crusade would be against the heavy hand of Abraham Lincoln. Southern politicians and journalists prophesied a war that would last less than six months, where one good Southerner could whip many Yankees, and where all the blood that would be shed in the war could be soaked up by one pocket-handkerchief. Induced by the hype, Tennessee boys thronged to enlistment sites across their counties. Soon, companies such as the Hickman Guards, the Dickson County Slashers, and the Maury Greys were filled with the requisite number of men needed to staff their companies. These companies were then consolidated into regiments of infantry, cavalry, and batteries of artillery.

Despite the selections of defensive positions on the twin rivers and the response to Harris's call for volunteers, Tennessee was largely unprepared for war. Nevertheless, in an outcome much different than a February referendum, by popular vote, on June 8, 1861, Tennesseans voted to leave the Union.[41]

Gaining Tennessee was a massive windfall for the Confederacy. With Tennessee's

Brigadier General Lloyd Tilghman superseded Colonel Adolphus Heiman as commander of the twin river forts in November 1861 (Alabama Department of Archives and History, Q132).

secession, the Confederacy won substantial and much-needed resources. The addition of the Middle Tennessee iron industry to the Southern war effort, in and of itself, was immense. In the decade preceding the Civil War, iron production of the major furnaces in just three Middle Tennessee counties (Stewart, Montgomery, and Dickson) yielded an annual total in 1852 of over 16,300 tons of pig iron.[42] Additionally, there were other major production facilities located up the Cumberland River between Dover and Nashville, which could serve the Southern war effort. The Cheatham, Watson, and Company (Sycamore Powder Mills), located in nearby Cheatham County, produced gunpowder for both small arms and artillery. The Whitfield, Bradley, and Company (the Clarksville Foundry), cast cannons. The T.M. Brennan & Company in Nashville produced numerous items, including cannons, artillery rounds, and various other military stores. Other Nashville firms, such as Sharp and Hamilton, produced cavalry sabers, and Ellis and Moore manufactured cannonballs.[43]

Not only was Tennessee valuable for her resources, but gaining Tennessee as a Confederate state, now moved the border of the Confederacy some one hundred miles further north away from Mississippi, Alabama, and Georgia. While good for the deep-South states, it made Tennessee in her unpreparedness ripe for the picking.

Tennessee's decision to unite with the Confederacy placed her on the chessboard of war as an objective, which must now be eliminated as the northern plan of war was focusing a significant part of their strategy to subdue the South by driving down the Mississippi River and her tributaries. In their way now lay Tennessee with three open avenues of invasion—the Mississippi, Tennessee, and Cumberland rivers.

As the clock ticked past the spring and into the summer of 1861, each passing day brought Tennessee closer to imminent danger. Despite the urgency to construct adequate defensive works, the month of July saw little progress on the construction of Tennessee's river defenses. At Fort Donelson, in June, when the 10th Tennessee Infantry was moved over to the Tennessee River to work on the fortifications of Fort Henry, only fourteen men were left to man the defenses at Camp Donelson.[44]

In the meantime, in the distant east, July brought the first large-scale clash of the armies and the rude awakening that both sides had grievously misjudged the potential severity of the crisis. On the rolling hills of Manassas Junction, Virginia, on July 21, scarcely six weeks after Tennessee's secession, 60,000 Americans—fathers, sons, brothers, neighbors, and friends, with growing animosity toward each other, faced off in lines of battle. When the rattle of musketry and thunder of artillery were ended, some 4,800 killed and wounded littered the ground. This inaugural battle shocked the nation as the citizenry of both sides began to see that the war might last longer and be a much bloodier affair than politicians had earlier envisaged. The bloody clash at Manassas was only the beginning of a long brutal war where the names of Fort Donelson, Shiloh, Antietam, Gettysburg, Chickamauga, the Wilderness, and Franklin would haunt the American consciousness for decades to come, and where of the extent of the slaughter would grow in severity as the losses of singular battles would exceed the casualties of the entire Mexican War.

2

"There was not more than half enough men on all boats at Cairo"

May 1861–January 1862

The dust of the battered walls of Fort Sumter had barely settled when both sides began gearing up in earnest for the inevitable conflict. While the Military and Financial Board of Tennessee began making defensive preparations on the Mississippi, Tennessee, and Cumberland rivers to fend off a likely Northern invasion, in Washington, D.C., the Federal government was making preparations to bring the defiant Southern states to their knees.

By the opening days of May, Lieutenant General Winfield Scott, the senior U.S. Army general, put forth his plan to destroy the Confederacy. Scott, known as "Old Fuss and Feathers" due to his persistence in adhering to proper military etiquette, was born on June 13, 1786, near Petersburg, Virginia. President Thomas Jefferson appointed him to the army in 1808. Scott, age seventy-four, had by the time of the Civil War, commanded the army for twenty years. This man, a veteran of the War of 1812 and the Mexican War, was no novice.[1] His "Anaconda Plan," as it was called, was a simple, straight-forward scheme to dismantle the Confederacy and slowly strangle her into submission. Gary D. Joiner recognizes that Scott "saw with remarkable clarity what the Union must do to win a conflict with the southern states."[2] Unlike most of his contemporaries, Scott perceived that the war would be long and bloody. He also realized that the most strategic area lay not in the intervening 100 miles between Washington, D.C., and Richmond, but rather in the Mississippi Valley.[3] Part of Scott's proposal entailed a strong Union naval blockade of Southern seaports, while a decisive movement was aimed down the Mississippi River to split the Confederacy in twain. With Tennessee's recent alignment with the Confederacy, the Federals now aimed their sights down her interior rivers. Utilizing these avenues would allow them to rip the heart out of the Volunteer State. As Federal armies prepared to drive down the Mississippi and her primary tributaries, their plan would include the utilization of a fleet of steam-powered riverine gunboats. Myron Smith comments, "This was the famous western river-based 'Anaconda Plan.' It was often ridiculed, would not be fast or simple to apply, but, in the end was, with modifications, followed as the basis of the Union's war-fighting master strategy."[4]

Even though the plan called for an inland amphibious component, there were two significant challenges to this part of the plan. First, the United States government at the time did not have a suitable boat in its naval arsenal for this type of operation. Second, the army, not the navy, had jurisdiction over the inland rivers. After much consideration, it was determined that a fleet of riverine gunboats would be developed, and this fleet would be commanded and crewed by naval personnel. Still, the boats would fall under the control of the army.

The new river gunboats would look very different than almost any other vessel in the U.S. Navy. In reality, perhaps they resembled turtles more than ships; thus, they were nicknamed "Pook's turtles," so named after their designer Samuel Pook. Intended solely for use on the Mississippi River and its tributaries, Pook designed a boat based on the commercial vessels then employed on the Western waters, armed with heavy guns, and protected by a sloped armored casemate. In the end, the Federal government produced a highly effective weapon to assist in the drive to split the Confederacy in half.

To achieve Scott's objectives, land and naval forces would disembark from bases in Missouri and Illinois and penetrate the South's interior by moving down the Mississippi River with additional excursions into Kentucky and Tennessee along the Tennessee and Cumberland rivers. A second push would begin in the Gulf of Mexico to capture New Orleans and push up the Mississippi from that point and link up with the forces headed south. By splitting the South down the Mississippi, the Federals would deny the Confederacy access to the troops and resources of the Trans-Mississippi.

In late April 1861, Secretary of the Navy Gideon Welles was contemplating a suitable plan to develop an inland navy and devise a strategy to practically execute Scott's concept of splitting the South down the Mississippi. It is interesting that the same week that Tennessee Governor Isham Harris commissioned Engineer Adna Anderson to locate defensive positions on the Tennessee and Cumberland rivers, Secretary Gideon Welles received a letter from James B. Eads, an inventor, and entrepreneur from St. Louis, Missouri, proposing a strategy to accomplish just such an undertaking.

James Buchanan Eads, named for his mother's cousin, President James Buchanan, had already become wealthy with his riverine inventions. Mostly self-educated, Eads began his career as a purser on a Mississippi riverboat. In time, Eads began inventing equipment to salvage cargo from sunken wrecks which had met with disaster on the perilous waters. At age 22, he designed a salvage boat and a diving bell, which he used to recover valuable freight from the bottom of the rivers.

At the time of the Civil War, Eads, recognized as one of the most knowledgeable men about the Mississippi River, began considering how the North could wrest control of the rivers from the South. Eads formulated a plan that would utilize

James B. Eads, the builder of the City Class ironclads (Naval History and Heritage Command, NH49790).

shallow-draft, steam-powered armored gunboats to operate on the western waters. In April, Eads presented his idea in the form of a letter to Gideon Welles.

Eads proposed the establishment of a base of operations at Cairo, Illinois, with gunboats capable of operating on the Ohio and Mississippi rivers. Eads also offered his *Submarine No. 7*, a snag boat, which he believed could be effectively converted into a suitable armed naval vessel for such use.

Eads wrote to Gideon Welles:

> The effect of this blockade would be most disastrous to the South, as it would effectually close the main artery through which flows her food. It would establish a tollgate through which alone her dutiable goods could enter, or through which her products could find their way to market. The only outlets or inlets which would remain to her would be the Tennessee and Cumberland rivers and the railroads from Louisville to Nashville and Chattanooga. The Tennessee and Cumberland rivers are navigable only by very small steamers, except in short seasons of high water. Their mouths can be easily commanded by batteries on the Illinois shore or by floating batteries. The railroad is very vulnerable, as one man could blow up a culvert or bridge and render it useless for the time being.
>
> If Kentucky were friendly to the Union, these three inlets could be effectually guarded; if she were unfriendly, their northern termini would be completely at our mercy. Once close them and the great Mississippi, and starvation is inevitable in less than six months.[5]

Welles was favorably impressed with Eads's proposal, but without the jurisdiction to undertake a shipbuilding program in the west, he forwarded Eads's letter to Secretary of War Simon B. Cameron.

In turn, Cameron, who was equally impressed with Eads's proposal, instructed General George B. McClellan, commanding the Department of the Ohio, to give final approval for the unprecedented operation. McClellan, unfamiliar with water-borne operations was also directed to work in consultation with a naval officer who would be sent west to advise on that purpose. The Secretary of War sent the following Special Order to General McClellan:

> Mr. James B. Eads, of St. Louis, has proposed as a means of defense and of active operations at Cairo and the rivers adjacent, the employment of the boats owned by the wrecking company of which he is a member, and has advised that said boats be taken by the Government and adequately armed and equipped for that service. The Government here deeming very favorably of the proposition, but unwilling to decide positively upon the matter without the knowledge and approval of the general in command of that department, it is ordered that the subject be referred to General McClellan, who will consult with Mr. Eads and with such naval officer as the Navy Department may send out for that purpose, and then, as he shall find best, take order for the proper preparation of the boats.[6]

To form the "brown water navy" as the fleet of gunboats would be called, Commander John Rodgers was transferred west on May 16, to work with McClellan "in regard to the expediency of establishing a naval armament on the Mississippi and Ohio Rivers."[7] The forty-nine-year-old Rodgers was then serving in the east and was the son of the famous Commodore John Rodgers. In 1821, Rodgers had been appointed a midshipman. He was stationed in the Mediterranean and led an expedition of naval infantry and marines during the Seminole Wars. In the 1850s, he commanded the North Pacific Exploring and Surveying Expedition.[8] Recently, Rodgers had been captured by Virginia State Militia, but since Virginia had not yet seceded, he was released. Rodger's next orders were unusual. Joiner comments, "Rodger's orders were peculiar for a naval officer. He was to report to McClellan with the intent of establishing a naval presence on the Mississippi and/or Ohio rivers to blockade commerce."[9]

Welles gave the following instructions to Rodgers:

> You will proceed to Cincinnati, Ohio, or the headquarters of General McClellan, where [ever] they may be, and report to that officer in regard to the expediency of establishing a naval armament on the Mississippi and Ohio rivers, or either of them, with a view of blockading or interdicting communication and interchanges with the States that are in insurrection.
>
> This interior nonintercourse is under the direction and regulation of the Army, and your movements will therefore be governed in a great degree by General McClellan, the officer in command, with whom you will put yourself in immediate communication. He will give such orders and requisitions as the case to him shall seem necessary, you acting in conjunction with and subordinate to him.
>
> Whatever naval armament and crew may be necessary to carry into effect the objects here indicated, you will call for by proper requisition.[10]

While Rodgers was heading to St. Louis to report to McClellan, Secretary of the Navy, Gideon Welles, ordered Naval Contractor Samuel Moore Pook, at the Washington Naval Yard, to proceed to Cairo to work with Rodgers.[11] Upon Pook's arrival, Rodgers was absent. In Rodger's absence, Pook met with Eads, who conveyed his ideas regarding the shallow-draft gunboats for river warfare. Pook, Eads, and Rodgers realized that the conventional ships then in the Navy's arsenal would be inadequate to fulfill the demands of riverine warfare on the Mississippi. Conversely, as Eads had proposed, the wide, flat-bottomed steamers already in use in commercial interests were ideally suited to navigate the shallow waters of the western rivers.

After hearing Eads's ideas, Pook, impressed with the concept, set to work designing the plans for "the most famous gunboat fleet in U.S. history, forever to be known as 'Pook's Turtles.'"[12] Upon Rodger's return, he met with Pook and McClellan, proposing that there initially needed to be three gunboats on the Mississippi River to protect Cairo from Southern incursion. McClellan and Pook concurred, and Rodgers purchased the *A.O. Tyler, Lexington,* and *Conestoga.* After remodeling and armament, the three gunboats cost approximately $34,000 each.[13]

By the end of May, heavily armed fortifications had been erected to guard the junction of the Ohio and Mississippi rivers. Approximately six weeks later, on July 17, Congress approved one million dollars for the "gunboats on the western rivers."[14]

Authorities soon realized that three gunboats would be inadequate to execute the war on the western waters. Therefore, engineers set to work to design a heavily armed shallow draft vessel with a centrally located paddlewheel surrounded by armor casing, and massive gun platforms that could effectively navigate the western rivers. John Lenthall, the chief of the Bureau of Construction, Equipment, and Repair, submitted initial concepts to Rodgers and Pook. Lenthall's plans were promising, although, in the end, Pook made substantial revisions.

Lenthall proposed to General Joseph Totten, the army's chief engineer, that the military needed heavily armed, shallow draft, paddlewheel vessels, drawing about five feet.[15] General Totten immediately saw the wisdom of Lenthall's proposal and forwarded the letter to General Winfield Scott. Like Totten, Scott also recognized the necessity of the proposed boats in the achievement of his plan. Scott was so favorable to the proposed gunboat plans that he recommended that sixteen gunboats be acquired for these purposes.[16]

Despite the progress, Rodgers faced many challenges. Rumors, Congressional complaints, miscommunication, and communication delays caused increasing problems for him. When word reached Gideon Welles of the gunboat purchases, he exploded. Welles, not realizing that the authority to purchase the three gunboats came from McClellan, supposed that Rodgers had acted of his own accord. Welles censuring Rodgers stated, "The movements on the Mississippi are under the direction and control of the Army. All purchases of boats for army movements must be made by the War Department. You are not authorized to make requisitions except for armament and crew."[17]

The following day, Welles fired off another letter of censure:

Your letter of the 8th instant, the first that has reached the Department from you, was received to-day. The requisitions for gunboats, for which you state you have contracted, are without authority from this Department. You were directed to proceed West and report to General McClellan, commanding the forces on the upper Mississippi, and it was distinctly stated in your instructions that that officer would make the necessary requisitions. The movement in that quarter pertains to the Army and not the Navy. Nor must the two branches of service become complicated and embarrassed by separate action or any attempt at a combined movement on the rivers of the interior. You are, then, subordinate to the general in command, to aid, advise, and cooperate with him in crossing or navigating the rivers or in arming and equipping the boats required for the army on the Western waters. Should naval armaments be wanted for any of the boats, or crews to manage them, you were specifically authorized to make requisition for either or both, but nothing further. The Department can not recognize or sanction any contract for boats. They are not wanted for naval purposes. If they are required for the Army, those whose business and duty it is to procure them will make requisitions on the War Department. There has been and is great sensitiveness among the boatmen and others on the Western rivers in relation to the water craft that might be required for the Army, and it was an especial object of the Department in framing your instructions to so restrict them as to avoid jealousy. Repeated applications have been made to the Department in regard to your movements and powers by Members of Congress and others, to all of whom unequivocal answers have been given that you were not authorized by this Department to purchase or build boats or make contracts. You were promptly telegraphed, immediately on the receipt of your first letter informing of your operations, this Department can not respond to your requisitions for money to purchase boats, nor with our limited number of officers can we spare any such number as are proposed for interior operations. Boatmen who navigate Western rivers must be selected, and, for the management of river boats, would doubtless be quite as serviceable as experienced seamen. The employment of men and their subsistence, together with the necessary engineers, pilots, firemen, etc., for the army movements, including the steamers, properly belong to the Army; and whatever you may do as regards them or either of them will be under the direction of the general in chief and by requisitions on and at the expense of the War Department. Should not your services or those of Mr. Pook be required by the War Department, you will be at liberty to return to this city.[18]

Unlike the verbosity of his censure, Rodgers sent a direct and terse reply: "General McClellan has approved the bills for the steamboats. The written approval of a superior officer makes an act of purchase his own."[19]

The job of fitting the three timber-clads just purchased was unprecedented. No one in the U.S. Navy had ever attempted converting river steamers of such magnitude into gunboats. Nevertheless, Pook was up to the challenge, and he got busy designing the changes. The modifications entailed utilizing five-inch oak sections to protect the crew and guns. Beams and timbers were put into place to support the immense weight of the guns.

While work progressed on converting the *Tyler*, *Lexington*, and *Conestoga*, Lieutenant Roger Stembel and Master Joshua Bishop began recruiting crews. Meanwhile, Lieutenant Seth Ledyard Phelps went to Louisville, initially to move the boats to Cairo due to the dropping water of the Ohio. When Phelps arrived in Louisville, he realized the river had already dropped too much to move the boats. To further complicate matters, he found several issues with the conversions. Phelps spent the summer correcting the problems with the timber-clads. Next, issues with arming the boats arose in requisitioning the guns from the army. The *Conestoga* was armed with 32-pounder smoothbores, and the *Tyler* and *Lexington* were armed with two 32-pounder smoothbores and four 8-inch smoothbores.[20]

Rodger's problems accelerated when General McClellan was reassigned, moving from the Department of the Ohio to take Irvin McDowell's place as commander of the Army of the Potomac. McClellan's successor for the Department of the Ohio was John C. Fremont, the legendary "pathfinder" and 1856 Republican presidential candidate.

Unlike his predecessor, Fremont was not in favor of the gunboats and began pursuing a different agenda. Fremont ordered sixteen 9-inch "naval shell guns" and thirty 8-inch mortars "of army pattern."[21] Compounding Rodger's problems was Fremont's characteristic stubbornness. While an asset to him during his pathfinding days, it now became a detriment. Joiner points out that Fremont "was stubborn to the point of abstractness."[22] Joiner further observes that Fremont, wanting to play by his own rules, soon ran afoul of Montgomery Meigs, Quartermaster General of the U.S. Army. Fremont resented anyone in Washington second-guessing him. Moreover, Meigs happened to be Rodger's brother-in-law. As a result, since Meigs was not present, the disdain Fremont had for Meigs was displaced on Rodgers.[23]

Things became even more difficult for Rodgers in June as he rejected Eads's proposal to buy his *Submarine No. 7*, for conversion to an ironclad. Fremont bought the boat anyway and gave the contract to Eads for conversion. Under Eads's direction, *Submarine No. 7* soon became the USS *Benton*.

Amid growing difficulties, Secretary of the Navy Gideon Welles decided to replace Rodgers. On August 30, Rodgers received orders to transfer his command to Captain Andrew Hull Foote.[24] Foote received the following orders:

> You have been selected to take command of the naval operations upon the Western waters, now organizing under the direction of the War Department.
> You will therefore proceed to St. Louis, Mo., with all practicable dispatch, and place yourself in communication with Major-General John C. Fremont, U.S. Army who commands the Army of the West. You will cooperate fully and freely with him as to your movements. Requisitions must be made upon the War Department through General Fremont, and whatever the Army can not furnish the Navy will endeavor to supply, having due regard to the operations on the coast.
> The Western movement is of the greatest importance, and the Department assigns you this duty, having full confidence in your zeal, fidelity, and judgment.[25]

In 1861, Andrew Hull Foote was a promising Naval officer. His naval career spanned several decades and covered a wide range of experiences. Early in his career, he had served in the Mediterranean. Later, assigned to the USS *John Adams*, Foote had circumnavigated the globe. In a subsequent assignment on the USS *Perry*, he cruised the African coast as it suppressed the slave trade. When Foote was promoted to commander, he was assigned to the USS *Portsmouth* as part of the East India Squadron. Finally, in the days just before the war, he was in command of the Brooklyn Navy Yard. Also, Foote, personally, was a deeply Christian man. He was "an avowed abolitionist" and was "well known for his opposition to flogging," states Barbara Tomblin.[26] In June 1861, Foote was promoted to the rank of captain and was transferred west.

While Rodgers spent the summer trying to navigate the tricky political waters with Fremont, the development of the ironclad gunboats moved forward. Initial drafts had been submitted to Welles by John Lenthall. In turn, Welles presented the concepts to Samuel Pook. After reviewing the submissions, Pook determined that the drafts were fundamentally sound, but made several modifications and innovations to the designs, utilizing the structural elements of the commercial boats of the western rivers.

One of the primary modifications for the gunboats was the adaptation from a side-wheeler to a sternwheeler. This reasoning transferred the paddlewheel inside the vessel, totally enclosed, which would help protect it from enemy fire. Other structural changes were employed as well. While Pook's concept maintained a conventional forward part of the boat, the aft would be constructed in a catamaran fashion. To accomplish this, Pook slightly lengthened and significantly widened the proposed plans.

By July 18, Pook's plans had been approved by the army, and on August 5, the office of the quartermaster general opened bids to construct the new gunboats. In just a few days, Eads was awarded the contract to construct the ironclads.

The contract called for seven boats instead of Scott's proposed sixteen and stipulated the ships were to be completed by October 10, a mere sixty-five days. After Eads was awarded the contract, he began constructing the new "City-class" gunboats, so named after the cities central to their creation. The boats were the *Cairo, Carondelet, Cincinnati, Louisville, Mound City, Pittsburgh,* and *St. Louis.*

Once awarded the contract, Eads set about his monumental mission of constructing the seven gunboats. To accomplish his task, he would need carpenters, lumber, iron, and subsistence for the workers on top of a shipyard to construct the vessels. There was no single shipyard in the west that could handle a project of such enormity. The industrious Eads employed, "five sawmills, a rolling mill, and two foundries in and near St. Louis to prepare lumber, iron plating, and machinery."[27] Eads leased the largest shipyard in the area, the Carondelet Marine Railway and Dry Dock Company at Carondelet, Missouri, eleven miles south of St. Louis, to construct the *Benton, Carondelet, Louisville,*

Flag Officer Andrew Hull Foote commanded a successful sortie with his gunboats resulting in the capitulation of Fort Henry on February 6, 1862. At Fort Donelson, much to everyone's surprise, Foote's vaunted gunboats were pummeled by the Confederate River Batteries (Naval History and Heritage Command, NH 49586).

Construction of City Class gunboats at St. Louis, MO. In late 1861 (Naval History and Heritage Command, 165-C-703).

Gunboat construction at Carondelet, MO, in late 1861 (Naval History and Heritage Command, 165-C-702).

Pittsburgh, and *St. Louis*. The *Cairo*, *Cincinnati*, and *Mound City* were built upriver at the Hambleton, Collier, and Company dry docks in Mound City, Illinois. Once a boat was built, it was taken downriver to Cairo, Illinois, where it was outfitted with ordnance. Figure 1. shows the ordnance of the four city-class gunboats that moved against Fort Donelson in February 1862.

	32-pounder 42 cwt	8-inch 63 cwt	Army 42-pounder Rifle	12-pounder Boat Howitzer	12-pounder Rifle
St. Louis	7	2	4	-	1
Carondelet	6	3	4	1	-
Pittsburgh	6	3	4	-	-
Louisville	6	3	4	1	-

Figure 1. Armament of Gunboats, January 1862[28]

Eads was unable to meet the October 10 deadline. But the *St. Louis* was commissioned on October 12, and the *Carondelet* came ten days later. By January 1862, the seven sisters, as the City-class gunboats were called, were launched, with the *Essex* (another ironclad, but not of the city-class variety) following in February.[29]

H. Allen Gosnell describes the final characteristics of the City-class ironclads as they were launched:

The seven sister ironclads had the following features: 512 tons and 6 feet draft at full load; two horizontal high-pressure engines, each with one cylinder 22 inches in diameter and 6-foot stroke, driving a 22-foot wheel which operated in a 60-by-18-foot horizontal opening in the deck aft; five horizontal, cylindrical return-flue boilers 24 feet in length and 3 feet in diameter, necessarily having only one furnace per boiler; speed, 6 to 7 knots "through the water." ... The front of the casemate was protected by 2½ inches of iron backed by 20 inches of oak; the sides abreast of the engines and boilers were covered with 2½ inches of iron, the steam plant not being below the waterline. The remainder, including the wheel, was unprotected.[30]

Joiner adds:

These seven vessels initially looked almost identical, differentiated only by different colored bands near the tops of their tall chimneys: *Cairo*, gray; *Carondelet*, red; *Cincinnati*, blue; *Louisville*, green; *Mound City*, orange (not officially confirmed); *Pittsburg*, light brown; and *St. Louis*, yellow. The officers at times added additional adornments. In two photographs, the *Mound City* bears a five-pointed star between her chimneys directly below her colored stripe. After a name change to the *Baron De Kalb* later in the war, the *St. Louis* displayed a device similar to the Masonic emblem hanging from the spreader bar between its chimneys.[31]

Once construction on the boats began, the next challenge facing Foote was obtaining crew members for the western navy. Ed Bearss duly noted, "Manpower would plague the western navy throughout the Civil War. Even before a keel of one of the new ironclads touched water, Foote was pleading with the navy and war departments for recruits."[32] Foote recruited heavily to obtain the necessary men. Recruiting stations established in Chicago, Milwaukee, Cincinnati, and Cleveland netted only about 100 men.[33] In the opening days of December, Foote was still in desperate need of crews. In a dispatch to the navy department on December 5, the Flag Officer requested another 1,000 men.[34] By December 10, Foote reported the offer of 1,000 men from Captain

Howard, formerly of the Revenue Service, but Foote lacked the funds to pay advances and expenses.[35] Foote's continual pleas for men to the navy department were rebuffed, as Secretary Welles succinctly replied that the matter had been referred to the War Department "it being considered the duty of the Army to furnish the men."[36] General Grant, also trying to alleviate the manpower shortage, authorized men in the army who were "river or seafaring men" to be transferred to the gunboats.[37] Despite Foote's best efforts to the contrary, one of the gunboat crewmen wrote, "There was not more than half enough men on all boats at Cairo."[38]

By February 3, 1862, with the river rising, Flag Officer Foote with four ironclads, the *Essex*, and three city-class ironclads, the *St. Louis*, the *Carondelet*, and the *Cincinnati*, and with three timber-clads, the *Conestoga*, *Tyler*, and *Lexington* headed South. Along with the flotilla, General Ulysses S. Grant moved with two infantry divisions, one under the political appointee Brigadier General John A. McClernand and the other under the professional soldier, Grant's old West Point commandant, Brigadier General Charles Ferguson Smith. In total, Grant moved south with about fifteen thousand men. By February 4, Foote's gunboats were within a few miles of Fort Henry, staged just beyond Panther Island, waiting for Grant's forces to get into position.

Brigadier General Ulysses S. Grant, in early 1862, was a little-known general of volunteers. He achieved notoriety as he successfully moved against Forts Henry and Donelson in February 1862. His victory at Fort Donelson gained him the moniker of Unconditional Surrender Grant (Naval History and Heritage Command, NH63768).

3

"The people of Kentucky are profoundly astonished"

August–September 1861

From the initial threat of hostilities, Tennessee leaders recognized the possibility of a Federal invasion along her major rivers. Their great hope was if Kentucky did not side with the South, that she would at least be able to maintain her neutrality. Either way, in their reasoning, Kentucky would provide a much-needed buffer for the Volunteer State. In reality, Kentucky's hope of neutrality was only a pipe dream as the state's situation was a sectional quagmire. Both Lincoln and Davis desperately needed Kentucky. Describing the value of Kentucky to the Union war effort, Abraham Lincoln purportedly stated, "I hope to have God on my side, but I must have Kentucky."[1]

Much to the disappointment and detriment of Tennessee, Kentucky's neutrality did not last long. In August, the circumstances that would force Kentucky's hand began lining up. Both Federals and Confederates were actively recruiting Kentuckians for their sides. Several Kentuckians, notably, Robert Johnson, William T. Withers, Robert J. Breckenridge, Lloyd Tilghman, and Simon Bolivar Buckner enlisted Kentucky volunteers at Camp Boone, a Confederate enlistment and training camp located on the Guthrie Road, just three and a half miles south of the Kentucky state line near Clarksville in Montgomery County, Tennessee. On August 6, the Federals were more brazen as they established Camp Dick Robinson, a Federal recruitment and training base near Danville, Kentucky. Writing to Kentucky Governor Beriah Magoffin, on August 30, Tennessee Governor Isham Harris, pointed out these flagrant Federal incursions against the Kentucky Commonwealth. Harris writes, "It is with profound interest and regret that I have witnessed recently the open violation of the neutrality of Kentucky by the Government of the United States, by the establishment of military encampments and other warlike preparation within the territorial limits and jurisdiction of your State."[2]

Despite blatant Federal activity in Kentucky, an intolerable Confederate infraction was about to occur under the authority of the Western Department Commander, Major General Leonidas Polk. Polk had an interesting background, one that hardly qualified him to serve as a junior officer, much less a major general (and thereafter as lieutenant general), but such was the character of volunteer armies. Perhaps Polk's most distinguishing qualification was his close friendship with Confederate President Jefferson Davis. Steven Woodworth insightfully pointed out, "Besides being a basically incompetent general, Polk had the added fault of hating to take orders."[3]

Leonidas Polk was born in Raleigh, North Carolina, on April 10, 1806. His grandfather Thomas and father William were both officers in the Revolutionary War. At age fifteen, Polk was a student at the University of North Carolina. However, Polk intending to follow in the military tradition of his family, received an appointment to West Point. Polk entered the Academy in 1823. At West Point, Polk made close friends with Cadet Jefferson Davis.[4]

Polk was graduated from the Military Academy on July 1, 1827, and was commissioned a brevet 2nd lieutenant and assigned to the artillery. However, within five months, Polk had resigned his commission (December 1, 1827).[5]

While a student at West Point, a life-changing event occurred. Cadet Polk, under religious conviction, became a follower of Christ and was baptized by Charles P. McIlvaine, West Point's Episcopal chaplain. Polk's conversion quickly and significantly altered his plans. After resigning from the army, for a while, Polk helped his father and brother operate their plantations in North Carolina, but he soon entered the Virginia Theological Seminary and pursued the ministry. First, moving to Tennessee, he established his plantation, "Ashwood," in Maury County. Polk became an influential churchman and served as the Missionary Bishop of the Southwest for the Episcopal Church. Later, Polk moved to Louisiana and then back to Sewanee, Tennessee, where he established the University of the South.[6]

With the coming of the Civil War, Polk exchanged his vestments for the soldier's uniform and offered his services to the Confederacy. On June 25, 1861, Polk, who had only served five months as a brevet 2nd lieutenant thirty-four years earlier, now received an appointment to major general and took command of the Western Department.[7] Despite deliberate Federal activity in Kentucky since early August, the powder keg was irreversibly lit when Major General Polk, on September 3, 1861, occupied Columbus. Polk was strongly influenced by his very persuasive subordinate, Brigadier General Gideon J. Pillow, who had advocated seizing Columbus as early as May 13. As a result, Polk cast aside political concerns regarding Kentucky neutrality, for what he believed was a strategic necessity.[8]

Polk believed Columbus, Kentucky, was the Gibraltar of the Mississippi River, and as such, he thought it was critical to the defense of the State of Tennessee. Timothy Smith explains, "Polk dreamily viewed that locale as the end-all and be-all bastion that would stop any Federal movement along the Mississippi River."[9] Smith Continues, "Polk saw a major bastion at Columbus as the key to the defense of the Mississippi Valley, and in his hopes of achieving that, he began to experience fears that were not there. He grew anxious that the Federals would capture Columbus to deprive the Confederacy of perhaps the best defensive area north of Vicksburg, Mississippi."[10] To accomplish his chief goal of preventing any Federal move down the Mississippi, Polk authorized Brigadier General Gideon Pillow to seize and to fortify Columbus and Hickman, Kentucky. Stanley Horn explains, "By this time Polk had both eyes on Columbus because of the suspicious and threatening movements of Federal troops in its vicinity. General Grant at Cairo on September 2 had dispatched a land and naval force to occupy Belmont, Missouri, straight across the river from Columbus. Polk considered this a sufficiently overt act to justify taking possession of Columbus, which he promptly did."[11]

Kentucky was already on edge. Their August elections resulted in a Unionist legislature since the secessionists boycotted. Despite earlier Union incursions into Kentucky, Polk's overt act provided justification for the Kentucky Commonwealth to end her neutrality.

Regardless of Polk's intentions, his action of seizing Columbus and Hickman sent

Brigadier General Gideon Pillow, a man who was known for his egotism and abrasive manner, assumed command of Fort Donelson on February 9, 1862 (Alabama Department of Archives and History, Q209).

Governor Harris of Tennessee into a tailspin. The day following Polk's forays, Harris began firing off letters to President Davis, Governor Magoffin of Kentucky, and General Polk. On September 4, Harris wrote President Jefferson Davis, informing him, "Confederate troops commanded by Genl Pillow landed at Hickman Kentucky last night. I regard the movement as unfortunate, calculated to injure our cause within the State. Unless necessary there would it not be well to order their immediate withdrawal?"[12] He next fired off a telegram to General Polk. Harris stated, "Just learned that Pillow's command is at Hickman. This is unfortunate as the President and myself are pledged to respect the Neutrality of Kentucky. I hope they will be withdrawn immediately unless their presence there is an absolute necessity."[13] Next, in an attempt to do damage control with the State of Kentucky, Harris wrote Governor Magoffin, "The Confederate troops that landed at Hickman Kentucky did so without my knowledge, or consent, and I am satisfied without knowledge or consent of the President. I have telegraphed President Davis urging their immediate withdrawal."[14] In addition to Harris's reproof, Polk received a scathing reprimand from John M. Johnston, "Chairman of Committee, State of Kentucky." Johnston thus rebuked Polk:

> Sir, I have the honor to enclose herewith a resolution of the Senate of Kentucky, adopted by that body upon the reception of intelligence of military occupation of Hickman, Chalk Bank, and Columbus by the Confederate troops under your command. I need not say that the people of Kentucky are profoundly astonished that such an act should have been committed by the Confederate States, and especially that they should have been the first to do so with an equipped and regularly organized army.[15]

Despite the objections, Polk remained unmoved in his convictions and began heavily fortifying the positions.

Brigadier General Ulysses S. Grant, commanding the District of Southern Missouri, immediately seized on Polk's overt act and countered on September 6, by taking Paducah and Smithland. Paducah was a critical strategic point at the junction of the Ohio and Tennessee Rivers, and Smithland, thirteen miles upstream, is where the Cumberland River flows into the Ohio. Grant now had possession of the mouths of both the Tennessee and Cumberland rivers.

On September 13, despite hopes of having the Ohio River as a protective barrier to the north, what little security Tennessee thought she had with the Commonwealth's neutrality, came crashing down as the Kentucky legislature voted to end neutrality and side with the Union.

Two days later, on September 15, President Jefferson Davis placed General Albert Sidney Johnston in command of Department Number 2. In taking command, Johnston superseded Leonidas Polk as department commander, but Polk was given command of the Western Department's 1st division, which included responsibility for Forts Henry and Donelson. Interestingly, in July 1861, Polk had superseded his fellow Maury Countian, General Gideon Pillow, as commander. Even though in this case, Polk had urged Davis to place Johnston in command of the department, this tradition of commanders superseding another, while the former was left in place as subordinate, is a routine that would be executed time and again in the Western Department throughout the summer, fall, and winter, leading up to the Battle of Fort Donelson. With the egos involved in this cadre of officers, this practice would fuel jealousy, selfishness, hurt feelings, resentment, and uncooperative spirits among many of the upper key Confederate leaders in the department. In time, Gideon Pillow, who will later be superseded again, will lead the herd in damaged egos and

General Albert Sidney Johnston was given the responsibility of commanding Department #2, a massive area, and was given few resources to accomplish his assignment (Alabama Department of Archives and History, Q6915).

unwilling cooperation. This custom will figure prominently in the communication and command failures which will significantly impact the outcome of Fort Donelson.

Johnston, superseding Polk, assumed command of the department. By all estimations, Johnston's assignment was a tough one. Department Number 2 was an expansive territory with overwhelming problems.[16] The massive department stretched from the Appalachian Mountains in the east to the Indian Territory to the west. However, Johnston was a life-long friend of President Davis, and as in the case of Davis and Leonidas Polk, despite competency, Davis never forgot his friends. Timothy Smith describes well Johnston's relationship with the Confederate president, "Theirs was a friendship much like Polk and Davis's, the two having attended Transylvania University in Kentucky and

West Point together."[17] Later, when Davis was Secretary of War, he appointed Johnston colonel of the newly formed 2nd United States Cavalry. Like Polk, Johnston "reaped the rewards of knowing well a president who never forgot his acquaintances, whether or not they were competent," concludes Smith.[18] When criticism arose against Johnston, Davis was adamant about his old friend's abilities exclaiming, "I know Sidney Johnston well. If he is not a general, we had better give up the war, for we have no general."[19]

Despite the hype about Johnston, his task was, in all practicality, an impossibility. Gary Joiner summed it up well, "For the Rebels, it was simply a matter of too much land to control and too few troops to hold it."[20]

Perhaps one of the most significant challenges facing Johnston, was his own short-comings. Thomas Lawrence Connelly gives further insight into the new commander's personality:

> The most persistent of all factors which made Johnston's command structure weak was his personality. As far as human nature was concerned, Johnston seemed to live in a world to himself. He was never able to establish rapport with his sub-commanders, and never really grasped their personalities or command problems. Somehow, he never felt the "pulse" of the Army's command system. He was insensible to command friction in the department, such as the quibblings of Polk and Pillow.[21]

Despite the challenges, Johnston took command of the department, established his headquarters at Bowling Green, and got busy assembling his staff.

One of the critical appointments to Johnston's staff was the position of chief engineer. First Lieutenant Joseph Dixon, a man who served as an engineer in the U.S. Army, was selected to fill this role. Dixon was described as "a young engineer of extraordinary skill, courage, and character."[22]

The twenty-five-year-old Dixon was a native of Athens, Tennessee. Dixon received an appointment to West Point and graduated third of twenty-seven cadets in the class of 1858. As a brevet 2nd lieutenant of Topographical Engineers, he was assigned to duties in the Northwest Territories.[23] In 1860, he was stationed at Fort Vancouver, Washington.[24] When his home state of Tennessee seceded, Dixon resigned his commission in the U.S. Army on June 28, 1861.[25] Traveling to Richmond, Virginia, with other officers to offer his services to the Confederacy, he received a commission as 1st lieutenant on September 9. He was assigned duty as the chief engineer in the Western Department.[26]

By September 17, Dixon was on the job. Johnston ordered the young engineer to "make an examination of the works at Forts Henry and Donelson and to report upon them."[27] In a survey conducted shortly after assuming his position, Dixon reported that even though Fort Henry was not located "at the most favorable position, that it was a strong work, and instead of abandoning it and building at another place, he advised that it should be completed and other works constructed on the high lands just above the fort on the opposite side of the river."[28] Dixon, giving his opinion on Fort Donelson, reported: "a better position might have been chosen, for the fortifications on that river, yet, under the circumstances then surrounding our command, it would be better to retain and strengthen the position chosen."[29] In finishing the assignment, Dixon made surveys for additional works at Fort Donelson. Once Dixon's initial assignment was complete, due to the significant shortage of engineers, he was sent to Columbus, Kentucky, to work on the fortifications there, leaving the Cumberland River fortifications with but little attention.

4

"To arms!
Fellow countrymen, to arms!"

Late September–October 1861

Many challenges faced Albert Sidney Johnston in developing strong defenses for the Western Department. One of the pressing obstacles was the shortage of manpower. Within days of assuming command, Johnston entreated Governor Harris for an additional 30,000 Tennessee recruits. At Johnston's request, on September 26, Harris issued his second call for volunteers.[1] In Harris's proclamation, he petitioned his Tennesseans: "Whereas the Government of the Confederate States has called upon me through General Albert Sidney Johnston, for thirty-thousand troops, for immediate service in addition to those already in the field, it becomes my duty to proclaim to the gallant citizens of Tennessee that their country demands their services."[2] Exacerbating the man power shortage was the scarcity of arms. To help alleviate the crisis, Harris asked his volunteers to supply their own weapons, which "will be replaced by furnishing the troops with the regular army gun at the earliest practicable period."[3]

As the Governor concluded his proclamation, Harris appealed, "To arms! Fellow countrymen, to arms. Let there be no delay. The insolent mercenaries of the Federal government are threatening an invasion of our homes, from every exposed point along our borders."[4]

While Tennesseans were responding to Harris's call for volunteers throughout the fall of 1861, the Nashville Ordnance Department was a hub of activity as it attempted the arduous task of acquiring gunpowder, military equipment such as saddles, sabers, harness, canteens, knapsacks, cannon and associated equipment, as well as cartridge boxes, percussion caps, rifles, and ammunition. To accomplish this overwhelming task, the Ordnance Depot, directed by Captain Moses H. Wright, then located at the State Capitol, made known the government's desire to enter into contracts with "responsible parties" for manufacturing military goods by posting advertisements in local papers.[5] As Tennessee began turning "plowshares into swords,"[6] soon the depot entered into agreements with various local firms such as the T.M. Brennan Company, Sharp and Hamilton, Ellis & Moore, E.R. Glascock, the State Penitentiary, J.E. Logwood (the Military Storekeeper at Memphis who was forwarding things from the Memphis Ordnance Depot), and many others.

While Harris raised troops, the Nashville Ordnance Department geared up to supply them, and Johnston assembled his staff, at least some attention was now being directed to the twin river fortifications. Up to this point, little had been done to prepare the defenses at Fort Donelson. Back in May, the 10th Tennessee Infantry, a regiment of Middle Tennessee Irishmen, commanded by Colonel Adolphus Heiman and Lieutenant Colonel Randal W. MacGavock was organized at what would become Fort Henry.[7] The location, known as Kirkman's Old Landing, earlier in the month, was selected by Colonel Bushrod Johnson, and the defensive lines for Fort Henry had been laid off by Lieutenant Wilbur Foster of the engineers.[8] The ready labor force the army found in these Irish volunteers was immediately employed as they were quickly put to work building the fort. Lieutenant Foster said that the Irishmen began work on Fort Henry on Friday, June 14, with the first gun mounted on Friday, July 12.[9]

While the men of the 10th regiment worked on Fort Henry, Heiman also sent detachments to Camp Donelson to complete the works that Adna Anderson had laid off and had been started but abandoned by the work party from the Cumberland Iron Works some time before. In the coming weeks, these Irishmen constructed the parapets of what would be known as the Upper Battery and the positions for a four-gun battery on the ridge overlooking the Cumberland River.[10] Once the Upper Battery works were complete, Reuben Ross, a West Point graduate and captain of the Tennessee Artillery Corps, was sent, likely sometime in July,[11] to mount the first guns at Camp Donelson.[12] The guns that Ross mounted were two very unimpressive 32-pounder naval carronades (also called howitzers or sea-coast howitzers in other reports) on "casemate chassis and carriages."[13] Ross gives his opinion of the position, "it was in a faulty position rendered so by commanding only the river and opposite shore."[14]

The Upper Battery at Fort Donelson was the first position constructed. It was built in the summer of 1861 by members of the 10th Tennessee Infantry. Originally the position mounted the two 32-pounder Naval Carronades. The 6.4-inch rifled columbiad arrived on January 23, 1862, just a few weeks before the Federal attack on the River Batteries (authors' photograph).

Ordnance report of Lieutenant W.O. Watts identifying that the two 32-pounder howitzers (naval carronades) were mounted on casemate carriages (service record of W. Ormsby Watts).

These naval carronades, like many other 32-pounders which would eventually be sent to Donelson, likely originated from the Gosport (Norfolk) Naval Yard, which had been captured by Virginia State troops on April 21, 1861. The spoils of war given up by the naval yard were immense. The Confederates seized over 1,000 pieces of heavy artillery from 11-inch guns down to 32-pounders, along with thousands of shot and shell and 2,000 barrels of powder.[15] These captured guns would be sent to various locations across the south, such as Columbus, Kentucky, Forts Henry and Donelson, and Port Hudson, Louisiana.[16]

After the detachment of the 10th Tennessee completed their assignment and the carronades were mounted in the Upper Battery, work at Camp Donelson once again ceased. From summer to fall, Camp Donelson had been "entirely abandoned," stated Heiman.[17]

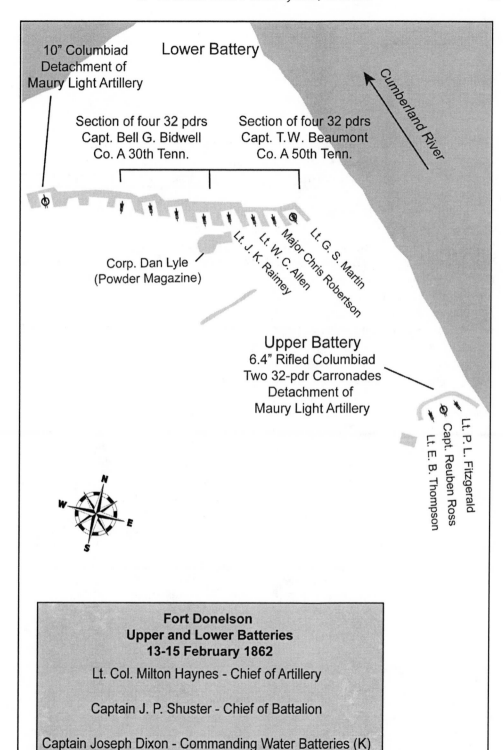

10" Columbiad
Detachment of
Maury Light Artillery

Lower Battery

Cumberland River

Section of four 32 pdrs
Capt. Bell G. Bidwell
Co. A 30th Tenn.

Section of four 32 pdrs
Capt. T.W. Beaumont
Co. A 50th Tenn.

Corp. Dan Lyle
(Powder Magazine)

Lt. J. K. Raimey

Lt. W. C. Allen

Major Chris Robertson

Lt. G. S. Martin

Upper Battery
6.4" Rifled Columbiad
Two 32-pdr Carronades
Detachment of
Maury Light Artillery

Lt. P. L. Fitzgerald

Capt. Reuben Ross

Lt. E. B. Thompson

N
W
E
S

Fort Donelson
Upper and Lower Batteries
13-15 February 1862

Lt. Col. Milton Haynes - Chief of Artillery

Captain J. P. Shuster - Chief of Battalion

Captain Joseph Dixon - Commanding Water Batteries (K)

Captain Jacob Culbertson - Commanding Water Batteries

After an approximate five-month interlude, a focus on the Donelson defenses was once again renewed. October brought the arrival of three infantry companies. One of the first companies to arrive was Captain Thomas Beaumont's Dunlap Greys. In time, they would become Company A, 50th Tennessee Infantry, and would play a conspicuous role defending the Fort Donelson river batteries.

The thirty-one-year-old Thomas Beaumont was a native of Clarksville, Tennessee, a burgeoning town just upstream from Dover. Thomas was the son of Henry F. Beaumont, a prominent tobacco merchant.[18] Beaumont studied law and was a member of the bar in Montgomery County.[19] Despite a promising law career, Beaumont made journalism his profession, and for two years, 1858–60, he was an associate editor with the Nashville *Banner*.[20]

In March 1860, following his stint as a newspaper editor, Beaumont and Gustavus A. Henry (future Confederate Senator) traveled with other well-known citizens making speeches at barbeques and events in small communities across Montgomery, Dickson, Benton, and Humphreys Counties. Several of the speakers afterward became Confederate officers, including Alfred Robb, James E. Bailey, and William A. Quarles, all of whom would be engaged in the defense of Fort Donelson.[21]

In the summer of 1861, just before Harris's second call for troops, Brigadier General W.H. Carroll of the Provisional Army of the State of Tennessee authorized the well-known Beaumont to raise a company of infantry. Beaumont began recruiting efforts in July at Antioch Church Campground six miles outside of Clarksville, and by August 12, he began enlisting in Clarksville. By the end of August, recruiting efforts for Beaumont's company were occurring at Antioch Campground, Clarksville, at Cunningham Mills in the northern end of neighboring Dickson County, and around the Narrows of the Harpeth in nearby Cheatham County.[22]

Dickson Countian, Christopher Robertson, assisted Beaumont by enrolling men in Dickson County and the Harpeth River area of Cheatham County. Christopher Wills Robertson, a native of Dickson County, was the son of Benjamin C. Robertson, a wealthy businessman and farmer and his wife Ann G. Napier Robertson. Their large family home, "Harpeth Hall," was located on the Harpeth River northeast of Charlotte, the county seat. His family was related to General James Robertson, known as the Father of Tennessee, and were some of the first to settle in the area. Christopher studied law and was graduated with high honors in the 1859 class of Cumberland University at Lebanon, Tennessee.[23]

After weeks of recruiting, the organization of the Dunlap Greys was completed on September 16, 1861. Upon the organization of the company, Thomas W. Beaumont was elected captain and Christopher W. Robertson, 1st lieutenant.

Around the first of October, the "Dunlap Greys" passed through Clarksville, where they were treated to a sumptuous feast by local tobacconist Hugh Dunlap.[24] From here, they proceeded on to Fort Donelson. Upon arrival, they made their camp above the Upper Battery, and as some of the first troops to arrive at Fort Donelson, they were quickly put to work constructing gun emplacements.

In addition to the arrival of a few infantry companies, around the first of part of October, Colonel Adolphus Heiman, then commanding Forts Henry and Donelson, began sending qualified people from Fort Henry to assist in organizing and training the few men who had arrived at Donelson on the heavy guns then present. Heiman first detached 1st Lieutenant W. Ormsby Watts of Taylor's Battery, then stationed at Fort Henry, to go to Donelson to train men.[25]

Since there were no artillerymen present at Fort Donelson, Watts began training Beaumont's infantrymen on the 32-pounder carronades. Colonel Heiman, reporting to his division commander, Major General Leonidas Polk at Columbus, Kentucky, wrote, "No artillery force whatsoever is there; but I have detached Lieutenant Watts, of Captain Taylor's company, to instruct such men of the companies there to serve the guns as may be best fitted for that purpose."[26]

The Confederates were not getting their river defenses in order any too soon. By October 4, the Federal navy began making reconnaissance excursions up the Tennessee River. Lieutenant Seth Ledyard Phelps, commanding the four-gun timber-clad *Conestoga*, took the gunboat within two and a half miles of Fort Henry, where he was able to examine the fortifications. A week later, on October 11, Lieutenant Phelps took his timber-clad sixty miles up the Cumberland, making it as far as Ingram's Shoals. Phelps had penetrated deep into Confederate territory on both rivers.[27]

By October 7, Lieutenant Watts had assumed his duties as the Ordnance Officer at Fort Donelson. Watts had enlisted in Captain Jesse Taylor's Artillery Battery at Nashville, Tennessee, on May 14, 1861. Within a few months of enlisting, Watts was serving as 1st lieutenant.[28] Later, his commanding officer Brigadier General Lloyd Tilghman would write, "Lieutenant Watts is the coolest officer under fire I ever met with."[29]

Upon his arrival at Donelson, Watts recorded the ordnance on hand at the fort: two 32-pounder howitzers mounted on casemate chassis, four bronze 6-pounder guns on field carriages, two 9-pounder guns on truck wheels, one hundred four rounds for the 6-pounders, thirty-three rounds for the 9-pounders, and one hundred cartridges and ninety balls for the 32-pounders.[30]

As the armament at Donelson was now being increased, additional 32-pounders were expected to arrive. General Johnston, on October 8, directed General Polk to send Lieutenant Joseph Dixon, his chief engineer, to mount the guns at Fort Donelson for the "defense of the river."[31]

Following orders, Lieutenant Dixon proceeded to Fort Donelson. Although Dixon was sent to Donelson with instructions to mount the guns, he was often called to Fort Henry. As a result of being pulled in many directions, Dixon's effectiveness was greatly hampered.

As the Southerners continued efforts to strengthen the situation at Fort Donelson, 1st Lieutenant Hugh Lawson Bedford received orders to report to Fort Donelson

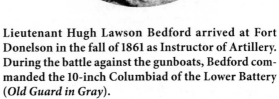

Lieutenant Hugh Lawson Bedford arrived at Fort Donelson in the fall of 1861 as Instructor of Artillery. During the battle against the gunboats, Bedford commanded the 10-inch Columbiad of the Lower Battery (*Old Guard in Gray*).

as Instructor of Artillery.[32] When Bedford received his orders to go to Donelson, he was given clear instructions about the critical nature of his assignment. Bedford recalls, "Colonel E.W. Munford aide to General Johnston, informed me that he was instructed by his chief to impress upon me that the Cumberland River cut his rear, and the occupation of Bowling Green was dependent on the proper guarding of that stream."[33]

Hugh Lawson Bedford was born on June 11, 1836, and was the son of Benjamin Watkins Bedford and Martha Ann Whyte. His paternal grandfather was Captain Thomas Bedford, a Revolutionary War veteran, and the one for whom Bedford County, Tennessee, was named. His maternal grandfather, Honorable Robert Whyte, served as a judge on the Supreme Court of Tennessee. Although born in Fayette County, Tennessee, Hugh was raised in Panola County, Mississippi. Entering the University of Mississippi and taking the classical course, he then attended Kentucky Military Institute studying civil engineering under Colonel E.W. Morgan, graduating in 1855. He read law under Judge J.P. Caruthers and took the full law course at Cumberland University in Lebanon, Tennessee, graduating in 1858.[34] Hugh and his older brother Harry Hill Bedford, also a graduate of Cumberland University, opened a law office in Memphis, Tennessee, but Harry soon became ill and passed away on July 10, 1858. Hugh continued to practice law until the war began.[35]

When Lieutenant Bedford arrived at Fort Donelson, he found that the defenses were unfinished and that Lieutenant Joseph Dixon, the engineer in charge, was often called away to Fort Henry, where he was also supervising the works. Not only did Bedford discover the works unfinished, but he found the green Confederate troops highly excited by the Federal reconnaissance incursions up the Cumberland. Bedford writes, "At the time of my arrival, there was considerable excitement at the Fort. Smoke was seen rising a few miles down the river, the long-roll was being beat, and there was hurrying to and fro; companies were getting under arms and into line with the rapidity of zealots, though wanting in the precision of veterans."[36]

Out of the nervousness of the raw recruits often came occurrences of a ridiculous nature. One such incident happened in the fall of 1861 after Captain Thomas Beaumont's company had arrived. At this time, Dr. James H. McNeilly, a Presbyterian minister from nearby Dickson County, availed himself to the staff of Captain Beaumont. Beaumont, McNeilly, and 1st Lieutenant Christopher Robertson formed a "mess" and shared food and sleeping arrangements, with Robertson's body servant cooking for them.[37] McNeilly related that in those early days, many of the customs of home had not been given up. Some of the traditions included wearing long white nightshirts to bed. McNeilly describes:

> One day it was rumored that the gunboats were in the river below us, and were coming up. About midnight, while all were sleeping soundly, the long roll began to beat in the company stationed on the riverbank. At once there was a stir in the camp; officers were calling the men to fall in; there was hurrying to and fro. Captain Beaumont was always when on duty in faultless dress…. Quickly, he put on his uniform, buckled on his sword, and stepped out of his tent to take command of his company.
>
> But the men had not been as thoughtful as he. They sprang up and grasped their muskets, and formed a line in front of their tents, but every man of them had forgotten to put on their trousers, and they stood there in the starlight, in their nightclothes like "sheeted ghosts," trembling with cold and excitement. As the captain and I stepped out, and his eye glanced along the line, his sense of propriety got the best of his military ardor, and he shouted out his first command, "Confound your fool souls, go and put on your breeches!"[38]

McNeilly concludes, "By that time the alarm was found to be false, and with laughter and jokes we all went back to bed. But the 'shirt tail gang' which comprised most of the men, enjoyed the ridiculous situation."[39]

To bring a greater sense of organization to the raw troops which were gathered at Donelson, on October 12, General Polk detached Lieutenant Colonel Randal MacGavock from the 10th Tennessee Infantry, then at Fort Henry, to take command and to organize them into a battalion.[40]

The red-haired, fourth-generation Irishman, Randal William MacGavock,[41] was born in Nashville, Tennessee, on August 10, 1826. His grandfather, Randal MacGavock, had served as the mayor of Nashville in 1824. Young MacGavock entered the University of Nashville in 1843. Upon graduation in 1846, MacGavock entered Harvard Law School and completed his residency on February 21, 1849. Returning to Nashville, he practiced law and was involved in the political scene. In his grandfather's footsteps, he served as the mayor of Nashville in 1858–59. At the coming of the Civil War, MacGavock was serving as captain of a Tennessee Home Guard company, comprised entirely of Irishmen, known as the Sons of Erin. This home guard unit soon became Company H, 10th Tennessee, a regiment consisting mainly of Middle Tennessee Irishmen. Upon organization, the regiment elected the well-known Prussian-born Nashville architect, Adolphus Heiman, as colonel and former Nashville mayor, Randal W. MacGavock, lieutenant colonel.[42]

When MacGavock arrived at Camp Donelson, he found the three companies of infantry. There were Captain Thomas W. Beaumont's Dunlap Greys (men from Dickson, Cheatham, and Montgomery counties); Captain George W. Stacker's Company, and Captain Samuel Graham's Company, both from Stewart County. These companies would later become companies A, B, and D of the 50th Tennessee Infantry Regiment.[43]

As MacGavock took over at Fort Donelson, he was instructed to "remain in vigilant command."[44] In expectation of the arrival of additional 32-pounders from Clarksville, MacGavock requested that a detachment of Taylor's Battery be sent from Fort Henry to man the heavy ordnance. Colonel Heiman felt that he could not concede to MacGavock's request. Three primary issues led him to this decision. First, the Federals had already begun increasing their activity up the Tennessee River. Second, there was no Federal activity on the Cumberland. Third, he didn't believe the Donelson defenses could be effectively held.[45]

As Beaumont's men worked to strengthen the fortifications, their work was soon interrupted. On Monday, October 14, the company, sixty strong, under command of 1st Lieutenant Chris Robertson, was sent to reinforce Fort Henry due to the threat of Federal gunboats.[46]

Despite his numerous duties, by October 16, Lieutenant Dixon was engaged in moving four 32-pounders from Clarksville to Fort Donelson. These guns had been initially transferred from Memphis three weeks earlier.[47]

Even though some progress was being made at Fort Donelson, it was not enough. As Dixon was moving the guns, an urgent request arrived at Johnston's Bowling Green headquarters from Senator Gustavus A. Henry, who resided in nearby Clarksville. In his note, Henry implored Johnston to send "one regiment" from Hopkinsville to Fort Donelson. No doubt Phelps's excursion up both the Tennessee and Cumberland Rivers caused Senator Henry great concern about the Donelson defenses as he informed Johnston, "It seems to me there is no part of the whole West so exposed as the valley of the Cumberland."

Henry concluded his request, "Excuse my anxiety about this matter, for I think the danger is not only great, but that there is no time to be lost to avert it."[48]

The day following Senator Henry's communication to Johnston, Lieutenant Colonel Randal MacGavock at Fort Donelson sent the general additional intelligence. MacGavock informed his chief that a gunboat reached Eddyville, Kentucky, the day before at noon, and landed 200 cavalry and had taken possession of the town. Eddyville was a town in Kentucky approximately fifty miles north of Fort Donelson. "We are in a defenseless condition here, having only three companies of raw recruits, poorly armed, and not one artillerist to manage what heavy guns we have," stated MacGavock.[49]

That same day (October 17), Johnston fired off a message to Fort Donelson's division commander, Major General Leonidas Polk, at Columbus, Kentucky, ordering him to "hasten the armament of the works at Fort Donelson." Johnston continues, "The operations of the enemy on the Tennessee show that the necessity of interrupting the Cumberland is urgent."[50]

Senator Henry also sent Polk an urgent message, similar to the one he penned to Johnston the previous day. Henry, decrying the state of preparedness at Donelson, wrote, "I beg leave to draw your attention to the defenseless condition of the Cumberland River. From here (Nashville) to Smithland (the town at the confluence of the Cumberland and Ohio Rivers) there are not 300 soldiers in arms. One small fort—Donelson—3 miles below the town of Dover, with four guns is all we have to rely on."[51] Henry's message conveyed his anxiety as he described the desperate situation:

> The four 32-pounder guns cannot yet be put in battery, nor are there now any soldiers there who know anything about artillery service. Wood, Lewis. & Co. have very valuable property on the river a few miles above Fort Donelson—the Cumberland Rolling Mills—now engaged in manufacturing iron for the Confederate States, which could be destroyed any night. Its machinery could not be reinstated now, and the public loss would be irreparable. The bridge at Clarksville over the Cumberland River could also be destroyed, which would sever all connection with West Tennessee, and this loss could not be repaired at a cost of $200,000. If the river keeps up Nashville itself is not safe.[52]

Henry concluded, "I am now more fully impressed with [the] danger, and cannot too urgently urge you to send prompt relief to us."[53]

On Friday, October 18, Colonel Heiman submitted a report to Major General Leonidas Polk and Governor Harris on the defenses being constructed at the river forts. Heiman states that under order of General Leonidas Polk, he [Heiman] is still in command of both Fort Henry and Fort Donelson. He described Fort Henry as a "bastion fort inclosing a little over three acres" with an armament of six 32 pounders, two 12 pounders, and one 6 pounder field piece. The force there consisted of the 10th Tennessee with an aggregate of 820 men and Captain Taylor's Company of Artillery with 50 men.[54]

Heiman went on to describe the lack of progress at Fort Donelson:

> The defenses on the Cumberland have so far been almost entirely overlooked. It is true a little fort was constructed 1 mile below Dover by my regiment, in which were placed two 32-pounder sea-coast howitzers, which have a very good range down the river, but from the hemmed-in position of this work it is entirely worthless.
>
> To hold a place against even a small force would require a great deal of additional work on the crest of a ridge which immediately overlooks this work, called the fort.[55]

The situation at Donelson was indeed bleak. To this point, the only guns mounted

Captain Bell G. Bidwell commanded Company A, 30th Tennessee. Bidwell's company crewed a section of four 32-pounders in the Lower Battery (*Confederate Veteran*).

were the two 32-pounder carronades, "or ship's guns." Colonel Heiman said they "have a very good range down the river," but Captain Bell G. Bidwell of the 30th Tennessee, who would arrive in the coming weeks, had a differing opinion as he said, they "were worthless there or anywhere else."[56] Four additional 32-pounder siege guns had been obtained, but there was no one to mount them. Even though Donelson had been mostly abandoned, Colonel Heiman sent Lieutenant Watts to train men on the artillery and Lieutenant Colonel Randal MacGavock to begin organizing the companies who were arriving there into a battalion. Additionally, Heiman recommended the construction of earthworks on the crest of the hill overlooking the river batteries to hold the place "even against a small force."[57]

The Confederate authorities in Johnston's department were acutely aware of the perilous deficiencies at Fort Donelson. However, it is interesting to note that despite the critical nature of the situation, neither Division Commander Leonidas Polk nor Department Commander Albert Sidney Johnston ever set foot on the Cumberland River defenses.

By this time, Lieutenant Dixon was making a little progress in bolstering the Donelson earthworks. After moving the four 32-pounders from Clarksville, each gun weighing roughly 7,000 pounds, Dixon was able to get them mounted in the works on the ridge which had been laid out by Anderson in May. This position is known as the "alternate position."[58]

The infantrymen, now under MacGavock's command, formed fatigue parties that worked to mount the guns under Dixon's supervision. The details set these four 32-pounders on front-pintle carriages *en barbette*.[59] To install the guns, the work parties laid down beams in a semi-circular pattern on top of which they nailed the boards, which served as the traverse arc. This front-pintle mounting system was employed for each of the four guns. Sergeant James C. Cook of Captain Harrison C. Lockhart's company (later Company H, 50th Tennessee), recorded on October 18, that the four 32-pounders had just arrived. The following day, Cook said they had one of the guns on a log sled being pulled by "nine yoke of oxen" and "could not move it at all."[60] The detail finally succeeded in getting the gun mounted on the carriage.

The following day, Sunday, October 20, Sergeant Cook, and his party were still at work trying to get the 32-pounders moved from the landing and mounted. Cook had requested a log wagon to help move the heavy guns. After the log wagon arrived, the guns were moved easier. Cook describes, "Still at work at these heavy guns. Got the log wagon.

I succeeded in getting all those large guns up today. Got one of them mounted about 11 o'clock at night."[61]

While Dixon made improvements at Fort Donelson, the Federal threat continued growing. On October 19, Brigadier General J.L. Alcorn, commanding the Confederate camp near Hopkinsville, Kentucky, reported to General Johnston additional "reliable information" on the movements of the enemy at Eddyville, Kentucky, only sixty miles distant. Alcorn states, "The gunboat steamed up to the town and steamed back again. A company or squad of 25 cavalry from Smithland marched within 4 miles of Eddyville, took all of the double-barreled guns they could find, robbed some women of their jewelry, seized several horses and mules, destroyed some property, insulted some women, captured one citizen as prisoner, and returned to Smithland, from whence they came."[62]

In the meantime (on October 17), Major Jeremy F. Gilmer had been appointed Chief Engineer of the Western Department, superseding Lieutenant Dixon. Gilmer, a very respected and efficient engineer, reported to Johnston's headquarters at Bowling Green.

Jeremy Francis Gilmer was capable and qualified for his task and eventually rose to the rank of major general in the Confederate army. Gilmer was born in Guilford County, North Carolina, on February 23, 1818.[63] Gilmer was graduated from the United States Military Academy at West Point in 1839.[64] He ranked fourth in his class just behind Henry W. Halleck.[65] Upon graduation, he served as a 2nd lieutenant of engineers, and in 1853 was promoted to captain. By the time of the Civil War, Gilmer was in command of

The alternate position originally mounted four 32-pounder smoothbores. It was determined that the guns could not be brought to bear on any gunboats moving up the river, so the Lower Battery was constructed, and the four 32-pounders were moved (authors' photograph).

the fortifications at San Francisco. On June 29, 1861, he resigned his commission in the U.S. Army, and the very respected engineer was appointed to Johnston's staff.[66]

Johnston realized the great value of Nashville to the Confederate war effort. The T.M. Brennan Company alone reported during this period the capacity to produce "fifteen guns a week, viz. twelve field guns, 6 and 12 pounders, and three siege and garrison guns up to 32-pounders." Brennan added that he could "turn out about ten tons of shot and shell a day."[67] As Gilmer assumed his duties, in an October 26 communication, Johnston instructed his Chief Engineer to arrange works for the "defense and obstruction of the river at Donelson, Clarksville, and Nashville." Money was not to be a concern in these defensive preparations. Special attention was to be focused on a "plan of defensive works for Nashville," and Johnston added, "urge them forward by all means."[68]

Meanwhile, at Fort Donelson, after all the work to get them mounted, it was discovered that the guns mounted in the alternate battery on the ridge overlooking the Cumberland River were too high to engage the gunboats effectively. After consideration, Dixon decided to move the four guns further down the hill toward the river. He soon had work parties building a new line of parapets that would come to be known as the Lower Battery.[69]

To make things easier for his engineer, Johnston sent a letter to Governor Harris at Nashville introducing Major J.F. Gilmer, C.S. Corps of Engineers, who had as his chief object to examine the country below Nashville to determine upon "the most eligible sites for the erection of such works as will completely defend the city from all approaches of the enemy by means of the river."[70]

Original position of the right section of 32-pounders of the Lower Battery. The guns in these positions were manned by Company A, 50th Tennessee commanded by Captain Thomas W. Beaumont (authors' photograph).

The left section of four 32-pounder smoothbores crewed by Company A, 30th Tennessee, commanded by Captain Bell G. Bidwell (authors' photograph).

As part of the Confederate defensive strategy, they would try to obstruct the river by sinking rock-filled boats at natural sandbars which made shallow points in the river. Dixon was charged with obstructing the river at Ingram's Shoals thirty-five miles downstream from Fort Donelson and at Lineport thirteen miles downstream.

At 3:00 p.m. on October 26, Captain Dixon left Fort Donelson with an expedition to obstruct the navigation of the Cumberland River at Ingram's Shoals. A squadron of cavalry numbering 115 men under Major David Campbell Kelley left for the Shoals the day before to scout the area and protect the expedition. Dixon was accompanied by a detachment of Captain Maney's Light Artillery Company of 40 men and four guns, and two companies of infantry (170 men) commanded by Captain Young.[71]

At the end of the month, Johnston directed Polk to keep a vigilant eye on the Tennessee River. Johnston told Polk, if possible, to fortify opposite of Fort Henry to protect it from being taken by the enemy and that Lieutenant Dixon, familiar with the country, will be able to point out the proper position.[72]

On the last day of October, Johnston again sent an urgent message to General Polk at Columbus. Johnston wrote,

> Your front and particularly your right flank, requires incessant watching, and may at any moment demand all the force at your disposal. The Cumberland and Tennessee Rivers afford lines of transportation by which an army may turn your right with ease and rapidity, and any surplus you may be able to spare from the left flank on the Mississippi can well be used to secure you against such movements.[73]

5

"Push forward the completion of the works and their armament with the utmost activity"

November 1861

Conditions at Fort Donelson, by the opening of November, had improved little, if any. Writing from his home in Clarksville, Senator Gustavus A. Henry sent another harried report to General Johnston. Henry had just returned from an inspection of Forts Henry and Donelson with Major Jeremy Gilmer. The Senator once again complained about the lack of progress made as Fort Donelson was in "very bad condition."[1] Henry railed that no work had been done "of any account."[2] Though he was hopeful that Lieutenant Dixon, whom he described as "a young officer of great energy," would soon have Fort Donelson adequately defended.[3]

During this time, as ordered, Major Gilmer focused his energy on the defense of Clarksville. Clarksville was essential to the Confederate war effort as the town was a major strategic transportation and communications hub. Lending to Clarksville's significance was its location on the Cumberland River and the presence of the Memphis, Clarksville, and Louisville railroad. Also, the town and outlying areas were significant due to its rich agricultural and iron manufacturing capabilities.

As Gilmer attended to his duties laying out the Clarksville defenses, the work of moving forward the defenses of Fort Donelson were left to Lieutenant Dixon. As Major Gilmer surveyed the area for the security of Clarksville, General Johnston sent him some much-needed support. Johnston ordered Brigadier General Lloyd Tilghman, commanding forces at Hopkinsville, Kentucky, to move his troops to Clarksville. Once at Clarksville, Tilghman was to have his men engage in constructing the works that Engineer Gilmer had laid out. The Maury Artillery, a light artillery battery raised in September, comprised mainly of men from northwest Maury County, Tennessee, were sent to join Tilghman as well.[4]

By the second day of the month, Lieutenant Colonel Milton Haynes of the Tennessee Artillery Corps reported to General Johnston that the obstruction of the Cumberland at Ingram's Shoals had been completed. Haynes reported that "three barges, '120 by 27 by 8, filled with stone'" and also two smaller ones were sunk near the bar.[5] Haynes assured Johnston that the obstructions would be effective against the gunboats for any rise less than 12 feet over the present stage. The boats contained 1,200 tons of stone, and the vessels themselves were made of 6-inch scantling. Further mentioning that it might be possible in a few weeks that the current which sets in over the head of the bar between the sunken boats may wash out a channel which could easily be closed by sinking a small boat in the new channel.[6]

Meanwhile, downstream at the shoals as Dixon finished his work, a Federal gunboat approached. W.B. Machen at Princeton, Kentucky, reported to General Lloyd Tilghman at Clarksville notifying him that the gunboat advanced up to the obstruction on the Cumberland and fired "a good many heavy guns, but for what purpose not known" and that "She is a new boat, and has the appearance of being much more formidable than those heretofore seen in the river, mounting much heavier guns."[7] Likewise, Lieutenant Dixon reported seeing the gunboat as he completed his work.[8]

The reports were concerning. Federal activity down the twin rivers was indeed intensifying. On October 30, Commander William David Porter and his boat the *New Era* passed up the Cumberland River. The *New Era* arrived at Ingram's Shoals at 6 a.m. on the following day. Porter reported that he "found the river completely obstructed by sunken coal barges."[9] Porter believed the Confederates abandoned their work approximately an hour before his arrival and had left "in such haste that part of their work was unfinished."[10]

Despite all of Dixon's efforts to the contrary, and only three days after Colonel Haynes's report assuring Johnston of the completion of the obstructions, on November 5, Lieutenant Seth Ledyard Phelps with the *Conestoga* rendered the Ingram Shoals obstructions ineffective as he was able to pass over them. Phelps states, "I succeeded in passing with this vessel over the stone boats sunk by the rebels upon Ingram's Shoals, in the Cumberland River, 7 miles above Eddyville, and also others laid at the channel near the head of Line Island, 2 miles below the Tennessee State line, crushing one by running upon it, and proceeded up to within a few miles of Dover."[11]

As Gilmer continued his duties at Clarksville, he studied the best possible places to defend the city. In a November 3, report to Lieutenant Colonel W.W. Mackall, Johnston's Assistant Adjutant General, he recommended that the defenses for Clarksville should begin as far down as Fort Donelson. Gilmer stated, "Our efforts for resisting gunboats should be concentrated there, and to this end Captain Dixon will do everything in his power to hasten forward the works at that point."[12] Gilmer went on to give his entire opinion of the matter; he fully believed there were many advantages to constructing defenses thirteen miles beyond Donelson at Lineport.[13] Nevertheless, in Gilmer's view, since the defenses at Donelson were "partially built, and the place susceptible of a good defense landward, I advised Captain Dixon to retain the position and construct the additional defenses as rapidly as possible."[14] With the submission of Gilmer's findings, the position intended to protect the cities of Clarksville and Nashville from Federal invasion on the Cumberland River was now firmly fixed at Fort Donelson. As Gilmer closed his correspondence with Mackall, realizing the enormity of his task, the major requested Mackall "to send him written authority to employ negro labor for throwing up defenses at Nashville, Clarksville, and Fort Donelson, as well as at all other points where defensive works may be found necessary."[15]

As part of his plan to stop any move up the Cumberland toward Clarksville and Nashville by Federal gunboats, while at Clarksville, Gilmer employed T.J. Glenn, a competent engineer, to build an obstruction just below and under the guns of Fort Donelson.[16] Glenn's instructions were to locate the obstructions approximately 1,000 to 1,200 yards below the river batteries. Glenn was ordered to sink trees, by attaching anchors of big rocks to their roots, thereby sinking them in their upright positions, so that the tops would rise above the water.[17]

The following day (Monday, November 4), Gilmer writing again to Mackall, requested additional guns for a proper defense at Donelson. The engineer informed Mackall that at present, there were only four 32-pounders and the two naval carronades. The major shared his belief that this armament was insufficient "against a fleet of gunboats."[18] Gilmer had determined that an adequate defense of Fort Donelson, would require the number of guns to be doubled.[19] Gilmer recommended "4 additional 32-pounders and 2 of heavier caliber, 8 inch Columbiads, or long range Parrott guns, all with garrison carriages."[20]

After further planning, Major Gilmer and Lieutenant Dixon[21] ordered an abatis to be made to protect the rear at Fort Donelson. Due to a scarcity of supplies, on November 5, as "we have not a sufficient number of axes," Lieutenant Colonel Randal MacGavock submitted a requisition for 60 axes and helves to accomplish the assignment.[22]

MacGavock also reported that he had five companies of infantry "tolerably armed but not so well drilled" and that "we have there now Colonel [Nathan B.] Forrest's command of cavalry, one company of light artillery, [Maney's Battery] with seven guns, and a sufficient amount of heavy guns."[23]

While trying to bolster their Western defenses, Jefferson Davis, who was running unopposed, was officially elected president of the Confederacy. On the same day as the election, Davis received an unexpected letter of resignation from 1st Division commander Major General Leonidas Polk at Columbus, dated November 6. In the communication, Polk explained that he was reluctant to assume the position to begin with, but now that "our mutual friend" Johnston is in place, Polk asked to be allowed to "resume my former pursuits."[24] In the letter, Polk, referring to Johnston's ability, states, "a more judicious selection could not have been made."[25]

Before Davis could respond to Polk, two significant events occurred. The first, Federal troops, on November 7, under Brigadier General Ulysses S. Grant, attacked Confederate positions across from Columbus, Kentucky, at Belmont, Missouri. In the end, the battle achieved little, only giving men of both sides their baptism of fire. In a telegraph to President Davis, Polk claimed: "a complete rout" on the part of Grant's troops.[26] Second, four days after the Battle of Belmont, Polk and two staff members were inspecting their positions at Columbus. As Polk watched a demonstration of the biggest gun on his line, the "Lady Polk," a massive 6.4-inch rifled columbiad, produced at the Tredegar Iron Works, the gun exploded. Unlike many of the crew, Polk's life was spared, but he was wounded to the point of having to relinquish command temporarily. With Polk's incapacitation, Brigadier General Gideon Pillow took command of the 1st Division. A major of the 11th Louisiana, serving at Columbus, shared his observations of Polk and Pillow, "I see Genls. Polk and Pillow from time to time, they are both very polite to me always; the army has no confidence in either of them."[27]

By November 12, Davis had rejected Polk's resignation. The President stated, "You are master of the subjects involved in the defense of the Mississippi and its contiguous territory. You have just won a victory which gives you fresh claim to the affection and confidence of your troops."[28] At Davis's urging, Polk retained his command, but for the time being, he needed time to recuperate from his injuries.

In the meantime, despite Dixon's efforts, progress at Fort Donelson remained at a standstill. On Thursday, November 7, Senator Henry once again decried the state of affairs. Henry began by stating that the "condition of things at Fort Donelson demand immediate attention."[29] Henry pointed out that there were only "about 800 cavalry and 500 infantry and a great want of organization and drill."[30] Henry pushed for the deployment of 500 additional infantry to the fort. The Senator went on to complain that since his last letter, seven days earlier, no progress had been made to protect the guns. Henry anticipated that no work would be done until additional troops were sent there. Henry found Lieutenant Dixon to be "ready and willing to work," but he was not equipped with adequate resources to get his job done.[31]

Despite the outcries for men, arms, and the sorry state of affairs at Fort Donelson, General Johnston, who was more focused on his Bowling Green defenses, obviously not comprehending the reality of the conditions of the Cumberland River fortification, wrote to Richmond on November 8, claiming that the Donelson garrison "is in a state of defense, having, besides other guns of less caliber, four 32 pounders, and a sufficient garrison."[32]

A week later, Governor Harris informed General Johnston that he had conferred fully with Senator Henry about the defenses on the Cumberland below the Cumberland Iron Works. Harris reminded the general, "Such work not only involves the protection of the citizens in that quarter, but the protection of the iron works which are at this time an absolute national necessity."[33]

By the middle of November, Colonel Heiman was still in command at Forts Henry and Donelson. General Leonidas Polk realized that it would be advantageous to have a man with greater military aptitude and experience to command the twin river defenses. Polk had his eye set on Brigadier General Lloyd Tilghman then commanding at Clarksville.[34] Tilghman, a resident of Paducah, Kentucky, had just recently been promoted to brigadier general (October 18).[35] Tilghman was an 1836 graduate of West Point, and even though he resigned from the service the same year, he did serve in the Mexican War. He had extensive experience as a construction engineer on several railroads.[36] Upon appointment to brigadier general, Tilghman was assigned by General Johnston to the command of the troops at Hopkinsville, Kentucky, then was sent to Clarksville, Tennessee.[37]

During the next week, Johnston began to realize that many problems were fronting his Cumberland river garrison. On November 17, nine days after his favorable report to Richmond, Johnston ordered Brigadier General Lloyd Tilghman to take command at Forts Henry and Donelson. Tilghman was instructed to "push forward the completion of the works and their armament with the utmost activity."[38] This order came as a result of great dissatisfaction with the progress at Fort Donelson and the resulting pressure from Senator Henry and Governor Harris. In the communication, Johnston's adjutant, W.W. Mackall, stated, "The general [Johnston] regrets to hear that there has been heretofore gross negligence in this respect—the commander at Fort Donelson [MacGavock] away from his post nightly and the officer in charge of the field batteries frequently absent [Dixon]."[39] As Mackall continued his instructions to Tilghman, he emphatically stated, "you will push forward the completion of the works and their armament with the utmost activity, and to this end will apply to the citizens of the surrounding country for assistance in labor, for which you will give them certificates for the amounts due for such labor."[40]

By November 18, the idea of utilizing slave labor was considered as a possible workforce in the construction of the Fort Donelson defenses. Major Gilmer expressed his opinion, "In imminent danger, the brigadier-general commanding Forts Donelson and

Henry might be authorized to press all neighborhood negro labor into service, but under other circumstances I do not think that the labor of troops and slaves can be combined to any advantage."[41] Writing a few days later, Gilmer reiterated, that "In regard to labor, I would suggest that the batteries at Fort Donelson can be completed sooner by the troops, perhaps, than if an effort were made to collect negroes for the purpose from the surrounding country."[42]

Apparently, there was some attempt to impress slaves in the area for work on the Donelson defenses. Writing from Humphreys County the following month, a citizen, Henry Yarbrough wrote,

> We have had a draft among the negroes here to go to Fort Donaldson to ditch. They made a call for 130 from this County, and when they were counted up there was but 146 in the County. Esq., C.E. Harris detailed every negro in the County, leaving one at every place where they have negroes. So there was 3 of mine detailed to go. I was a little too sharp for them. I called in Dr. Wilkerson, gave them some physic, and then gave me a certificate. I enclosed it to Gen. Tillman and kept my sick negroes at home, so you understand how that trick was worked off.[43]

On the night of November 19, a company of infantry, commanded by Captain Cyrus A. Sugg, left Clarksville on a steamer to "join McGavock's battalion."[44] Third Lieutenant Charles Tyler said they left Clarksville at 10:00 p.m. After a four-hour journey down the Cumberland, they arrived at the landing at Fort Donelson at 2:00 a.m. On arrival, Tyler remembered climbing "the muddy hill to the fort" and then "prepared to play our part in the great drama."[45]

By November 21, Lieutenant Dixon informed Gilmer that the emplacements of the Lower Battery were now complete and that he was preparing to mount the 32-pounders in their permanent places. Dixon writes,

> I have completed the new battery on the river, and I am at present preparing to mount the pieces in it. I have also laid out a little work on the ridge about 100 yards back of the encampment, and have mounted the two 9-pounders there. I have had the trees felled around the encampment so as to form a very good abatis. That portion of the field where the dragoons were encamped when you were here I will cause to be obstructed by *trous-de-loup* and dragging small trees over the open space. I wish you would get the general to give an order to press labor, for it cannot be obtained here any other way.[46]

Expressing his concern for finishing the works, Dixon added, "There are not more than 200 troops here fit for duty; all the rest are sick or have leave of absence."[47]

In this same communication, Dixon informed Gilmer that he [Dixon] had received direct orders from Brigadier General Pillow, who was still temporarily commanding the division, to leave his duties at Fort Donelson and to report to Fort Henry. Upon arrival at Fort Henry, Dixon was to survey a site across the Tennessee River [to become Fort Heiman] that would protect Fort Henry's flank.[48]

This incident is demonstrative of the miscommunication which occurred in the Confederate command structure. Brigadier General Gideon Pillow took it upon himself to issue orders to Lieutenant Dixon, bypassing Chief Engineer Gilmer. As Gilmer heard about this blatant disregard of his authority, he was greatly angered. In response, Gilmer immediately fired off communication to General Johnston's headquarters requesting that Pillow be reined in as orders should be sent through the proper channels in the future.[49]

Since Dixon was overwhelmed with his duties, and the mounting of the guns was given a higher priority than training the men who serve them, Lieutenant Hugh L.

Bedford, who had been sent to Donelson as the instructor of artillery, volunteered to get the guns mounted in the new lower battery.[50]

To strengthen the fortifications against Federal advance up the Tennessee River, General Pillow appealed to the Alabama defense committee to assist in constructing defensive works. Pillow implored, "If Alabama will furnish the means of constructing these works and the forces to garrison them, with arms, &c. the troops from that State will be placed in them, thus allowing her to hold the keys of the gate-way into her own territory."[51]

Dixon did receive some good news. The Alabama defense committee recognized the value of Pillow's request and informed Lieutenant Dixon that a contingent from Alabama would soon be added to his workforce. Gilmer writes, "He was at the same time informed that a large force of slaves, with troops to protect them, from Alabama, would report to him for the work, which was to be pushed to completion as early as possible."[52]

It took Tilghman about a week to complete his duties at Clarksville and assume command of Forts Henry and Donelson. Tilghman arrived at the twin rivers on November 21.

Upon arrival, Tilghman found the soldiers at Fort Donelson engaged in the back-breaking labor of felling trees for the abatis above the river batteries. That evening, Lieutenant Colonel MacGavock recorded this brief but descriptive entry in his diary: "passed the whole day at Ft. Donelson superintending the work on the fortifications."[53]

The day following Tilghman's arrival (November 22), he surveyed the situation at both Forts Henry and Donelson. Tilghman reporting to Johnston's headquarters, stated, "[I] do not admire the aspect of things. I must have more heavy guns for both places at once, not less than four for each; one also of long range for each, say sixty-fours [6.4-inch rifles]."[54]

On November 23, Lieutenant Colonel MacGavock arrived at General Johnston's headquarters at Bowling Green. In a nighttime conference with the general, MacGavock laid out the situation at Fort Donelson. MacGavock stated, "I laid before him the defenseless condition of the Cumberland."[55] In response, Johnston immediately ordered Colonel John W. Head's 30th Tennessee Infantry to Fort Donelson.[56]

Much like General Pillow's earlier interference with Lieutenant Dixon, Brigadier General Tilghman now stopped Mr. Glenn's work on the Cumberland River obstructions below the Water Battery. Gilmer was again furious at these interruptions and interference with his work. Gilmer instructed Lieutenant Dixon to "not let his [Mr. Glenn's] operations be interfered with."[57]

To maintain the defenses, the troops gathered at Fort Donelson would require much of the resources collected and distributed from the Nashville Depot. Cheatham, Watson, & Company, later known as the Sycamore Powder Mills, provided much if not all of the gunpowder for the River Batteries.[58] In the three months of September through November 1861, the powder mill provided 192,550 pounds of cannon gunpowder to the Nashville Ordnance Department.[59] While the Cheatham, Watson, & Company were producing gunpowder, Ellis & Moore and Company in Nashville were producing 32-pounder solid shot, and the Tennessee State Penitentiary produced many artillery related items, including shoes, ammunition boxes, cannon rammers, sponges, handspikes, water buckets, and sabots.[60]

On November 27, MacGavock arrived at Fort Donelson with Head's regiment. Following MacGavock, the 30th Tennessee left the steamer at the landing, entered the fort, and in proximity with the other companies gathered there, made camp above the river batteries. As Private Joseph Hinkle of Company A, 30th Tennessee, surveyed the surroundings, he emphatically concluded, "I looked upon Fort Donelson as a death-trap."[61]

Wesley Smith Dorris of the 30th Tennessee remarked, "We disembarked from the boat [the *General Anderson*] stretched our tents dispared [disparaged] our humble meal and lay down for the night. Morning came with torrents of Rain falling which continued for several days having no plank nor straw in our tents but having to lay on the wet ground."[62] Private Joseph Hinkle, described his plight after arriving at Fort Donelson:

> When the troops were all embarked upon the boats we pulled out for Fort Donelson, and arriving there, we went into quarters and slept upon the damp ground. That night, still being unwell, I drank a cup of briar-root tea, and the next morning I was all broken out with the measles. After suffering for several days and not improving much, I asked permission from Captain Bidwell to return home until I should get better. I hardly know how I got on the boat at Fort Donelson, but I did get on it, and made out to get home. It was extremely cold weather. If exposure would kill a man with the measles I ought to have died.[63]

On entering the camp, MacGavock discovered the measles had decimated the infantry companies under his command. MacGavock found many men on the sick list and learned that many had died. However, MacGavock seemed to be encouraged as he noted in his journal that General Lloyd Tilghman has taken command of the river forts and that "he seems to be a man of great energy of character and a good soldier."[64]

As MacGavock settled back into his duties, he refocused on his work of forming a new regiment. To raise more troops, MacGavock posted a recruiting advertisement in the November 28 issue of the *Nashville Union and American*:

> Attention Volunteers
>
> In compliance with an order issued by Gens. JOHNSTON & POLK, I am now forming a regiment at Ft. Donelson to serve twelve months. Six well-armed and equipped companies are now in camp and I need four more companies to complete the regiment. Captains of companies who desire to get into a regiment will please report to me at this post, or to Lt. George Jones at the Sewanee House, Nashville.
>
> Lt. Col. R.W. McGavock Commanding at Ft. Donelson[65]

The advertisement looks to be at odds with the actual condition of the soldiers already at Fort Donelson. The six "well-armed and equipped" companies seemed to be quite a stretch from the actual state of things. Nevertheless, from this time until late December, MacGavock put his energy into raising the companies needed for the new regiment.

6

"It has nothing to prepossess a man favorably unless wind is a recommendation"

December 1861

"It has nothing to prepossess a man favorably unless wind is a recommendation," stated an unimpressed William Maurey, as he marched into Fort Donelson at 8:00 a.m. on December 10, 1861.[1] Maurey's company, from Springfield, Tennessee, commanded by Captain Matthew Fyke, had just arrived and was part of the buildup occurring at the Cumberland River bastion.[2] As Fyke's Robertson Countians climbed the hill into the fort, they were greeted by the barren, windswept terrain, which was by then starting to take the shape of a military encampment.

Tilghman, by this time, had completed a thorough survey of the defenses of both Forts Henry and Donelson. He was in the process of making a complete report, but in a preliminary statement, he sent his observations to E.D. Blake, Assistant Adjutant General for the 1st Division of the Western Department. Similar to his November 22, communication to Johnston, Tilghman wrote, "I will state here, however, that it is but too plain that instant and powerful steps must be taken to strengthen not only the two forts in the way of work, but the armament must be increased in number of pieces of artillery as well as in weight of metal."[3]

Following Tilghman's plea for additional guns, on November 24, Gilmer instructed Dixon to extend the parapet of the lower battery as one to two other 32-pounder guns would be sent there.[4] Major Gilmer then appealed to Captain Moses H. Wright, directing the Nashville Ordnance Department, for additional armament for Fort Donelson and Clarksville. Gilmer requested "four 8-inch columbiads or, if these are not to be had, then other guns of long range, four 32-pounder guns all to be delivered at Clarksville, Tenn., with platforms, chassis and carriages complete, also 50 rounds of ammunition."[5] The 8-inch columbiads were unobtainable, but by December 4, the four 32-pounders had arrived at Clarksville, and at least two of them were being forwarded to Lieutenant Dixon at Fort Donelson.[6]

As Dixon made the adjustments to lengthen the parapets of the Lower Battery, work crews followed the plans and extended them up the rise from the river and then across the lower base of the ridge. Sometime around mid- to late December, four additional 32-pounder guns arrived at Fort Donelson and were mounted in the works.[7]

As the fatigue parties labored on these works, they dug into the hillside, and as they removed soil, it was heaped in piles to the front to form a straight parapet "with twelve traverses to protect the guns."[8] The result was a parapet approximately 16 feet wide at the base and almost 9 feet wide at the top. Archaeologist Lee Hanson gives additional detail, "It was 4 feet high on the interior with a 96° interior slope and 40° exterior slope. The top of the parapet sloped 8° away from the gun position."[9]

By December 2, the encampment had started taking shape. Private Wesley Dorris of the 30th Tennessee described,

> We did a great deal of work clearing up the ground for our encampment and other purposes and the 2nd of December found us arranged reglgentally [regimentally] in our tents and soon got straw and plank for our tents had some very wet weather while we were in our tents which made it very disagreeable to us some few had stoves and some made places which were beneficial as it was now dead of winter.[10]

Within the week, Dorris reported that they had received orders "to procede to build winter quarters the work progressed as the weather was now good which was fortionate for us."[11] Major Gilmer, writing to his wife back in Savannah, Georgia, also described the warmth of the season, "for the past week we have had very warm unseasonable weather; but today (December 11) winter seems to be upon us again. Being nearly mid-winter we must expect snow and ice soon."[12]

As fortifications continued to go up, on December 10, Tilghman received a letter from 1860 presidential candidate John Bell of the Cumberland Iron Works. Apparently, Bell had been pointed with Tilghman in previous communications stressing the importance of the ironworks to the Confederacy and alleging that Tilghman and Johnston were not taking its defense with the seriousness it deserved. However, by the time of the letter, Bell seems to have changed his opinion and was satisfied with the defensive measures being taken.[13]

The following day, to further strengthen the position on the rivers, Johnston received some much-desired news from Lieutenant Colonel Josiah Gorgas, Chief of the Confederate Ordnance Bureau in Richmond. Gorgas informed the general that he had ordered two 10-inch columbiad smoothbores and one 5.82-inch rifled columbiad to be delivered via Captain Wright at Nashville. Later in the month, on December 24, Lieutenant Colonel Gorgas informed Johnston that he was sending two more 32-pounders for the Cumberland and Tennessee rivers.[14]

Christmas Eve at Fort Donelson was business as usual. On this day, ten companies, mostly from nearby Montgomery and Dickson counties, were organized into the 49th Tennessee regiment and elected James E. Bailey colonel and his law partner, Alfred Robb, lieutenant colonel. Wesley Dorris of the 30th Tennessee wrote, "Christmas eave but looks little like it."[15] Dorris went on to complain that General Tilghman had issued an order "prohibiting female visitors." "Gross humaity [humanity]," exclaimed Dorris.[16]

As the 49th Tennessee was completing its organization, Lieutenant Colonel Randal MacGavock's assignment of organizing a regiment was completed. On December 24, while the 49th Tennessee was electing officers, MacGavock turned over ten full companies to General Tilghman for formal organization into a regiment. Tilghman, following militia regulations of the time, called an election for colonel. Before leaving Fort Donelson to return to the 10th Tennessee at Fort Henry, MacGavock gave a "brief but soul stirring speech" in which he set forth the circumstances that brought him to raise the regiment and told the companies to be particular in electing their field officers as their comfort in camp and safety in battle depended on it.[17]

Even though MacGavock was not technically a candidate, he said his name was "used."[18] Much to MacGavock's surprise, Captain George W. Stacker was elected colonel of the new regiment. According to MacGavock, the reason Stacker secured the office was that his company and those of Captain Cyrus A. Sugg, and Captain Harrison C. Lockhart formed a "combination between them," and the three companies voted solidly for Stacker.[19] Although MacGavock was not a candidate, he was nominated and received "nearly half the votes of the regiment, and that of nine-tenths of the officers, all of the old companies, and every sick man in the hospital voted for me," stated MacGavock.[20] He added that "great dissatisfaction prevailed about the result and General Tilghman was very angry, because he knew that Stacker was incompetent to command the regiment."[21] With Stacker's election, the regiment was designated the 50th Tennessee.

Two days after the election, MacGavock wrote that Captain Sugg was elected lieutenant colonel and Captain Lockhart, major. MacGavock stated, "The latter named individual was the chief mover in the combination. He acted with great duplicity towards me.... I denounced him a scoundrel before his own company."[22] The following day, Lieutenant Colonel MacGavock left Fort Donelson to rejoin the 10th Tennessee Regiment at Fort Henry.

A few days later, General Tilghman remarked that "the regiments of Colonels Bailey and Stacker have only just organized, and freed now somewhat from feeling themselves bound to court the goodwill of their men in order to secure their election, aided by a positive order against granting any furloughs, I hope to be able to restore matters to a more wholesome state."[23]

The garrison troops of Fort Donelson were formed into a brigade commanded by Colonel John W. Head of the 30th Tennessee. The brigade was comprised of the 30th Tennessee, commanded by Major J.J. Turner; the 49th Tennessee commanded by Colonel James E. Bailey; and the 50th Tennessee, commanded by Colonel George Stacker.

After organization, the men of the 30th, 49th, and 50th regiments near the opening of 1862 were daily employed "building quarters, commissaries, and quartermaster buildings, roads, fortifications, and water batteries."[24] Lieutenant Hugh Bedford explains,

> The work for the completion of the defenses and for the comfort of the soldiers, was pushed on as rapidly as the means at hand would permit. There was no lagging, nor lukewarmness, nor shirking of duty. As one of the many evidences of the zeal manifested by the garrison, I would state that whenever a detail for work of any magnitude was made from any of the regiments, a field officer usually accompanied it, in order to secure promptness and concert of action. This, I believe, was the invariable rule with the 49th Tenn.[25]

Toward the end of the year, General Johnston sent 1st Lieutenant Jacob Culbertson, then acting as Chief of Artillery at Bowling Green, to Fort Donelson to assist with the heavy artillery.

The thirty-three-year-old Kentucky native graduated seventh in his 1850 West Point class. Upon graduation, Culbertson was appointed 2nd Lieutenant on December 11, 1850, and entered service with the 4th U.S. Artillery. He was promoted to 1st lieutenant on February 14, 1856, and served in that capacity until he resigned from the U.S. Army on January 10, 1857.[26] During his time with the 4th Artillery, he was stationed at Fort Columbus, New York Harbor; Fort Mackinac, Michigan; Fort Brown, Texas; and Fort McRae, Florida.[27]

Culbertson was appointed 1st lieutenant of the Artillery Corps on October 16, 1861,

A replica cabin constructed at Fort Donelson similar to the quarters which housed the Confederate troops (authors' photograph).

and reported to General Albert Sidney Johnston. At Fort Donelson January 13, 1862, General Lloyd Tilghman reported to Headquarters at Bowling Green, Kentucky, that Lieutenant Culbertson was there and acting as Chief of Artillery. Tilghman stated, "His ability is unquestionable and his services invaluable and indispensable."[28] Tilghman cautioned that as a lieutenant in the regular army, Culbertson is ranked by all of the Captains forming the artillery battalion, and the situation "is not as conducive to the best interests of the service as I would desire."[29] Tilghman recommended Culbertson to be promoted to Captain in the Provisional Army.[30] On January 29, Culbertson was promoted to the rank of temporary major for service with volunteer troops. It's possible this communication did not reach him, as he was known as "Captain Culbertson" and signed as "Captain of Artillery, Commanding Batteries."[31]

Through December, the men at Fort Donelson were busily engaged in the back-breaking manual labor of chopping wood, digging trenches, building huts and fortifications, and mounting guns. Wesley Smith Dorris commented that on January 3, "we have got into our quarters and have to drill 4 hours each day principally in the manel [manual] of arms."[32] This was hardly what they had imagined themselves signing up for a few months earlier. Yet, the safety of their state and even their very lives depended on it. As 1861 came to a close, perhaps the solemn words of a private of the 49th Tennessee betray the sadness of the soldier's heart: "Nothing to cheer or enliven."[33]

7

"I think we can tan them
up here if they come"

January 1862

The New Year dawned on the rivers with increased enemy activity, calls for more men and supplies, and a sense of urgency to strengthen the fortifications and mount heavier guns. Throughout January, artillery, ammunition, and supplies began flowing in almost daily from the Nashville Ordnance Depot.

On the first day of the year, Lieutenant Jacob Culbertson received for the 32-pounders at Fort Donelson a shipment of 96 blank cartridges containing 6 pounds of powder each and 343 rounds of solid shot. E.R. Glascock made the cartridges, and the solid shot were made by Ellis & Moore and T.M. Brennan all of Nashville. Before the end of the first week of January, another 154 32-pounder shells with attached wooden sabots were received by Culbertson at Donelson.[1]

By January 2, Tilghman was encouraged as he conveyed "favorable progress in all matters under my command."[2] Tilghman also expressed optimism as he reported, "A most satisfactory progress has been made in the main fortification, an enclosed work. A few more days will close up the gap and give us a very good work."[3] As Tilghman continued, he reported that he still had nearly 2,000 unarmed men in his command. The general explained that the unarmed men at Donelson were insufficient "to man one-half of the lines within the fortification, much less to effect anything at points which command my whole work."[4] Tilghman continued by saying that the entire command was now comfortably housed for the winter. "The houses are admirable built, well suited, and present an appearance of real comfort that will compare favorable with any command in the field."[5]

To further increase Tilghman's sense of preparedness, on the same day that he informed his superiors of satisfactory progress, a piece of super heavy ordnance arrived at Fort Donelson. A massive 10-inch columbiad had been sent to Lieutenant Culbertson at Fort Donelson from Captain Lardner Gibbon at the Tredegar Iron Works by way of the Nashville Ordnance Depot.[6] An iron carriage and chassis accompanied the columbiad along with other necessary components for mounting, including eight traverse segments, a center ring, a pintle plate, a pintle pin, an elevating screw, and eight tie plates. Also, in the shipment were necessary items for firing the gun, such as two priming wires, a gunner's gimlet, two maneuvering handspikes, and two roller handspikes.[7] The detail struggled to unload the six and a half ton columbiad and move it from the landing to mount in the river batteries. While the columbiad was being unloaded, Lieutenant Colonel Gorgas,

Letter from Lieutenant Colonel Josiah Gorgas to General Leonidas Polk at Columbus, Kentucky. This letter informs Polk that a 6.4-inch rifled columbiad is being sent to replace the "Lady Polk," a 6.4-inch rifled columbiad which exploded. Gorgas is careful to point out that this gun has been "well proved" and was constructed "of different kinds of iron from the 6.4-inch columbiad last sent you." Despite the differences, this gun, the "Belmont" also exploded at Island No. 10 (Josiah Gorgas service record).

Chief of the Confederate Ordnance Bureau, notified General Albert Sidney Johnston that he had ordered a 6.4-inch rifled columbiad to be sent to Nashville from Tredegar.[8]

The Confederates were not getting their river defenses in shape any too soon as on January 6, U.S. Navy Lieutenant Seth Ledyard Phelps, commanding the timber-clad

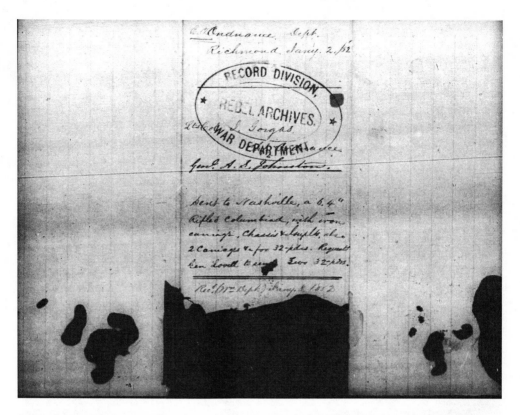

Letter from Lieutenant Colonel Josiah Gorgas, chief of the Confederate Ordnance Bureau, dated January 2, 1862, informing General Albert Sidney Johnston that a 6.4-inch rifled columbiad is being sent to Nashville (Josiah Gorgas service record).

Conestoga, undertook an excursion toward Fort Henry and made it as far as the Tennessee state line. Phelps reported:

> The rebels are industriously perfecting their means of defense both at Dover and Fort Henry. At Fort Donelson (near Dover) they have placed obstructions in the river, 1½ miles below their battery, on the left bank and in the bend where the battery comes in sight. These obstructions consist of trees chained together and sunk across the river with the butts upstream, the heads floating near the surface, and are pointed. Placed as they are reported to be, any attempt to remove them must be made under a severe fire and where there is very little room for covering boats. The bend is a very sharp one and the river not more than 150 yards wide. The battery upon the right bank is upon a hill one-half mile back from the river and considerably below the fort upon the left bank. It can be seen, I am told, but 1 mile. Four weeks since they had four 32s mounted on the hill, and had a large force of negroes at work. The fire of gunboats here would be at a bad angle. On these narrow streams, with their usually contracted channels, it would appear to me very necessary to have the assistance of mortars in reducing earthworks as strong and complete as those on the Tennessee and Cumberland have been made. The forts are placed, especially on the Cumberland, where no very great range can be had, and they can only be attacked in one narrow and fixed line. Shot can dismount their guns (all en barbette), nothing more. Our shell must burst at the moment, or they pass harmless, while there is little room to regulate distance nicely.[9]

The following Monday, January 6, a substantial shipment of 154 32-pounder shells, attached to wooden sabots, arrived. A week later, Culbertson began receiving

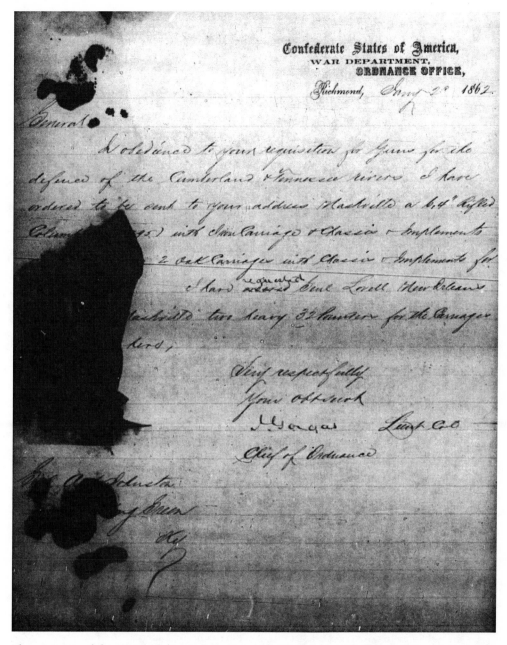

The contents of the Gorgas letter to Johnston identify the identification of the 6.4-inch rifle as #1295. The gun was sent with iron carriage, chassis, and implements (Josiah Gorgas service record).

ammunition for the columbiad. The Nashville Ordnance Depot had sent forty-eight 10-inch solid shot and fifty-two 10-inch shells. Ellis & Moore produced the solid shot, and the shells were made by T.M. Brennan, both of Nashville.[10]

On January 7, Lieutenant Colonel MacGavock wrote in his journal that an Alabama regiment (27th Alabama) had recently arrived and were encamped near Coleman's Hill (the location which would become Fort Heiman), "which is above and opposite the fort

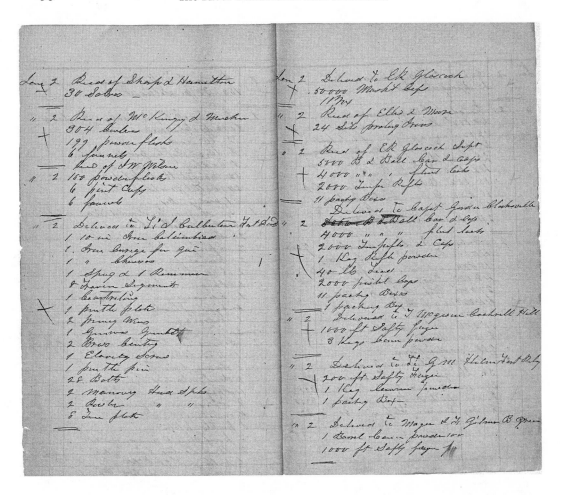

Records from the Nashville Ordnance Department on January 2, 1862, show the 10-inch columbiad delivered to Lieutenant Jacob Culbertson at Fort Donelson (Record of Receipts and Deliveries, 1861–1865).

and where they propose making a fortification." MacGavock went on to state that "Several hundred negroes are there to work on the fortifications."[11]

As work crawled forward, the weather was uncooperative. MacGavock complained, "This has been an exceedingly inclement and disagreeable day, both above and under foot."[12] Despite the nasty weather, a detachment of the Alabama soldiers and "negroes" were sent to Dover to construct telegraph lines between Forts Henry and Donelson.[13]

As the month progressed, within the four days of January 15–18, Culbertson continued to receive daily deliveries from the Ordnance Depot. These shipments contained additional stores for the 32-pounders and the 10-inch columbiad. For the 32-pounders, 100 blank cartridges were received containing six pounds of powder each, 254 fuses for the 32-pounder shells, 1,000 small friction primers, 500 large friction primers, and 37 stands of grapeshot. For the 10-inch columbiad, there were 90 blank cartridges, each containing sixteen pounds of powder, and ten blank rounds containing twenty-pound charges, 50 fuse plugs, and 130 paper fuses (fifty 20-second fuses, fifty 28-second fuses, and thirty 36-second fuses). Culbertson also received ordnance for the 8-inch gun, commanded by Lieutenant Peter Stankiewicz. These included 50 8-inch fixed shells, 50 8-inch fuse plugs, and 80 8-inch paper fuses. The shipment was concluded with 990 friction primers and 25 signal rockets.[14]

To further bolster the Tennessee defenses, on January 15, Lieutenant Colonel Milton Haynes of the Tennessee Artillery Corps received orders from Major General Leonidas Polk to leave Columbus, Kentucky, and to report to Brigadier General Tilghman at Fort Henry.[15]

By the time of the Civil War, Milton Andrews Haynes was an experienced soldier. Lieutenant Hugh Bedford called him "an accomplished artillerist."[16] He was graduated eighteenth in the West Point Class of 1838.[17] Upon graduation, he was commissioned a brevet 2nd lieutenant and assigned to the U.S. 3rd Artillery. Haynes was promoted to 2nd lieutenant on July 7, 1838.[18] Second Lieutenant Haynes served in the Florida War (1838–39) but resigned from the army on September 30, 1839.[19]

After leaving the army, Haynes returned to Tennessee and pursued a law career, with a six-year stint as a lawyer in Nashville (1840–46). While working in this occupation, he also served part of the time serving as the Assistant Adjutant General of the Tennessee Militia (1844–46).[20] With the coming of the Mexican War, Haynes again entered military service, enlisting on May 28, 1846, and served as captain of Company E, 1st Tennessee Mounted Infantry.[21]

At the outbreak of the Civil War, Haynes once again answered the call to arms. In May 1861, Haynes was commissioned a lieutenant colonel of the Tennessee Artillery Corps.[22] As Haynes assumed his role, he wrote a military manual for Tennessee troops, *Instructions in Field Artillery, Horse, and Foot.*[23]

Upon Haynes's arrival at Fort Henry, he was appointed chief of artillery and sent to Fort Donelson to take command of the guns there, while Tilghman attended to the artillery at Fort Henry. Haynes arrived at Fort Donelson on January 16. At Donelson, Haynes found only one artillery company, Maney's Light Artillery. In addition to Maney's Battery, there were two volunteer infantry companies under captains Beaumont and Bidwell. Beaumont's company had earlier been "slightly and imperfectly trained" by Lieutenant Watts of Taylor's Battery and received some instruction from Lieutenant Bedford as he had been attending to engineering duties.[24] Bidwell's company had to this point received no training on the guns.[25]

Bidwell's company was comprised of men from Robertson County who had enlisted at Springfield and went into camp at Red Springs in adjacent Macon County, where they were sworn into service. Bell G. Bidwell was elected captain of this company, which when the regiment was organized, became Company A, 30th Tennessee Infantry. Bidwell grew up in Robertson County and studied medicine at the University of Nashville but decided upon a career in law and in 1860 graduated from the law school at Cumberland University, Lebanon, Tennessee.[26] The 30th Tennessee regiment was organized October 22, at Red Springs, Macon County, Tennessee. Being ordered to Fort Donelson, the regiment arrived there with Lieutenant Colonel MacGavock on November 27, 1861.[27]

Haynes organized Maney's Battery and Beaumont's and Bidwell's infantry companies into a provisional artillery battalion. To get some training for the gunners, Haynes's requested that Major General Polk send artillery instructors from Columbus. In response, Polk sent Lieutenants George S. Martin and J.J. McDaniel.[28]

The forty-year-old 1st Lieutenant James J. McDaniel was a veteran of the Mexican War. He enlisted in Nashville on May 28, 1846, in Company L, 1st Tennessee Infantry, and gained the rank of 1st sergeant.[29] At the beginning of the Civil War, McDaniel enlisted in Nashville on 1 October 1, 1861, in the Nelson Artillery, and on October 28, was commissioned a 1st lieutenant and stationed at Columbus, Kentucky.[30]

George Saunders Martin, born January 3, 1840, was the son of George W. Martin and Narcissa Pillow (daughter of Gideon Pillow, Sr., and Anne Payne, and younger sister of General Gideon J. Pillow). The Pillows were prominent citizens of Maury County, Tennessee.[31] George was admitted to the Western Military Institute in Nashville, Tennessee, on January 27, 1856. He was listed in the Register of Cadets 1856–57 as a sergeant in the Sophomore class from Columbia, Tennessee.[32]

In May 1861, Martin volunteered for service in Columbia, Tennessee, and was elected 2nd corporal in Captain William R. Johnston's Company H, 1st (Feild's) Tennessee Infantry. By July, he had transferred to the artillery service, and on July 18, at Fort Pillow on the Mississippi River, he was appointed 2nd lieutenant. Martin was promoted to 1st lieutenant on August 12, 1861.[33]

Under the watchful eye of Lieutenant Colonel Haynes, lieutenants Martin and McDaniel began a thorough drilling schedule for Beaumont's and Bidwell's infantrymen. Bidwell's company was assigned to the Water Battery on January 16, 1862. Captain Bidwell stated,

> I was detached by order of General Tilghman, from the Thirtieth Tennessee Regiment for heavy artillery service about one month … before the attack on the fort. My company had at that time never drilled in heavy artillery nor knew anything about it, and I myself had never directed my attention to that branch of the service; but with the assistance of yourself [Captain Culbertson], Captain Dixon, and Lieutenants Martin and McDaniel, I was enabled to arrive at a tolerable degree of proficiency for myself and company by the time of the attack on the fort.[34]

After training on the guns for only one day, Wesley Smith Dorris of the 30th Tennessee stated they "Improved very fast in the art of gunnery."[35]

Haynes supervised, as Martin and McDaniel vigorously transformed these infantrymen into artillerymen. As the boys learned gunnery skills, firing at targets 1,000, 1,500, and 2,000 yards, they learned to elevate the guns correctly for the varying ranges.[36] These gunners also put chalk marks on the trees to help estimate the ranges.[37] In addition to their instruction in artillery, "every man in the battalion of artillery, nearly 300, who was fit for duty, was required to labor in mounting the guns, repairing and finishing the merlons, embrasures, and platforms," reported Haynes.[38]

On January 18, Private G.T. Williams of Bidwell's company, in a letter to his cousin, wrote, "We have changed our positions since you have heard from us last and have charge of the heavy artillery."[39] With confidence in their position, Williams stated, "I think we can tan them up here if they come."[40]

On January 19, MacGavock recorded in his journal that General Tilghman had just returned from Fort Donelson with the news that "Bushrod R. Johnson of the military school at Nashville" had arrived and assumed command of Fort Donelson as a brigadier general. MacGavock remarked that "This is an acquisition to the service and such a man is particularly needed among raw recruits."[41]

MacGavock, still raw from the election results with the 50th Tennessee noted that "Col. Stacker has resigned his commission today. Poor fellow, I pity him. He allowed himself to be made a fool of by those who wished to ride into position with the strength his company gave in a combination. Having accomplished this end they now force him to give way. Leaving his regiment at this time when danger is near and when he was ordered to Ft. Henry will ruin him."[42]

Several days later, MacGavock learned that after an election to fill the vacancy left by Stacker's resignation that Cyrus A. Sugg was elected colonel and H.C. Lockhart, lieutenant colonel. MacGavock recorded that he was visited by many officers of the 50th Tennessee Regiment, who expressed great dissatisfaction with the election results. According to MacGavock, they intended to petition Sugg and Lockhart to decline the positions. If they refused, the disgruntled officers planned to file a formal protest. (Evidently, they were unsuccessful in the effort as both Sugg and Lockhart remained in position).[43]

Throughout January, the Federal threat on the twin rivers escalated. On Tuesday, January 21, the Confederate steamer *Dunbar* was fired on about ten miles below Fort Henry. The boat turned about and was able to outdistance the gunboat, which allegedly fired at her 22 times.[44]

The Yankee gunboat reappeared nearer Fort Henry at about 11:00 a.m. the following day, firing from a point below Panther Island. One shell burst inside Fort Henry, and another passed through the chimneys of a steamer near the fort. The action caused one Confederate at Fort Henry to observe, "Their guns are very heavy and they have good artillerists. No one was hurt."[45]

As the Nashville Ordnance Depot continued supplying the defenses at Dover, on January 23, some three weeks after the 10-inch columbiad arrived, a massive 6.4-inch rifled columbiad (#1295) reached Fort Donelson from the Tredegar Iron Works in Virginia.[46] At Tredegar, a few of the 10-inch columbiad tubes were rifled to 6.4 inches.[47]

The reproduction 6.4-inch rifle of the Upper Battery showing the iron carriage manufactured by the Paulson Brothers Ordnance Corporation (authors' photograph).

Reuben Ross said that the 10-inch columbiad and the 6.4-inch rifle "appeared to have been cast in the same mould."[48] The gigantic tube, alone weighing 14,850 pounds,[49] was cast on November 4, 1861.[50] The barrel was accompanied by an iron gun carriage, chassis, a center ring, and according to the records, pintle and pintle plate, along with tie plates, 28 bolts, an elevating screw, handspikes, a linstock, a rammer, staves, a gunsight, and sponge, all manufactured at Tredegar.[51] Along with the big rifled gun, another 50 rounds of 32-pounder grapeshot and 960 large friction primers were delivered.[52]

Lieutenant Colonel Milton Haynes, commanding the batteries, wasted no time in mounting the 6.4-inch rifled columbiad. Haynes had the gun placed in the Upper Battery, where it had a great command of the river and a good line of sight to the bend where the gunboats would emerge. As Haynes had his men wrestling with the heavy iron gun carriage, chassis, and tube to get them in place, progress came to a halt when it was discovered that the pintle and pintle plate were missing. Without these two critical components, the gun could not be mounted. Haynes immediately sent his adjutant, Lieutenant George T. Moorman, to Nashville to obtain the required parts.[53] Moorman returned from Nashville on February 10, with the needed components. The big rifle was mounted in the Upper Battery and was put in working order the following day.[54]

In the meantime, General Johnston had sent Captain Jacob Powhatan Shuster to assist Haynes with the heavy batteries. Shuster entered the service early in the war; a date of commission as captain is not recorded. Haynes mentioned him as "formerly of the U.S. Navy," but the position in which he served in the pre-war navy is unknown.[55]

Upon Shuster's arrival, Haynes appointed him "chief of the battalion." As

The Tredegar Iron Works in Richmond, Virginia supplied the 10-inch Columbiad and the 6.4-inch rifled columbiad to the Fort Donelson River Batteries. National Archives Records Administration (NARA-528978).

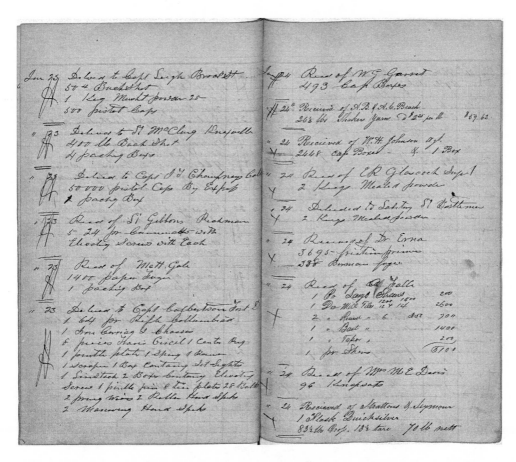

Records from the Nashville Ordnance Department on January 23, 1862, showing the delivery of the "64-pdr rifled columbiad" (6.4-inch rifled columbiad) to Captain Jacob Culbertson at Fort Donelson (Record of Receipts and Deliveries, 1861–1865).

ammunition arrived from Nashville, Shuster began getting it into the magazine. Next, he assigned fifteen men to each gun and appointed the chief of the piece. Haynes said that each man was given "his place at the gun, and their duties explained to them in case of an attack by day or night."[56] At this point, Maney's battery was detached from the battalion and took a position further to the left in the rifle pits.[57]

Meanwhile, on January 24, at Fort Henry, "torpedoes and submarine batteries" were placed near Panther Island and the 10-inch columbiad and the 5.82-inch Rifle (24-pounder rifle) were test-fired. MacGavock described the shots as the best yet from the fort and that the balls went below the island, a distance of about three miles.[58]

On January 25, news of the Confederate defeat at Mill Springs, Kentucky, and the death of Brigadier General Felix Zollicoffer were confirmed. Lieutenant Colonel MacGavock recorded in his journal, "Poor Zollicoffer, he was a brave man and died like a hero."[59]

As the news was arriving regarding Zollicoffer's death at Mill Springs, work on the fortifications of nearby Clarksville was progressing. Mr. Edward B. Sayer of the Engineer Department reported to Major Gilmer that with his workforce of 200 slaves and 50 soldiers, work was "progressing very well."[60]

Lieutenant Colonel Milton Haynes, on this date, submitted a large requisition for additional ordnance stores and implements for the Fort Donelson batteries to Brigadier General Tilghman. Haynes asked for 24 priming wires, 18 vent punches, 18 linstocks and port fires, 18 lanyards with knobs on the handles, 18 brooms for the batteries, 4 gunner's levels, 12 battery magazine lanterns, and 1 set of blacksmith tools. He specifically requested implements for the 10-inch columbiad: 1 sponge, 1 rammer, 1 budge barrel, 1 pair of shell hooks, and 1 vent cover. For the 8-inch howitzer, Haynes asked for 1 sponge, 1 rammer, and 1 pair of sleeves.[61]

Through the end of January, ordnance shipments continued arriving at Fort Donelson. Second Lieutenant R.L. Cobb[62] received 61 6.4-inch rifled shells copper cup made by T.M. Brennan at Nashville.[63]

With the 10-inch columbiad, mounted in the number 11 position, anchoring the western end of the Lower Battery and the 6.4-inch rifled columbiad installed in the Upper Battery, the Confederates must have been relieved to have these two heavy guns in their line. Even though unfired, they seemed ready to throw huge shells into any enemy ironclad that dared come into range. The jubilation did not last long; however, problems would soon arise.

8

"I have found out as mutch about the army as I want to"

February 1–11, 1862

At the beginning of February, the enemy began appearing on the twin rivers more frequently and in greater force. As a result, on February 3, General Tilghman and Chief Engineer Gilmer examined the positions at Fort Donelson. As the two studied the defenses, they realized that the works "required additions" to prevent the enemy from occupying positions from which they could threaten the river batteries.[1] In addition, Gilmer wrote, "It was also important that better protection should be made for the heavy guns (mounted for the defense of the river) by raising the parapet with sand bags between the guns to give greater protection to the gunners."[2] Over the next few days, fatigue parties were busy making the necessary modifications.

As the soldiers worked feverishly to improve the fortifications at Fort Donelson, the enemy neared Fort Henry. On February 4, drummers beat the long roll as Federal gunboats reached Marbury's Landing about four miles below the fort. Randal MacGavock described seeing the black coal smoke distinctly and later that night could see the enemy's campfires. "They have a brass band and regaled us with *Yankee Doodle*. I put our trust in God for he alone can preserve us in this our hour of trial," said MacGavock.[3]

Prepared or not, the time of trial had indeed arrived. At 10 a.m. on February 6, four Federal ironclads, the *Essex*, *Cincinnati*, *Carondelet*, and *St. Louis* with the timber-clads, *Tyler*, *Conestoga*, and *Lexington* in the rear, converged on Fort Henry. On the land, two divisions of infantry moved up the east and west banks of the Tennessee River toward Forts Henry and Heiman. The entire combined arms operation was under the command of the little-known Brigadier General Ulysses S. Grant. On the river, Flag Officer Foote, from his flagship *Cincinnati*, brought his ironclads in line-abreast with their heavy frontal armor and bow guns facing the fort. At 1,700 yards, they roared into action.[4]

In Fort Henry, amidst the bursting shells, the Rebel gunners of Taylor's Battery defiantly replied to the gunboats. General Lloyd Tilghman, commanding the fort, pulled off his frockcoat as he helped man the guns while the rising waters of the Tennessee River breached the fort. At 12:35 p.m., things started going from bad to worse for the artillerymen in Fort Henry. At that time, the 5.82-inch rifle burst as it was fired, killing three crew members and wounding others. Next, a Federal round struck one of the 32-pounders. In an unfortunate succession of events, a premature discharge of one of the 42-pounders killed three of its crew. Then, as matters grew steadily worse, the 10-inch columbiad was accidentally spiked as the gun was loaded with the priming wire still in the vent.[5]

The USS *Cincinnati*, one of the city-class ironclads, The *Cincinnati* served as Foote's flagship in the February 6, 1862, attack on Fort Henry (Naval History and Heritage Command, NH 63211).

Despite problems in the fort, the battle was not a one-sided affair. The Rebel batteries replied the best they could, and for a while, made the daring gunboats pay for every inch of river gained. The deep stentorian roar of gun reports resonated across the Tennessee River valley as the heavy artillery of both sides thundered and pealed. Amid the cacophony and muzzle flashes from the fort, the gunboats came on facing the iron-laden storm. As they did, the *Carondelet* and the *St. Louis* became interlocked. Then scenes of unimaginable horror erupted on the decks of the *Essex*, commanded by Commander William David "Dirty Bill" Porter.[6] As Fort Henry's guns pounded the *Essex*, one of the Confederate rounds passed through the number 2 porthole. On its journey, it took the head off of Masters Mate S.B. Britton and struck the boilers. As the boilers were perforated, hot pressurized steam sprayed out, scalding twenty-three sailors and nine soldiers.[7] Without steam power, the *Essex* dropped out of the fight. Undaunted, the intrepid flagship *Cincinnati* continued forward. With her bow guns, an 8-inch Dahlgren and 42-pounder Army Rifles blazing, she closed within 600 yards of Henry's works.[8]

As the Confederates slugged it out with the gunboats, Grant's infantry, sloshed through creeks and waded through the mud as they traversed the rough Middle Tennessee terrain. The divisions of C.F. Smith and John A. McClernand rushed to aid the gunboats, but their assistance was far too late in coming.

The prophecy of the local citizen, who months before warned about the area flooding, now came to pass as the rising Tennessee River breached the fort and poured in. By this time, Taylor's gun crews in the fort were serving their pieces in rising water. With most of their guns disabled and the river rising, Tilghman saw that Fort Henry's fate was sealed and asked for terms of surrender. Flag Officer Foote replied that any surrender must be unconditional. With but few options, Tilghman hoisted the white flag over Fort Henry. Before the surrender, except for the gunners of Taylor's Battery, Tilghman had the foresight to evacuate the remainder of Fort Henry's garrison to Fort Donelson. To signify the surrender, Foote sent Roger Stembel commander of the *Cincinnati* to confer with Tilghman. Stembel entered Fort Henry by taking a skiff through the sally port and across the parade ground. As the victorious Yankees took possession of the fort, they rifled through the things left behind by the fleeing Confederates. One Federal captain took Lieutenant Colonel MacGavock's diary.[9] As the guns at Fort Henry fell silent, Private William E. Maurey at Fort Donelson recorded in his diary, "A heavy battle is raging at Ft. Henry Lasting 1 hour & 15 Minutes."[10]

Meanwhile, back at Fort Donelson, under the supervision of Lieutenant Colonel Milton Haynes, the troops at the river batteries labored daily constructing the parapets and putting the finishing touches on the batteries. While they did, Captain Thomas Beaumont and Lieutenant Bedford supervised the construction of a new bomb-proof magazine.[11] Among the work parties was Captain Thomas Grigsby's company of the 49th Tennessee from Dickson County. As Grigsby's men cut trees for the works, a falling tree killed one of his privates.[12]

Even though the 10-inch columbiad at Fort Donelson had been mounted ten days earlier, it was not until February 6, that it was test-fired. The piece was loaded with a twenty-pound charge of powder. When fired, the recoil was so violent that the gun slammed backward against its hurters and threw the carriage off the pintle, causing severe damage to the iron barbette carriage. This same problem had occurred while test firing the 10-inch columbiad at Fort Henry.

As night closed, at about 8:00 p.m., Private W.E. Maurey took the time to write, "Ft Henry has been Surrendered, Gen'al Lloyd Tighlman a Prisoner."[13] Around midnight,

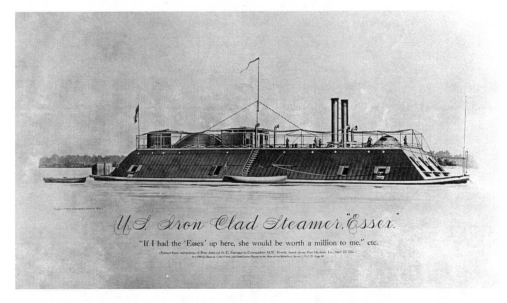

The USS *Essex*, a non-city-class ironclad commanded by Bill Porter, the *Essex* was engaged at Fort Henry on February 6, 1862, and took substantial damage (Naval History and Heritage Command, NH 54285).

the garrison troops of Fort Henry, two brigades under colonels Adolphus Heiman and Joseph Drake, consisting of an aggregate of about 2,600 men, arrived at Fort Donelson.[14] Even though Fort Henry was only twelve miles away, to effect their escape, the retreating troops were forced to take a more circuitous and exhausting route of twenty-two miles. By the next morning, a soldier of the garrison reported, "The troops at Ft. Henry made good their retreat to this place."[15] Wesley Smith Dorris observed, "On the 7th many of the men from fort Henry come in in a deplorable condition some without hats capes or guns purfectly drenched wading creeks and branches as the waters was up at this time."[16]

To remedy the recoil problem of the 10-inch columbiad, Haynes reasoned that for their most potent gun (to date) to be of any practical use, they would have to increase the gun's incline by raising its rear to reduce its backward force. To accomplish this, Haynes sent "a competent officer" to the Cumberland Rolling Mills, seven miles upstream, to have new rear traverse wheels cast. The new wheels were specified to be four inches larger in diameter than the originals. Within the week, the wheels were fabricated and taken to Donelson, where once installed, Haynes exclaimed the gun "worked like a charm."[17]

While Lieutenant Colonel Haynes was pleased with his engineering accomplishment regarding the effect the new wheels had on the columbiad, others were not similarly impressed. Lieutenant Bedford identified another problem. Bedford stated that even with the larger rear traverse wheels, the recoil against the counter-hurters was still of a sufficient force to cut ropes tied there as bumpers. "There was no alternative but to dismount the gun and lower the front half of the traverse circle, by this means the inclination of the chassis was so steep that the piece was in danger of getting away from the gunners when being run into battery, and of toppling off in front," stated Lieutenant Bedford.[18] Captain Bidwell was likewise unimpressed with the adjustments as he observed that the depression necessary to counter the recoil "was so great that it produced a valley or bed out of which the front wheels could not be rolled, thus diminishing very greatly the range of the gun right and left."[19]

After the disastrous defeat at Fort Henry, the Confederates at Fort Donelson continued increasing their defenses, anticipating hourly the arrival of Grant's land forces and Foote's vaunted gunboats. Lieutenant H.L. Bedford later wrote, "It must be remembered however that the great fear was of the gunboats. It was apprehended that their recent achievements at Fort Henry would be repeated at

Major Jeremy Gilmer became Johnston's chief engineer of Department #2. Gilmer oversaw the work of Lieutenant Joseph Dixon at Forts Henry and Donelson (American Civil War Museum, under the management of Virginia Museum of History & Culture, FIC2009.00660).

Donelson."[20] Major Jeremy Gilmer added, "The greatest danger, in my opinion, is from the gunboats, which appear to be well protected from our shot."[21]

On Saturday, two days after Fort Henry's fall, another load of ammunition arrived for the Fort Donelson river batteries. The shipment, addressed to Lieutenant R.L. Cobb,[22] included 10-inch shell straps, ten small tarpaulins, another 100 rounds of 32-pounder grape, 100 32-pounder shells, 204 6 pound 32-pounder blank cartridges, 50 10-inch columbiad shells, 75 sabots for 10-inch shells, and 100 paper fuzes.[23]

On Sunday, February 9, Brigadier General Gideon Johnson Pillow, under a directive from Department Commander Albert Sidney Johnston, assumed command of Fort Donelson.[24] This decision would turn out to be critical to the fate of Fort Donelson and its brave defenders.

Pillow was an interesting character. Stewart Sifakis wrote that Pillow was, "one of the most reprehensible men ever to wear the three stars and wreath of a Confederate general."[25] In the antebellum days, Pillow, a staunch Democrat, had strong political ties. Before President James K. Polk was elected to the White House, Pillow and Polk enjoyed a close relationship in their hometown in Maury County, Tennessee. After becoming president, and at the outbreak of the Mexican War, Polk appointed Pillow a brigadier general of volunteers, passing over more qualified West Point trained candidates. Pillow's appointment did nothing but gain him bitterness and resentment from others. Zachary Taylor, commander of U.S. forces, referred to Pillow as "that contemptible fellow."[26] Matters grew even worse, however, when Pillow demonstrated his lack of military knowledge by having breastworks constructed improperly. Nathaniel Hughes explains,

> While [Colonel William B.] Campbell's Tennesseans[27] were distinguishing themselves, a ditch was being constructed at Camargo that would become perhaps the most celebrated in American military history. Pillow's detractors, to the end of his life, told and retold the story of the ditch. Customarily such a ditch was dug at the front base of the wall to heighten the face of the parapet. Pillow, however, came up with the "happy idea of placing the ditch inside the breastwork."[28]

It was said that the regular officers "roared with laughter" whenever they recounted Pillow's folly.[29]

Despite misgivings, Pillow's political connections with President Polk gained him a promotion to major general. As the Mexican War progressed, Pillow, in one idiotic decision after another, continued to garner increasing resentment. After giving an order to deploy light artillery against heavier guns of the enemy, Lieutenant D.H. Hill (later a Confederate general and division commander in the Army of Northern Virginia) exclaimed, "Certainly, of all the absurd things that the ass Pillow has ever done this was the most silly. Human stupidity can go no further than this, the ordering of six and twelve pounders to batter a fort furnished with long sixteen, twenty-fours, and heavy mortars!!"[30] Unfortunately, Pillow's bad judgment did not end with the Mexican War, some of his most stupid decisions would come at Fort Donelson.

Between the wars, Pillow twice failed in his bid for vice president (1852 and 1856). When the Civil War broke out, Pillow was named the senior major general of the Provisional Army of Tennessee. While Pillow demonstrated his ineptitude in commanding combat troops, he did possess outstanding administrative and organizational abilities. As major general of the Provisional Army of Tennessee, he, along with Governor Isham Harris, played a significant role in organizing the state's provisional army. However, when

Tennessee troops were transferred to the Confederacy, Pillow was commissioned a briga- dier general in the Confederate army—a significant blow to his major general sized ego.[31]

Perhaps most telling was Grant's assessment of Pillow. Grant had served with Pil- low in the Mexican War and viewed Pillow as a "military buffoon" and "was the one Con- federate officer for whom Grant consistently and openly expressed personal contempt."[32]

In the early months of the war, Gideon Pillow again demonstrated great organiza- tional capacity at Columbus, Kentucky. Later, General Albert Sidney Johnston sent him and his division to Clarksville, Tennessee, where Pillow transformed the supply base "into a well-functioning distribution point."[33] After three months at Clarksville, on Feb- ruary 9, Pillow was ordered to assume overall command at Fort Donelson, superseding Brigadier General Bushrod Johnson, who had been sent there from Nashville only three days before. When Pillow arrived, he assigned Bushrod Johnson to command the Con- federate left.

The same day that Pillow was ordered to Donelson, additional supplies were deliv- ered to Lieutenant R.L. Cobb for the river batteries. This shipment included a budge barrel, 51 6.4-inch rifled shells, four vent punches, and eight rammers, sponges, and staves for the 32-pounders.[34]

Pillow arrived at Fort Donelson on Monday morning, February 10, and estab- lished his headquarters at the home of his aide, Major J.E. Rice. Lieutenant Colonel MacGavock gave his opinion of Pillow, "Gen. Gideon Pillow arrived here today and assumed the command of the forces. Troops are now beginning to come in from Hopkinsville and Bowling Green. I regret very much that Gen. Pillow has been placed in command, as I have no confi- dence in him as an officer."[35]

Despite opinions, the ever-energetic Pillow wasted no time learning the nature of the defensive works at Fort Donelson. Not satisfied with the state of things, Pil- low ordered the works pressed forward and ordered the lines extended around the town of Dover to protect the landing and stockpiles of stores accumulated there.[36] While Pillow pushed the defenses to com- pletion, Chief Engineer Gilmer reported on progress at the river batteries, "We are making herculean efforts to strengthen our parapets—making narrow embrasures with sand bags, and if we can have ten days we hope to make bomb-proofs over the guns."[37]

Pillow ordered a company of the 10th

Bushrod Johnson, as the chief engineer of the Provisional Army of the State of Tennes- see, rejected the proposed Tennessee River defenses selected by Anderson and Foster and instead selected the Kirkman Landing site with its susceptibility of flooding as the loca- tion of Fort Henry (Alabama Department of Archives and History, Q50).

Tennessee to join Beaumont's and Bidwell's companies at the River Batteries, but the Irishmen refused to take the position. MacGavock describes,

> Today Gen Pillow ordered that Capt Morgan's company of my regiment be assigned to duty in the fort as heavy artillerists. The men of the company did not want to go, saying that they had no practice in artillery and that they did not wish to separate themselves from their Regt. Upon being informed by their Capt of their disinclination to go, Gen Pillow rode out to my encampment, had Capt Morgan's Company drawn up into line, and made the following speech: "You are Irishmen and I know you will prove true to your adopted South. I come here to drive the Hessians from this neck of land between the rivers, and to replant the stars and bars upon the battlements of Fort Henry. I will never Surrender! The word is not in my vocabulary! I had Irishmen with me in the Mexican War—and at Belmont where they proved themselves equal to any of our soldiery. Many of you know me personally, *certainly all of you by reputation* and I want you to go now when I command you." Like good soldiers they went although they knew nothing about artillery. For some cause or other they returned to their Regt the same evening.[38]

On the same day that Pillow arrived at Fort Donelson, another brigadier general arrived on the scene to take command of the area. With his headquarters at Clarksville, Brigadier General John B. Floyd settled in and started making his assessment of the situation. How Pillow and Floyd could have wound up on the same command staff supersedes logic. Lieutenant Hugh Bedford states, "that General Johnston was unfortunate in the selection, or rather the grouping of his lieutenants, on this occasion, is beyond controversy."[39]

As bad as Pillow was, Floyd was his equal, if not worse. The fifty-five-year-old John Buchanan Floyd has been described as "one of the greatest rogues ever to serve in high position in both the U.S. and Confederate governments."[40] A Virginian by birth and a lawyer by profession, Floyd lost vast sums of money in a failed cotton planting venture after moving to Arkansas. Returning to Virginia, Floyd was elected to the Virginia house of delegates in 1847 and became governor of Virginia in 1848. Ezra J. Warner states that "as a reward for Floyd's political activities in the state election of 1855, President [James] Buchanan appointed him his secretary of war."[41] Floyd's stint as secretary of war was nothing short of a disaster. Sifakis explains, "During his tenure he became embroiled in a controversy over the misuse—possibly for personal purpose—of funds earmarked for

Brigadier General John B. Floyd, former Secretary of War under President James Buchanan, superseded Gideon Pillow as overall commander of Fort Donelson. Floyd arrived at Fort Donelson on February 14, the day the Federal ironclads made their attack on the River Batteries (Alabama Department of Archives and History, Q153).

the Indians." Additionally, Floyd was accused of transferring military goods from Northern arsenals and overstocking the arsenals in the South. Floyd resigned when President Buchanan refused to order Major Robert Anderson from Fort Sumter back to Fort Moultrie. Offering his services to the Confederacy, he was commissioned a brigadier general on May 23, 1861. Floyd first served in West Virginia but was transferred to Department #2, where he became a division commander.[42]

At the end of his first day at Fort Donelson, Pillow reported his progress to his immediate superior, John B. Floyd at Clarksville:

> I am pushing the work on my river batteries day and night; also on my field works and defensive line in the rear. In a week's time, if I am allowed that much, I will try very hard to make my batteries bombproof. I am now raising the parapets and strengthening them. I got my heavy rifle gun, 32-pounder,[43] and my 10-inch columbiad in position to-day, and tried them and the other guns in battery. The trial was most satisfactory. I need two additional heavy guns very much, and if I am not engaged by the enemy in three or four days I shall apply for the 42-pounders at Clarksville.
>
> It is certain that if I cannot hold this place, the two 42-pounders at Clarksville will not arrest his movement by Clarksville. Upon one thing you may rest assured, viz, that I will never surrender the position, and with God's help I mean to maintain it.[44]

In the meantime, Floyd had arrived at his conclusions about the prospects of holding Fort Donelson. Floyd began to scheme that the defense of the Cumberland River should be made at Cumberland City, by river some sixteen miles upstream from Fort Donelson and twenty miles downstream from Clarksville. In Floyd's estimation, only a token force "but no more" would be left at Fort Donelson to put up "all possible resistance."[45] Former Fort Donelson Park Historian Jimmy Jobe explains, "Cumberland City had railroad and river transportation which would increase the avenues of escape for Confederate forces if necessary. This is a clear indication of the mindset among Confederate leaders. They were only thinking about ways of leaving, rather than some way to stop Grant and Foote."[46] Part of the problem with this plan was, as Jobe continues, "Cumberland City had no defensive works, no heavy cannons to stop gunboats, only avenues of retreat."[47]

Floyd was so intent on executing his plan, he sent Brigadier General Simon B. Buckner on February 11, with instructions to evacuate Fort Donelson and join him at Cumberland City.[48] Buckner arrived at Donelson that evening. Pillow balked at such an idea and refused to send any troops back to Cumberland City until he had personally conferred with Floyd. As he stormed off to find Floyd at Cumberland City, Pillow left Buckner in command with instructions not to bring on an engagement. During Pillow's absence, Lieutenant Colonel Nathan Bedford Forrest reported the enemy advancing "with the view of enveloping our line."[49] By noon, Pillow had returned with the news that the fort would not be evacuated, and the "remaining troops from Cumberland City and Clarksville" would be forwarded to Fort Donelson.[50]

On Tuesday, February 11, after Pillow's return from Cumberland City, the Maury Light Artillery arrived by boat from Clarksville. Commanding the Maury Artillery was Captain Reuben R. Ross.

Reuben Reddick Ross was born in Montgomery County, Tennessee, on April 17, 1830. He was the son of Professor James H. Ross and Mary D. Barker Ross. He was named after his grandfather Elder Reuben Ross, an early Baptist minister in Montgomery County. His early education was under his father at the Masonic College in Clarksville, Tennessee.[51]

In July 1849, young Ross was accepted to the U.S. Military Academy at West Point. He was graduated in 1853, ranking 51 out of 52 cadets. Several of his classmates would become well known during the Civil War including, John Bell Hood, James McAllister Schofield, James B. McPherson, and Phillip H. Sheridan. Ross was commissioned a brevet 2nd lieutenant in the 1st U.S. Infantry and served until the following year when he tendered his resignation on January 24, 1854.[52]

After leaving the army in 1854, Ross later that year, married Miss Mary E. Herman in Christian County, Kentucky.[53] By 1861 the couple had three children, and in his father's footsteps, he was teaching school in Clarksville.[54]

As Governor Harris was raising troops for the imminent defense of Tennessee, Ross was among several men who were commissioned officers in the Provisional Army of the State of Tennessee. On May 17, 1861, Harris appointed Ross a captain in the Tennessee Artillery Corps.[55]

In late summer 1861, the War Department authorized Ross to raise a regiment of infantry. Ross raised three companies that were joined by others in Hopkinsville, Kentucky, to form the regiment that would become the 8th Kentucky Infantry. Senator Henry C. Burnett of Kentucky was elected colonel of the new regiment, and Ross was elected lieutenant colonel. Because of derogatory remarks made by a competitor to the War Department, Ross's commission to lieutenant colonel was withheld. The accusations were later proven false, and Ross was acquitted.[56] After this incident, Ross resumed his duties with the artillery corps training cannoneers at Hopkinsville, Kentucky. Perhaps one of the defining moments of Ross's military career occurred on January 7, 1862, when he was elected captain of the Maury Light Artillery, a company he had trained. The Maury Artillery was comprised of men mostly from the small town of Santa Fe and the Duck River area of northwestern Maury County, Tennessee.[57]

The Maury Artillery was raised in September 1861 when James Madison Sparkman, a well-to-do farmer, began recruiting men in the northwest section of Maury County for an artillery battery. These Maury County farm boys were competent riflemen and horsemen, most of them spending large amounts of time hunting in the Middle Tennessee woods. While enlisting these men into a company of cavalry or infantry would make sense, recruiting these plow boys into an artillery company was a bit more challenging, as most of them had never even seen a battery of field artillery. Moreover, if these country boys knew where their journey would take them and the dangerous situation in which they would soon face on the banks of the Cumberland River at Fort Donelson, doubtless many would have thought twice about enlisting.

On October 2, 1861, the men who had enlisted under Sparkman for the Maury Artillery assembled on the town square of Santa Fe, a quaint farming community in Maury County. It must have been a sight to behold as the men fell in line with their greatest soldierly bearing and tried to keep in step from the town square over to the Cumberland Presbyterian Church for religious services. As the company marched, Billy West began whistling *Dixie* while the drummer and fifer attempted to stay in time with him.[58]

The following day (October 3), the company again assembled on the square at Santa Fe. The men began their trip to the seat of war as they marched out of town and headed about seven miles southeast to Duck River Station, where they boarded the train for Camp Weakley, a camp of instruction near Nashville. However, once in Nashville, instead of going directly to Camp Weakley, the Maury Artillery was sent by steamboat to Clarksville, Tennessee, where they were bivouacked by October 6.[59]

Within a week of arriving at Clarksville, the Maury Artillery was redirected to Nashville, where, by October 14, they had reached Camp Weakley. Two days later, the men were sworn into service by their battalion commander, Captain George H. Monsarrat.[60] Even though J.M. Sparkman raised the company, he declined the position of captain. Sparkman felt that he lacked the experience to command the battery. In his place, Robert P. Griffith was elected captain. As it turns out, Griffith did not know anything about the artillery drill either, a problem that became readily apparent after the election. Despite Sparkman's humility, the men elected him 1st lieutenant, and held him in high esteem, much more so than their captain.[61] Private John Robison of the Maury Artillery commented on the great dissatisfaction the company had with Captain Griffith. "He is drunk one half of his time," stated Robison.[62] However, commenting on Sparkman, Private Robison said, "We would follow him further than are men in this world."[63]

On November 7, the battery, commanded by Captain R.P. Griffith, was back in Clarksville, "but in a very incomplete condition; thus six pieces, with harness for four teams; about ten rounds of fixed ammunition to each gun, and none of the etceteras."[64] Writing to his wife from Clarksville, a week later, Private Robison told her that the battery would soon be going to Hopkinsville, Kentucky.[65] Despite expected orders, a week later, on November 20, the Maury Artillery was still in Clarksville. Departure soon came, and within two days (November 22), the Maury Light Artillery had arrived in Hopkinsville, Kentucky.[66]

At Hopkinsville, Captain Reuben Ross and 1st Lieutenant William Dunlap drilled the raw artillerymen, trying to get them battle-ready.[67] Much to everyone's satisfaction, Captain R.P. Griffith resigned on December 6.[68]

By this time, the monotonous demands of drilling and soldiering were wearing on the boys. A wearied Private J.W. Robison stated, "I have found out as mutch about the army as I want to."[69] Soldier life was about to change as Captain Reuben Ross and the Maury Artillery were soon ordered to Fort Donelson, where they would be inexorably linked with the history of the river batteries.

9

"Don't you see
the gunboats coming?"

February 12, 1862

Captain Ross and the Maury Artillery arrived at Dover on Tuesday afternoon, February 11. As the unit unloaded horses, guns, limbers, and caissons at the Dover Landing, Captain Ross headed to the Rice House, about a block up from the dock, where he met with General Pillow. Pillow instructed Ross to take his battery to the left of the Confederate line and to "take position ... in his [Pillow's] brigade."[1] Ross gathered his men and proceeded to the specified location. Ross stated that they "had no sooner reached this position before orders came to all or most of the captains of light batteries to report at headquarters."[2]

As Ross returned to the Rice House with the other battery commanders, Pillow told them he needed one company to man the heavy batteries at the river. Pillow went on to inform the captains that it would be "the post of danger, but the post of honor."[3] Despite the danger, Ross eagerly volunteered his company for the assignment. Pillow instructed Ross to move his men to the heavy guns of the river batteries, where they would be under the immediate command of Captain Joseph Dixon.

Just days after the catastrophic defeat at Fort Henry and with the fear of the dreaded Federal gunboats arriving at any moment, Pillow reiterated to Ross that the position where his unit was being placed was "the post of great danger," but Ross replied to Pillow, "Yes," it is also "the post of great honor, and that's why we want it."[4]

Leaving the Rice House, Ross returned to his men and described the situation. As they listened, most of them agreed that "the post of honor was the one he wanted."[5] Ross then asked those who wished to serve on the big guns to take two paces forward. Everyone in the unit stepped forward except John Robison. Robison commented that he had volunteered to serve in the light artillery and did not wish to serve on the bigger guns. Robison's request was respected, and he and a few others were ordered to stay with the light battery and horses in Dover, while the rest of the company went down to take their positions at the river batteries.[6]

Ross's men then moved from the Confederate left and headed to the River batteries. As they crossed Indian Creek, entered the fort proper, they ascended the steep hill and passed through the camps of the 30th, 49th, and 50th Tennessee regiments. As they descended the hill at 8:30 in the morning, the Maury County boys saw the two batteries of enormous guns for the first time.

As the men took their places among the big guns, the consensus among the Maury Artillerists was that three-fourths of them would be killed in the river batteries.[7] All of the men manning the river batteries realized the danger of their assignment. Even Department Commander Albert Sidney Johnston expected a tragic outcome when he pessimistically wired Richmond, "I think the gunboats of the enemy will probably take Fort Donelson without the necessity of employing their land force in cooperation as seems to have been done at Fort Henry."[8] Like Johnston, the Rebel gunners also believed the most significant danger was from the gunboats and that "the land forces were safe if only the gunboats were driven back."[9] The gunboats must be stopped, and it was their job, no matter the cost, to stop them.

The battery to the right was called the Upper Battery. The half-moon shaped work housed the two naval carronades, mounted by Captain Ross eight months earlier, and the massive 6.4-inch rifled columbiad. On the left was the Lower Battery, so-called because it was slightly further down the river. The lower battery contained eight 32-pounder guns and the 10-inch columbiad. Captain Ross described the batteries,

> First and lowest down an eight gun battery of 32 pdrs, with a 10 inch Columbiad (128 lbs) on the left of them. These were placed in a strong but rough siege battery with natural earthen traverses mostly revetted with hurdles of sap wood. Capped between embrasure's with sandbags, embrasure's lined with Rawhide's. There were no bombproofs or roofs of any kind. The upper battery was a barbette battery without any traverses.[10]

Ross continued, "The rifle and Columbiad were cast apparently in the same mold, and were mounted upon the same carriage, a center-point chassis, carriage and chassis made of wrought and cast iron combined. They were most excellent guns and carriages."[11]

The 10-inch columbiad was manufactured by the Tredegar Iron Works of Richmond, Virginia. The columbiad anchored the extreme left of the Lower Battery. The gun was commanded by 1st Lieutenant Hugh L. Bedford, assisted by 1st Lieutenant J.M. Sparkman, and was crewed by a detachment of the Maury Tennessee Light Artillery (authors' photograph).

Behind the parapet and traverses of the Lower Battery, the men had constructed a communications trench, allowing passage in the rear of the batteries with access to the powder magazine, which was located on high ground near the center of the battery adjacent to Gun Position Number 5.[12]

It was late in the evening when Ross's Maury Artillery made it down to the battery and reported to Captain Joseph Dixon, who Pillow had assigned to command the batteries. Ross spent the remaining thirty or so minutes of daylight orienting his men to the heavy guns. The captain pointed out to the men the "different parts of the heavy guns and carriages they never having seen any before. I regretted I had not time to commence the drill that day."[13]

It is interesting to note that Pillow placed Lieutenant Dixon, an engineer, in charge of the river batteries. Lieutenant Bedford gives further detail,

> The artillery battalion as organized by Colonel Haynes was fully competent to serve the guns with success, but Gen Pillow deemed otherwise and proceeded to the mistake of assigning Lieut Dixon to the command of the heavy batteries, instead of attaching him to his personal staff and availing himself of that officer's familiarity as an engineer with the topography of the battle ground and of the surrounding country. The assignment was particularly unfortunate, inasmuch as Dixon was killed before the main fight and the batteries were not only deprived of his services for that occasion, but the Confederate army lost an able engineer.[14]

Now, with ample men, Captain Dixon started making assignments to the guns. Dixon placed Captain Jacob Culbertson in command of the 8-gun battery of 32-pounders. Of the infantry, Beaumont's company had received the most instruction on the heavy guns, as Lieutenant W.O. Watts had given them some training as early as October. Dixon assigned Company A, 50th Tennessee, 92 strong,[15] commanded by Captain Tom Beaumont to guns 1–4 on the right of the battery. Company A, 30th Tennessee, 84 men strong, commanded by Captain Bell G. Bidwell, crewed guns 5–8, just to Beaumont's left. The Maury Artillery with 103 men had charge of the 10-inch columbiad in the Lower Battery and the 6.4-inch rifle[16] and the two 32-pounder carronades in the Upper Battery. A detachment of the Maury Artillery was also assigned to the 8-inch howitzer and two 9-pounders just above the Lower Battery, commanded by Lieutenant Peter Stankiewicz.[17]

Gun position 1 was on the extreme right of the Lower Battery nearest the river and on the lowest tier. In preparing this position, the laborers laid seven sleepers in a circle and mounted the 32-pounder on a center-pintle chassis. This gun was one of only three to be mounted on a center-pintle. The others were the 10-inch columbiad, also of the Lower Battery, and the 6.4-inch rifle of the Upper Battery.[18] With the center-pintle mount, the gun could swivel 360° and could fire on boats should they attempt to pass the battery. Dixon assigned Lieutenant George S. Martin, the artillery instructor sent from Columbus, Kentucky, to command this gun.[19] Perhaps, Dixon believed that having one of the most experienced gunners commanding the gun on the extreme right flank of the battery by the river would prove beneficial.

Moving up the line, gun 2 was just to the left, and just slightly higher than gun 1. The construction of this emplacement was unique in that it was the only emplacement in which was constructed an actual gun platform. Hanson surmised, "It [the gun platform] was probably necessary to distribute the weight of the gun as much as possible to keep it from sinking into the fill."[20] Gun 2, a front-pintle mounted 32-pounder, was commanded

Private R.M. Crumpler (seated) and family. Crumpler, of Company A, 50th Tennessee, helped crew one of the 32-pounders of the Lower Battery. Crumpler, who was mentioned in Captain Thomas Beaumont's report for gallantry, escaped capture at Fort Donelson by crossing the river and making his way back to his home near the Narrows of the Harpeth (courtesy Ricky W. Robnett).

by Major Chris Robertson of the 50th Tennessee. Even though at this time Robertson was the major of the 50th Tennessee, he had helped Beaumont raise this company and volunteered to serve with his friends and neighbors.[21]

Ascending the rise, Gun Positions 3 and 4 were next in line. Both guns were mounted on front-pintle traverse arcs. During the digs, archaeologists uncovered piles of rocks near the parapet in both emplacements. These may have formed the base for the front pintle.[22] 2nd Lieutenant W.C. Allen commanded gun 3, and 3rd Lieutenant James K. Raimey commanded gun 4.[23] These four guns comprised Beaumont's battery. With the gun commanders in place, approximately fifteen men from the company were assigned to each gun.

Gun positions 5, 6, 7, and 8 extended down the crest of the ridge. Company A, 30th Tennessee, commanded by Captain Bell G. Bidwell, had charge of these four guns, all front-pintle mounted 32-pounders.[24] If Dixon made assignments to Bidwell's battery in a similar way as he did Beaumont's, Gun number 5, positioned just in front of the magazine, was likely commanded by 1st Lieutenant J.J. McDaniel, the other artillery instructor who had been sent by General Leonidas Polk from Columbus, Kentucky. Guns, 6, 7, and 8 were likely commanded by Bidwell's lieutenants, 1st Lieutenant W.J. Benson and 3rd Lieutenant Archie Thomas. Second Lieutenant J.M. Barbee was absent on sick leave during the battle.[25] It is unknown who may have commanded Bidwell's last gun.

Positions 9 and 10 had no guns mounted in them, possibly awaiting the two 42-pounders Pillow wanted to be shipped from Clarksville. No gun platforms were constructed in either position. It is interesting to note that Position 10 was used to gather ammunition for the columbiad during the battle. In the archaeological excavation, three 10-inch solid shots were uncovered in this location.[26]

Gun Position 11, anchoring the end of the lower battery, was erected on a center-pintle chassis located on the left flank of the lower battery. This position housed the massive 10-inch columbiad that had proved so challenging during the test firing. The construction of this emplacement is interesting. While one might have expected the Confederates to have erected a very solid gun platform to support the great weight and violent recoil of the columbiad, there was none. Instead, planks measuring about two inches thick served as sleepers. These were not put in a consistent pattern but were "erratically spaced around a center point."[27] In the center were located several iron bars, previously removed by modern soldiers from nearby Fort Campbell. Hanson notes, "All of this, even if there was an iron traverse rail, indicates a flimsy, hastily constructed traverse arc."[28] The team discovered one of the sleepers located in the front of the arc was tilted to the side and appeared to be set at an angle. Archaeologist Hanson stated, "It may have been driven under the rail to counteract the depression that developed during the battle ... or, more probably, it may have tilted and thus created the depression."[29]

The 10-inch columbiad was placed under the command of 1st Lieutenant Hugh Lawson Bedford, who had been sent to Fort Donelson back in October to assist as Instructor of Artillery. First Lieutenant Matt Sparkman and twenty men of the Maury Light Artillery were assigned to this gun. Afraid that the gun might again dismount itself because of the recoil, Bedford was given instructions to continue firing blank cartridges if the gun should come off its mounting in action.[30] Part of the crew of the 10-inch columbiad was 1st Lieutenant H.L. Bedford (commanding), 1st Lieutenant Matt Sparkman, George McKennon, Walter Whittaker, John A. Pigg, Jim Sowell and Tom Moore at the lanyard, Jim Hughes, Frank Smith, Felix Cook, with Sam Woody and Jasper Woody as spongemen.[31]

The Upper Battery was located about 150 yards southeast or upstream from the Lower Battery. The position had been constructed in a semi-circular or half-moon shaped design and was also called the half-moon battery. The earthwork, about 70 yards long, was revetted[32] with sapwood hurdles and planking. When constructed, the merlons were approximately two feet high, and the embrasures were five feet wide.[33] This emplacement housed a battery consisting of a magazine located on the west side of the Upper Battery, and a 6.4-inch rifled columbiad mounted on a center-pintle chassis, flanked by two 32-pounder carronades. Each carronade was mounted on a casemate carriage.[34] Captain Ross personally commanded the 6.4-inch rifle. His crew consisted of Sergeant Pat H. Cook, Corporal J.M. Dockery, Thomas H.B. Johnson, T.J. Mays, Billy Woody, Ben Godwin, and Mike Luckett.[35] To Ross's left, Brevet 2nd Lieutenant Elijah B. Thompson commanded one carronade, and to his right, 2nd Lieutenant P.L. "Len" Fitzgerald commanded the other.[36] Once all the gunners were assigned to their posts, the officers immediately began drilling the crews to familiarize them with the big guns.

While Dixon was getting his gunners situated in the River Batteries, additional reinforcements reached Fort Donelson. Brigadier General Simon B. Buckner and his division arrived. Buckner, a West Point trained professional soldier, was an old political enemy of Pillow. Buckner was assigned to command the Confederate right.[37] Part of his responsibility was to protect the river batteries from a land attack.

While Buckner's Division was approaching Fort Donelson from the east, a more sinister force was approaching from the west. By 8:00 a.m., 15,000 Federal troops were "put in motion" from Fort Henry.[38] C.F. Smith's Division advanced by the Ridge Road, and John McClernand's Division moved by the Telegraph Road. By noon Grant's men had invested the Rebel lines. John McClernand placed his division opposite the Confederate left, and C.F. Smith took a position opposite the Confederate right.[39]

Meanwhile, in the river batteries, the new heavy artillerists had drilled for only about half an hour when the ominous telltale sign of the dreaded gunboats could be seen in the distance. Captain Ross stated,

> I suppose we had drilled half an hour the detachments having learned to go through the manual of their pieces with tolerable facility, when Lt. Bedford appeared on the parapet of our work and approached me standing on the same about half way giving out the commands to the detachment. I noticed nothing unusual in his manner until touching me on the shoulder I observed the pallar and nervousness produced by some extraordinary sensation. He whispered to me that the gunboats were coming and to begin preparation to receive them.[40]

Private Joseph Hinkle of Bidwell's company said they had just "started to dinner when we met Captain Dickson [Dixon], who said: 'Get back to your guns and get ready—don't you see the gunboats coming?'"[41]

At this time, Ross sent Lieutenant Sparkman with the detail he had just trained on the 6.4-inch rifle to crew the columbiad. Quickly, Ross sent other men "preparing water barrels, budge barrels and ammunition while at the same time the rifle detachment was to be drilled for the first time."[42] Ross concluded, "Everything however was full of life and we were soon in as complete a state of readiness as our time and means allowed us."[43] The Rebel gunners scrambled to their posts, and nearing 1:00 p.m., a lone city-class ironclad, the *Carondelet*, made an appearance at long range. Commander Henry Walke commanding the *Carondelet* stated, "At 12:50 P.M., to unmask the silent enemy, and to announce my arrival to General Grant, I ordered the bow guns to be fired at the fort."[44]

"The air was perfectly still and we could see the unmistakable sign of our dreaded visitors made awful by the reputation for destructiveness they had acquired at Fort Henry. A faint column of black smoke showed the position of several gunboats and some said they saw rockets rise above the garrison in that direction," remembered Ross.[45] As the *Carondelet* nosed around the river bend north of the fort, for the first time, the Confederate gunners saw the dreaded ironclad come into view. One of the Confederate gunners observed, "The smoke exactly marked the progress of the boat and we knew when to expect her appearance. A low black mass soon glided beyond the point shaped exactly like that of a RR engine having two steamboat pipes at the upper part of the nose a V the fore and aft were shaped alike and were flat between."[46]

Maintaining her distance, the heavy bow guns of the *Carondelet* shattered the silence. On the Confederate side, everyone waited with great anticipation as the rounds from the Yankee ship screamed noisily overhead. Although loud and terrifying, the huge shells fell harmlessly beyond.[47] Captain Ross further described,

> I suppose we had drilled half an hour when Bedford came and notified me that the gunboats were coming. As I said before, Captain Culbertson had immediate command of the eight 32's. Only a single gunboat engaged us that morning. She appeared above the bend, took position, and opened fire on us. Though two and one-fourth miles off her shot and shell reached us with perfect facility. We mostly answered her with the rifle, firing only a few rounds from the Columbiad. The rifle did fine service, striking, with an elevation of thirteen and one-half degrees, probably four or five times out of the twelve or fifteen shots fired. She drew off after about forty-minutes's bombardment, and we saw no more of them that evening.[48]

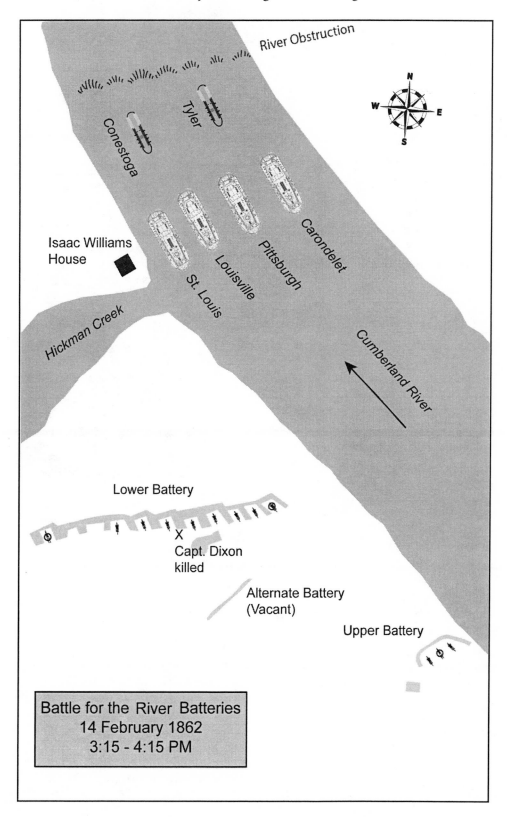

River Obstruction

Tyler

Conestoga

Carondelet

Pittsburgh

Louisville

St. Louis

Isaac Williams
House

Hickman Creek

Cumberland River

Lower Battery

X
Capt. Dixon
killed

Alternate Battery
(Vacant)

Upper Battery

Battle for the River Batteries
14 February 1862
3:15 - 4:15 PM

Captain Ross, commanding the 6.4-inch rifle, had never before fired a gun of such enormity. On first impressions, Ross noticed a marked difference between its report and that of the smooth bore "it being much clearer and more pointed in its report."[49] Using the pendulum hausse, Ross elevated the muzzle to 13½ degrees but could neither see nor hear anything of where the ball went.[50]

As the *Carondelet* come on, the Confederates watched as the gunboat halted. As she did, the Rebel artillerymen saw smoke pour from her front portholes. Several seconds later, the gunners instantly took cover as the gun reports made it upriver quickly followed by a loud "whizz" and "then came an awful crash about which time the ball or shell had come near enough for its whizz to be heard." It "was as pitiful a sound as could well be imagined," stated a Rebel gunner.[51]

With the battle on, the artillerymen, now in their first engagement, could not contain their excitement. As shot and shell from the *Carondelet* bracketed the battery, an anxious Reuben Ross contended that his men were almost "unmanageable," and he "could scarcely get my men to do their duty." To get the men on task, Ross "was compelled to use severe language."[52]

Commander Henry Walke commanded the USS *Carondelet*. The *Carondelet* took heavy casualties in the assault on the Fort Donelson River Batteries (Naval History and Heritage Command, NH 66752).

As the shells from the *Carondelet* came in, they exploded, sending shrapnel in every direction. A witness described, "After their shells would explode which they did in almost every conceivable place and position we could occasionally hear a report as of pistols firing in the air where the contents of the shell were passing."[53]

Eventually, the *Carondelet* withdrew. As she did, the Confederates quickly got busy drilling and strengthening the parapets with the assistance of the infantry. Ross commented, "We employed ourselves principally on the drill, and meanwhile secured valuable aid from the infantry Regiments, which constantly kept Strong detachments at work under charge of our lamented Capt. Dixon increasing the height of our embankments."[54]

While the River Batteries were having their first encounter with the *Carondelet*, Grant was taking the initiative to walk right up to Donelson's outer works. By February 12, Grant's men were getting into position to reduce the fort with little apprehensions of Confederate reprisal. Grant stated,

Commanded by Commander Henry Walke, the USS *Carondelet* made sorties against the Fort Donelson River Batteries on February 12 and 13, and in the main assault on Valentine's Day (Naval History and Heritage Command, NH 63376).

I had known General Pillow in Mexico, and judged that with any force, no matter how small, I could march up to within gunshot of any intrenchments he was given to hold. I said this to the officers of my staff at the time. I knew that Floyd was in command, but he was no soldier, and I judged that he would yield to Pillow's pretensions. I met, as I expected, no opposition in making the reconnoissance and, besides learning the topography of the country on the way and around Fort Donelson, found that there were two roads available for marching; one leading to the village of Dover, the other to Donelson.[55]

As the day closed, with the gunners having their first encounter with a Federal gunboat, Pillow, despite Grant's land forces investing his lines and the gunboats expected at any minute, seemed hopeful. Pillow writing to Johnston described his situation,

We shall have a battle in the morning. I think, certainly, and an attack by gunboats. The enemy are all around my position and within distance too close in with me in ten minutes march. One gunboat came today and fired fifteen or twenty shells and retired. We gave no reply. I have sent up to Cumberland City for Baldwin's two regiments. Feel sanguine of victory, though I am not fully ready. I have done all that it was possible to do, and think I will drive back the enemy.[56]

During this time frame, there was a great deal of chaos occurring in the Confederate high command. Pillow was working hard to build up Fort Donelson's defenses, which he had greatly improved. Timothy Smith writes, "By February 12, Gideon Pillow had his fort in the best conceivable shape he could, and had proven unshakable in the need to continue its defense. Ominous signs were nevertheless appearing on both land and water."[57] From that point, all available men were forwarded to Fort Donelson. As men were coming in, as Timothy Smith observed, "the independent Pillow was busily making Fort Donelson his own little fiefdom."[58]

10

"The boat was diabolically inspired and knew the most opportune times to annoy us"

February 13, 1862

Thursday morning, February 13, dawned a pleasant day. Wesley Smith Dorris stated, "Morning came beautiful and fare all quietly Resting on there arms."[1] As the sun rose, the gunners of the river batteries expected the advance of the Federal gunboat flotilla against their positions at any moment. Yet, as the morning progressed, no gunboat showed. Captain Ross took advantage of the silence to drill the men and to give the boys "some useful instruction in decreasing themselves from the enemys fire."[2] Ross also took advantage of the time to issue an order to correct their misbehavior of the previous day. Ross explained, "There was also an important order given them by me, in regard to what was of such a disappointment to us the day before—the disorder during the time of action. I made the rule that no man should speak above a whisper without permission from myself or one of the lieutenants. I encouraged them in being cool and deliberate when the fight came on and received from them every assurance that they would do so."[3]

Meanwhile, after commanding Fort Donelson for only five days, Pillow was superseded by the arrival of Brigadier General John Buchanan Floyd.[4] At daybreak, Floyd arrived and assumed overall command at Fort Donelson. Benjamin Cooling describes, "Like Pillow, Floyd was more the flamboyant politician than the great battle captain. He had bickered with superiors during the western Virginia campaign. He enjoyed the dubious distinction of having served as President James Buchanan's secretary of war just before the war, and Floyd earned the North's enmity for ostensibly stockpiling southern arsenals with war materiel."[5] Cooling continues,

> To this day, however, it remains a mystery just why Johnston sent this particular man to command the major portion of his western army, at the crucial battle, and at a place which even Floyd considered "illy chosen, out of position, and entirely indefensible by any re-inforcements which could be brought there to its support." What is equally strange was the fact that Floyd proceeded to stand and fight for that position for three long days.[6]

While all of this was transpiring, additional supplies arrived at Dover for the river batteries. The Nashville Ordnance Department sent 75 10-inch cannonballs and 50 32-pounder rifled shells (these were for the 6.4-inch rifle) in care of Lieutenant R.L. Cobb.[7]

Finally, by around 9:30 a.m., the *Carondelet* made her appearance. Lieutenant Bedford stated, "It really appeared that the boat was diabolically inspired and knew the most opportune times to annoy us."[8] Ross described, "I suppose I had passed into the sally port where all the garrison to the number of 3 regiments lay in their trenches, when the cry of gunboats fell upon my ears. Turning I saw the black column which showed that steam was getting up."[9]

The *Carondelet's* advance was in coordination with a land attack, Ross describes,

> I remained long enough to see that the main attack was upon our center, which was posted Heiman's Brigade. Walking down to my battery I found the gunboat nearly in sight and put things in trim for immediate action. I have the rifle loaded and start fires among us in case the friction primers should fail. I took a good look at the gunboat as she glided from the point of taking a short but deliberate sight at her through my telescope. She was, above water in shape, a low frustum[10] of a rectangular pyramid, with portholes in all four faces.[11]

The *Carondelet* was a formidable opponent. She was armed with a total of fourteen guns (six 32-pounders, three 8-inch guns, four 42-pounder Army rifles, and a 12-pounder).[12] As her gunners cut the fuses to explode at 10- and 15-second intervals, she came on, firing 139 rounds with her bow guns, an 8-inch Dahlgren, and two 42-pounder Army Rifles.[13] Ross describes,

> We expected an attack from the fleet early on Thursday morning, but only a single boat came up again. She was armed with powerful rifles, and it was easy to see that she was taking advantage of knowledge gained by the boat of Wednesday; for knowing where the rifle was situated, she fired fourteen rifle bombs in and about our battery in the course of about an hour and twenty minutes. Others she fired at the lower battery (I supposed at the Columbiad), and many promiscuously over the hill, on the top of which was situated the fort. These were elongated Parrot shells of 42 and maybe higher caliber.[14]

As noon approached, Lieutenant Bedford said that the *Carondelet* "delivered her fire with such accuracy that forbearance was no longer endurable." At this time, Lieutenant Dixon brought the 10-inch columbiad and the 6.4-inch rifle into the fight. Bedford watched closely as "the first shot from the Columbiad passed immediately over the boat, the second fell short, but the third was distinctly heard to strike. A cheer of course followed," stated Bedford.[15] Ross also describes, "I had not fired many rounds before a report shook the ground, as of a thunderbolt. I had first thought it was one of their huge shells which had fallen and exploded upon the outer edge, or maybe the top of our works. What was my surprise to find it was Sparkman and Bedford with their mammoth Columbiad helping me to sink their gunboats."[16]

As the rifle and columbiad fired on the *Carondelet*, Commander Walke stated, "a 128-pounder solid shot ... passed through our port casemate forward, and glancing over our barricade at the boilers, and again over the steam-drum, struck, and burst the steam-heater; and fell into the engine-room without striking any person, although the splinters wounded slightly some half-dozen of our crew."[17]

As shots continued to be exchanged, another round from the *Carondelet* plowed through the fortification on the hill killing Private James Beard, Company D, 50th Tennessee.[18] As the *Carondelet* continued her rate of fire, she sent another round bounding across the hill. This shot "passed through three strong cabins built of eight and ten-inch logs, mostly cutting their logs in two, then through a shanty, and finished by killing a mule. This, too, was at a distance from the huts of two and one-half miles."[19]

After banging away at each other for about an hour and a half, the damaged *Carondelet* began withdrawing. As she retired, still firing, one of her last rounds slammed

Location of the death of Captain Joseph Dixon. On February 13, as the batteries were engaging the *Carondelet*, Dixon was stooped over passing from Gun #5 to Gun #6 when a parting shot from the gunboat struck and dismounted Gun #6. A large bolt from the gun carriage broke loose and struck Dixon in the forehead, causing instant death (authors' photograph).

into the Lower Battery. The round, from one of her 42-pounder Army rifles, entered the embrasure of Gun number 6, striking the right cheek of the carriage, dismounting the gun and sending debris flying in all directions. At the time the projectile hit the gun, Lieutenant Dixon had just given the order, "fire the 8 guns, the 32 pndrs."[20] Dixon was bent over, making his way from Gun number 5 to Gun number 6, when a piece of a large bolt struck him on the left side of the head. Captain Bidwell described, "He was stooping, when a screw-tap struck him in the left temple, killing him instantly."[21] Captain Culbertson stated the shell that killed Dixon was "from a rifle," and Captain Ross identified it as an "elongated Parrott shell of 42 and maybe higher caliber."[22]

From the accounts, the round that killed Dixon was likely a Dyer shell fired from one of the 42-pounder Army rifles. Bidwell said that the shot "was descending when it struck the inner base of the embrasure, and turned upwards to the left, striking and shattering the right cheek of my second gun (gun #6). The gun was never fired, but was loaded when disabled. Several of my men were slightly stunned, but were not sufficiently injured to keep them from duty."[23] Major Chris Robertson further explained, "The gun at which he [Dixon] was standing had not fired a single time, when one of the cheeks of the carriage was struck by a shot from the enemy, dismounting the gun and throwing bolts and splinters in every direction. One of the iron bolt-heads struck Capt. Dixon carrying away the left side of his face and head killing him instantly."[24]

Down in the Upper Battery, Ross observed a great commotion:

I suppose we had fired half a dozen rounds when someone called my attention to a parcel of men on the hill going from the lower battery into the fort above. I inquired who it was killed, they answered Capt. Dixon our favorite Capt. Dixon. Poor fellow how I grieved at his loss. A cannonball entered the embrasure near which he happened to be stationed, knocked off a cheek from which a screw bolt flew out and killed him. The bolt struck him above the eyes smashing in the whole forehead. Of course the gun was dismounted.[25]

Upon Dixon's death, General Floyd sent an order to place the next in rank in command of the batteries. According to Captain Ross, this should have been him. However, due to miscommunication, command was given to Captain Culbertson. Ross explains,

Soon after dinner a courier came down to the fort with the order from Genl. Floyd to Col. Bailey to place the next in rank to Capt. Dixon in command of the heavy artillery. Bailey assigned to me a captain in the provisional Army, Culbertson an older graduate than myself and Lieutenant in the regular Army and had been at the fort some months and had drilled the eight gun battery of 32 pndrs. I concluded it best to let him retain command, especially as being old friends I knew he would in no way take injurious authority over me. All I cared for was to remain supreme in my own battery. I knew that he would do all that could be done with the 32 pndrs.[26]

Dixon's body was returned to his home in in Athens, Tennessee, where he was buried on February 16. A gifted engineer, Dixon was noted for his ability of getting more work out of volunteer troops than anyone who was at Fort Donelson and "the truest type of soldier that I have ever seen," stated Major Christopher Robertson. Robertson sadly concluded, "his loss was deeply felt by all."[27]

Joseph Hinkle of Company A, 30th Tennessee, was one of the crew members handling the number 5 gun, beside the one where Dixon was just killed. After the projectile struck the number 6 gun, killing Dixon, the round continued its deadly errand, bounding into the parapet of Hinkle's gun. Hinkle recalled that the impact of the round "covered the men up with dirt when it struck the ground, and the bombshell fell into the parapet."[28] There the deadly Federal projectile lay, ready to explode at any second. The awestruck Confederate artillerymen stood mesmerized, staring at the unexploded round. All of them thought to themselves their time had come. Finally, one of the boys got his wits about him and without regard to his own safety, picked up the shell and threw it out of the works. Hinkle states, "If it had exploded, we would have all been killed."[29]

Despite the commotion in the middle of their battery, the Confederates continued firing. As the guns of the Lower Battery fired at the lone gunboat, Captain Jacob Shuster, Chief of the Battalion, suffered a broken leg from standing too close to one of the 32-pounders when it was discharged.[30] Lieutenant Colonel Haynes had taken his place in the batteries. By this time, Haynes was unable to walk without the aid of crutches, and only then with great pain.[31]

Aside from Gun number 6 being dismounted, the columbiad also sustained damage, but not from Federal fire. The recoil of the monstrous gun continued to prove problematic. Bedford explains, "In this engagement the flange of one of the front traverse wheels of the Columbiad was crushed, and a segment of the front half of the traverse circle was cupped, both of which proved serious embarrassments in the action next day."[32]

With the *Carondelet's* withdrawal, men of the 49th Tennessee brought food and drink to the artillerymen and helped rebuild the battered works. Captain Ross complimented them, "in gradually improving the upper battery at all intervals between the bombardments."[33] Ross acknowledged, "Not a night, however cold and disagreeable, that their presence and encouraging words did not give evidence of their perseverance and patri-otism. In behalf of the artillerymen, I must acknowledge an obligation to them and the various captains of their regiments, which we hope to be able to repay. Our boys brought down ready-cooked provisions for us, and our meals were pleasant by being unexpected, and frequently caught us with fine appetites of which we were not conscious before."[34]

With the *Carondelet*, now out of sight, the men in the batteries lost no time in pre-paring for the next sortie. With the experience gained, Ross determined to fire at the gun-boat the next time with all of the guns when just enough of the boat was exposed to view coming around the bend. He planned to have all of the cannon fire simultaneously as he would watch the boats through his telescope.[35]

On the land, Grant tightened his lines beyond Donelson's outer works. Earlier in the day, Charles Ferguson Smith advanced against the Confederate right, held by Buckner. Buckner's line stood firm with Porter's Battery firing in support. Later in the day, McCler-nand launched an attack against one of the strongest parts of the Confederate line, a salient held by Adolphus Heiman's Brigade consisting of the 10th, 48th, and 53rd Ten-nessee, the 27th Alabama, and Maney's Tennessee Battery. Here, one of the most horrible events in the battle for Fort Donelson occurred. In the attacks against Maney's Battery, the Rebel guns punished their attackers, tearing considerable gaps in their lines. As the battle raged, the woods caught fire burning alive many of the Federal wounded. Private George O. Smith of Company F, 17th Illinois, of Colonel William R. Morrison's Brigade, stated, "The dry leaves took fire from the heavy firing and many of the wounded burned to death."[36] While the probing attacks on land occurred, Commander Walke stated, "the sound of distant firing being heard, we again attacked the fort, throwing in some 45 shell and receiving but little damage."[37]

Around 2:00 p.m., another column of black smoke around the riverbend gave notice to the Confederate gunners that another gunboat was approaching. Ross, ready to exe-cute his plan, intently watched the boat through his telescope. The captain, through a small break in the distant timber, watched as the boat passed, nearing the bend. As the shape of the boat filled the opening, Ross gave the order, "ready!" The gunners stretched their lanyards tight awaiting the command to fire. Soon, the bow of the *Carondelet* passed the brush of the distant point. As soon as the stacks of the gunboat cleared the timber, the command "fire!" brought the simultaneous deafening reports of the three guns of the Upper Battery. With the discharges, smoke boiled from the guns obscuring the effect of the volley. After this round, the gunners felt like the shots from the carronades were use-less, and so they were fired no more.[38]

Ross reasoned that if the guns were aimed correctly, they were bound to strike close to the boat's chimneys, which would be near the boilers. The gunners believed their vol-ley had been successful in deterring the boat as it "remained up only long enough to fire one round, and then fell back to load, as we supposed. Her firing, too, was the most inefficient we had yet seen on account of the hurry with which it appeared to be deliv-ered."[39] Ross continued,

> We loaded our rifle, and fired as fast as we could take aim. Each time as she returned we had the rifle aimed for her, firing at the same point of the boat. After the third return, she lay behind the brushwood out of view from our battery, and fired on the lower battery, which being to our left some rods, was still in her view. We turned the rifle upon the point behind which we could judge by the top of her chimneys she lay, and still fired on her. Again she moved lower down with her firing on the lower battery, and again we turned our rifle for her. She withdrew,

gradually driven off by it. Not one of her shot or shell did us harm. The 32-pdrs. had as yet fired none, the distance being too great for them, and the Columbiad had fired only a few times.[40]

Even though the day had been pleasant, clouds gathered, causing a gloomy overcast evening, soon rain set in. Before 8 p.m. with the falling thermometer, the rain transitioned into mixed precipitation, limiting sight to only a few yards. A member of the 30th Tennessee wrote, "In the evening it became cloudy turned cold and commenced Raining and soon in the night turned to snowing and we having to lay on our arms in the trenches was suffered in tensely [intensely]."[41] Spot Terrell of the 49th Tennessee commented, "the cold north wind was bloing and cutting our years [ears] and fingers we suffered a great deal from the Sevear cold and Snow that lay spread over the ground."[42]

After the engagement, the batteries were visited by Generals Floyd and Pillow. Pillow ordered that the dismounted gun where Dixon was killed, be remounted. Following orders, Lieutenant Colonel Haynes and Major Gilmer inspected the piece. After a thorough examination, Haynes ordered twelve artificers and carpenters to the task. Although working throughout the night in deplorable conditions, they were unable to remount the gun.[43]

By this time, Ross had left the battery and had ridden up to Dover to attend to some business matters. While the captain was away, the increasing darkness and snow, which continued to decrease visibility, caused him to realize that the Federals might use these worsening weather conditions to their advantage and attempt to pass the batteries. It also occurred to Ross that with their limited training and the short time they had been assigned to the heavy battery, he was the only one who knew how to aim the rifle. With these apprehensions, he hurried back to his gun.[44]

As Ross sped to the battery, his fear was amplified by the sounds of many whistles coming from downstream. As Ross passed the Dover cemetery, he became "sufficiently uneasy."[45] Ross described, "My alarm was much increased, soon after setting out on my return, at the sound of a concert of whistles of many different tones below the bend. Hurrying to the battery, I found that, though men were on the lookout, nothing further had taken place."[46]

As the captain arrived at the Upper Battery, he observed, "The snowy mist was then falling thick and the air rapidly turning cold, one could hardly see a few paces and I did not know at what time they might conclude to attempt the passage hoping to find us asleep or little watchful and possibly unable to resist the passage on account of the obscurity of the night."[47]

Attempting to discourage any move of the enemy, Ross decided to fire the rifle in the general direction of the riverbend. To prepare the gun, the boys brushed off the snow and removed the tarp and made the gun ready.[48] The crew sent two rounds down range in the direction of the boats' approach. Ross comments,

> To let them know we were on the lookout was the best thing I could think of and ordered the battery cleared for firing. The first two rounds we fired down the river as nearly in the different directions of the day firing as we were able the rain having destroyed all our chalk marks for night firing. The third and last round we placed in a loaded percussion shell pointed the gun 15 or 20 degrees to the right away over the forest gave it its highest elevation and fired with the hope of striking 3/4s or a mile below the bend.[49]

At 11:00 p.m. as the gunners in the batteries were suffering from the intense cold, Flag Officer Andrew H. Foote arrived, joining the *Carondelet*, with the remainder of his gunboat flotilla (three additional ironclads and two timber-clads) ready to attack the river batteries in earnest the next day. By 6:00 a.m., sixteen transports carrying about 16,000 troops to reinforce Grant had joined them.[50]

Foote's arrival around the bend was unknown to Ross. However, exercising due diligence, Ross detailed a "significant guard in the battery," after which he walked over to the shanty where Lieutenant Sparkman and his detachment were quartered. Just as Ross started, Captain McWhirter of General Pillows staff approached him "in sort of a mysterious manner" and handed him something Lieutenant Colonel Alfred Robb of the 49th Tennessee had sent. Robb had said it was "a piece of heavy artillery." Ross explains,

> I had no idea what it could be until he took it out when it turned out to be a fine large bottle of peach brandy. It was indeed a pleasant visitor. I called Lt. Fitzgerald and requesting his company walked on to see the other men. I found them all dead asleep and would not give them any of my fine brandy but kept it until I returned to the fort where I handed it over to my faithful detachment which I found watching around their rifle. I then prepared to lie down. The snow had ceased, and that already on the ground had frozen hard. A keen north wind was blowing with biting effect to ears and noses making one of the most sudden changes from summer warmth I had ever seen. Still I could hear the cracking of the muskets out on the line where our faithful boys were still holding the enemy at bay, though their clothing was wet and frozen on them.[51]

After keeping his men stationed at their guns all night, Captain Bidwell stated, "I remained all night at my guns, four 32-pounders, to which I had been assigned. The suffering from the severe cold was intense. I had to carry several of the men to quarters next morning so nearly frozen that they were unable to walk."[52]

Daybreak brought an end to the horrible night, the Federals, full of confidence at their recent victory at Fort Henry, were now ready to move up the Cumberland. They had the latest technology in their flotilla—the four new city-class ironclads. Flag Officer Foote was confident, and he had made proper preparations. The *Carondelet* had probed the positions three times within the last two days. With their land forces in motion, they were now ready to move on the fort.

11

"Come on you cowardly scoundrels, you are not at Fort Henry"

February 14, 1862

The sunrise of Valentine's Day, February 14, revealed the few inches of snow that had fallen the previous evening. Despite a beautiful sunny morning, the thermometer registered a bitter twelve degrees. The wind made the frigid conditions worse, causing great misery for the men of both sides. One of the Confederate gunners suffering in the River Battery complained, "I have seldom seen a more piercing wind than blew that morning."[1]

Lieutenant Colonel Haynes was suffering greatly from his leg wound. By the morning, Haynes was debilitated. As the inflammation in his leg increased, Surgeon Williams had him placed on board a steamer with other wounded soldiers and evacuated to Nashville.[2] With Dixon's death the previous day and Haynes' evacuation, the river batteries were without the much-needed experience of two of their higher-ranking officers.

By 8:30 a.m., much to everyone's surprise, no gunboat had yet appeared. Captain Ross surmised that the sun was "so bright that the fleet could not attack us, sunrise being immediately in the faces of the enemy."[3] Even though the gunboats had not advanced, Federal sharpshooters[4] had occupied the Isaac Williams's residence, a large frame house situated on a hill just across Hickman Creek a few hundred yards northwest of the Lower Battery.[5]

The sharpshooters, seeking targets of opportunity among the gunners, took careful aim as they sniped at the Rebel artillerists. Serving on one of Bidwell's guns (Gun #5) was Private Joseph Hinkle, then eighteen years old, from Springfield, Tennessee. In November, when the 30th Tennessee arrived at Fort Donelson, Private Hinkle had a severe case of the measles and received permission to return home until recovered. Having just returned to his company, he recalled, "The Federal sharpshooters got into a large frame house on a hill just across the backwater of the Cumberland River, and were firing on us, trying to pick off our gunners."[6] "We could not hear the report of their guns but could hear the whistling of minie balls as they passed near our heads," stated Hinkle.[7] Captain Culbertson, commanding the 32-pounders, ordered Hinkle's gun to fire at the house. Soon the 32-pounder roared into action, sending a few stands of grape downrange at the obstinate sharpshooters. After every discharge of the gun, a stand of 32-pounder grape, comprised of nine 2.8-inch diameter balls,[8] was loaded into the gun. Upon firing, the stand of grape would fly apart, turning the 32-pounder into a giant shotgun. After a few rounds of grape were "turned loose on the house," Private Hinkle jubilantly recalled, "you ought to have seen how the bluecoats pulled their freight."[9] Hinkle succinctly concluded, "They did not trouble us any more from that direction."[10]

Almost as soon as the gunners cleared the Federal sharpshooters from their front, Captain Ross recorded the time as 9:00 a.m.,[11] heavy columns of smoke pouring from the stacks of multiple Union transports were seen downriver two and a half miles away. Peering through his telescope, Ross could see the smokestacks of numerous transports below the bend of the river. As he looked closer, with the aid of the white snow silhouetting the dark uniforms of the soldiers, he could distinguish "a black continuous line of men passing the remote bend of the river. Cavalry and infantry in great numbers we found were debarking and marching inward to reinforce the enemy lines."[12]

While the reinforcements were offloading from the transports, Grant was in a morning conference with Flag Officer Foote aboard the *St. Louis*. In their meeting, Grant and Foote agreed to make a simultaneous attack against the Confederate positions. An observer stated that Grant "appeared to be confident of an easy victory."[13]

In the meantime, the Yankee sailors on the gunboats took the opportunity to reinforce their unarmored decks to withstand the plunging fire of the Confederate batteries. The sailors took anything that could deflect incoming fire, "'such as chains, lumber, and bags of coal,' and arranged them over the most vulnerable places."[14]

With the Federals pouring ashore in the distance, Ross firmly believed they could disrupt the landing with their big guns. He left his rifle and sought out Lieutenant Bedford at the columbiad. Bedford recalled that "Capt Ross became impatient to annoy them."[15] Ross proposed to Bedford that they interrupt the troop landing by throwing a few shells downriver. Bedford declined the request as he was cautious about firing on the enemy transports without orders. Ross, still eager to take advantage of the enemy boats grouped together, sought out Captain Culbertson commanding the battery. Culbertson also refused to fire on the landing troops without orders. Not to be outdone, Ross went to find Colonel James E. Bailey of the 49th Tennessee, who was at the time commanding the fort garrison. After Ross explained his proposition, Bailey was also unwilling to give the order without authorization from General Floyd. A courier was sent to Floyd's headquarters, and around 1:00 p.m., the messenger returned with verbal orders from the general to shell the troop landing. Bedford described, "In obedience to this order, we prepared to shell the smoke. A shell was inserted, the gun was given the proper elevation, the lanyard was pulled, and the missile went hissing over the bend of the river, plunged into a bank of smoke, and was lost to view. This was called by an army correspondent, claiming to have been on one of the gunboats, 'a shot of defiance.'"[16]

After a few rounds, columns of white steam indicated that the transports were moving further downstream. However, as the transports moved off, black smoke moving upstream was seen billowing around the bend.[17]

While the crew reloaded the columbiad, like Ross, Bedford now observed something more sinister as "the prow of a gun-boat made its appearance around the bend, quickly followed by three others, and arranging themselves in line of battle, steamed up to the attack."[18]

As Ross and Bedford watched, a little after 2:00 p.m., smoke billowed from behind the river bend, indicating multiple boats were moving upriver. One by one, the city-class ironclads *St. Louis*, *Louisville*, *Pittsburgh*, and *Carondelet* filed into view and positioned themselves line abreast, with the timber-clads *Tyler* and *Conestoga*, trailing behind. Commander Walke described,

On the 14th of February, Flag-Officer Foote, having instructed his officers, and prepared for battle, at one o'clock, p. m., hailed the "Carondelet," and ordered her with the other gunboats to follow the motions of the commanding officer. At 1.20, P.M., the flag-officer made general signal 958. At 2.10, p. m., he proceeded slowly up the river with the "St. Louis" (flag steamer), "Louisville" and "Pittsburg," and formed in the first order of steaming,—"St. Louis" on the extreme right, "Louisville" next, "Pittsburg" next, and "Carondelet" on the extreme left.[19]

From two and a quarter miles, Captain Henry Walke, commanding the *Carondelet*, took note of the Confederate river defenses. "The hills and woods on the west side of the river hid part of the enemy's formidable defenses, which were lightly covered with snow; but the black rows of heavy guns, pointing down on us, reminded me of the dismal-looking sepulchers cut in the rocky cliffs near Jerusalem, but far more repulsive."[20]

As they came on, a Federal sailor estimated their distance as a mile and a half from the fort and recorded the time as 2:48 when the first round was fired from the Water Battery. The mighty columbiad, anchoring the left of the Lower Battery, roared into action, "with a ricochet shot"—skipping across the water toward the waterline of one of the gunboats.[21] The sailor recalled that the round "struck the water about one hundred yards ahead of us."[22] The seaman continued, "Two minutes later another ball—a sixty-four pounder from the same battery—was fired at us, but dropped ahead about one hundred and fifty yards. Several shots were directed toward us but without effect before we opened fire."[23] A witness on board the *Louisville* described, "On we went, however, not a sound escaping from our crafts, except the slow puffing of the escape pipes and the cheery splashing of the paddle-wheels, while the enemy were busy awakening the

The city-class ironclad USS *Louisville* was commanded by Benjamin M. Dove (Naval History and Heritage Command, NH 96667).

dormant echoes with their cannonading, and agitating the swollen waters with their shot and shell, scattered in promiscuous profusion all around us."[24]

At 2:53 p.m., the flagship *St. Louis* opened fire. The shot roared toward the Confederate works but fell short, landing in the water within a few yards of the Lower Battery.[25] After the first round from the *St. Louis*, the other gunboats opened. Commander Benjamin Dove's *Louisville* did likewise. A sailor on board commented, "the flag officer let go his starboard bow rifle, and we followed him with ours, then the *Pittsburgh* and *Carondelet* followed suit, and the ball was really opened in earnest. Our first shots fell short; but a little more elevation of the guns remedied the failing, and the next round saw our balls and shells drop into uncomfortably close proximity to their batteries."[26] The *Carondelet* fired so rapidly that the Flag Officer instructed her to decrease her rate of fire.

At this point, the Confederates had only fired their columbiad and rifle. Just like at Fort Henry, things for the Confederates started going wrong almost immediately. While executing the loading sequence of the 6.4-inch rifle, the gunner used the priming wire to clear the vent of the rifle. Before the gunner finished clearing the vent, a nervous Mike Luckett sent the sponge in prematurely, bending the priming wire, thus spiking the piece. As the crew worked feverishly to remove the bent priming wire, Corporal Sam Jones tore the skin from his fingers as he desperately pulled at the obstruction. While Jones struggled in vain to unspike the gun with his bare hands, Lieutenant Marion Dockery ran to the tool chest over the hill to retrieve the pincers.[27]

The silence of the rifle demoralized the Rebel gunners in other parts of the battery. Lieutenant Bedford stated, "After the third discharge the rifle remained silent on account of becoming accidentally spiked. This had a bad effect on the men at the Columbiad, causing them considerable uneasiness for their comrades at the upper battery."[28]

For a while, the columbiad alone continued the action. Up to this point, the columbiad had fired only a few rounds. However, at every discharge, the low muttering earth-shaking discharge "added greatly to our courage by the hope which her tremendous report inspired."[29]

The 32-pounders continued reserving their fire. Captain Culbertson had been ordered by General Pillow to withhold the fire of the 32-pounders until the enemy had reached point-blank range. Culbertson complained, "This was opposed to my judgment, as it showed the enemy the positions of our two heavy guns, which I regarded as constituting our only hope."[30] Captain Bidwell stated, "We were ordered to hold our fire until they got within range of our 32-pounder. We remained perfectly silent, while they came over about 1½ miles, pouring a heavy fire of shot and shell upon us all the time."[31] Finally, the order to fire the 32-pounders was given. "The first round from that battery was fired at nearly the same time by all the guns, and the report was tremendous," stated Captain Ross.[32] "The cannonade was then at its utmost and beyond anything ever seen by any of the parties engaged. Not infrequently did all our guns open nearly together. The air above and around us was full of shot, solid, case [shot], and shell, while the river below too was almost a continuous spray."[33] One Confederate watching from the hill above observed, "A dence cloud of smoke arose from the battery while peale after peale are cleare as a bugler blast they sending terror and confusion on the enimys fleet at evry shot."[34]

By now, the rifle was back in action. The contest continued with the eleven guns of the batteries opposed to the twelve bow guns of the ironclads, supplemented by the *Tyler* and *Conestoga* in the rear. One witness noted, "As the boats drew nearer, the firing on both sides became faster, until it appeared as if the battle had dwindled into a contest of speed in firing."[35]

Against a single boat, the gunners in the batteries could screen themselves from incoming fire. Against six, however, any idea of trying to screen themselves was fruitless. It was now just stand and take it. At the rifle, Ross's men worked fervently to return fire, and Ross only stopped sighting the gun long enough to fire it.[36]

With the Federal flotilla closing, Ross picked out the left-hand boat (the *Carondelet*) as his target. After firing, "still they came on, apparently unharmed," reported Ross.[37] At this time, the *Carondelet* reached a point on the side of the bank, giving the impression that she was about to sink. With this supposed victory, Ross aimed the rifle at the *Pittsburgh*, the boat next in line. Ross's excitement was crushed as the *Carondelet* returned to her place in the formation and continued the advance.[38]

The four gunboats moving against the current maintained their line of battle and advanced slowly and steadily. At 3:15 p.m., the firing from both sides increased, the gunners rapidly loading and firing. A sailor from the *St. Louis* said, "Shell after shell was sent from our boat at intervals of less than five seconds. The enemy's fire had by this time become terrific. They were using thirty-two pound ball principally, and firing more frequently than we, and with great accuracy. Our fleet used twelve guns, each iron-clad boat working its three bow pieces. The *Conestoga* and *Tyler* kept about fifteen hundred yards in our rear, firing shell at long range. The *Conestoga* fired thirty-six eight-inch shell during the action; the *Tyler* sixty-one. Their distance from the fort was too great for effective working, but it kept a couple of the enemy's guns engaged during the greater part of the action, and thus diverted."[39]

The USS *Tyler* was the second supporting timber-clad for the naval assault on the Fort Donelson River Batteries (Naval History and Heritage Command, NH 49975).

Above the river batteries, troops of the fort's garrison watched the battle. A member of the 30th Tennessee described, "They opened a furious fire on the Fort and siege battery. Throwing bombs all over the Fort and out to the Rifle pits causing the boys to keep there eys open and sometimes to hug the ground."[40]

Captain Ross commanding the Upper Battery described the heavy fire they were under, "Though the bombardment was terrific, one shell cutting off the rear of a casemate carriage [of one of the carronades] within ten feet of the epaulement, another bursting within the fort so as to throw earth quite all over us, and any number of grape and fragments of shells passing around and through us."[41] Undaunted, Ross's men continued working their rifle. At the close explosion of one Federal round, it appeared that Lieutenant Len Fitzgerald and Private Gus Mays were killed. Ross recalled that one was standing on each side of him.[42] The boys quickly moved their fallen comrades to the powder magazine. Fortunately, neither Fitzgerald nor Mays was killed, just "jarred by the concussion."[43]

Problems plagued the Maury Artillerist as they labored diligently to load and fire the large rifle. As the boys rammed the elongated 68-pound projectile down the tube, due to fouling, the round stuck halfway. As Ross's boys pushed the rammer against the shell, it refused to budge. The situation was critical as the rifle was loaded with ten pounds of powder, and a 6.4-inch projectile was stuck halfway down the bore. Captain Ross described, "all efforts to drive it down with rammers had proved unavailing. The boats were advancing, and things were looking serious."[44] Since nothing else had worked, the boys decided to cut a sapling about six inches in diameter and try driving the shell down with a sledgehammer. Jim Johnson ran over the hill to fetch a sledgehammer. At the same time, Pat Cook, Marion Dockery, Tom Johnson, Tom Mays, and approximately eight others cut a sapling about the same diameter as the gun's bore and long enough to seat the round in the breech. The men soon returned to the gun with their log, and under incoming artillery fire, climbed on the works and drove the round home. With the thought of the bursting of the "Lady Polk" at Columbus, Kentucky, a few months earlier fresh in their minds, amazingly, when the lanyard was pulled, much to everyone's relief, the gun fired. After firing the round, the crew swabbed the bore with the sponge loosening the dirt and powder that had caked in the rifling. Using the "rifler," the boys cut additional debris from the bore. The barrel was sponged again and greased.[45]

If the bent priming wire and stuck round had not been trouble enough, Private Ben Godwin, working the number 1 position on the rifle, in the haste of withdrawing the rammer, accidentally flung the implement over the works. As the dumbfounded Godwin stood there rammerless, Captain Ross told him they had to have the rammer. Under a heavy barrage of incoming fire, Godwin climbed over the works, and "cooly walked" over to the water's edge, picked up the rammer, and headed back to the gun.[46] Just as Godwin was climbing back through the embrasure, rammer in hand, a Federal round hit the epaulement, tearing off several sandbags from the top row. Despite the close call and covering everyone in the vicinity with dirt, no one was injured.[47]

Down on the left of the lower battery at the columbiad, Bedford's men aggressively worked at rapid firing their massive 10-inch gun. Typically, the columbiad took five minutes to load and fire. However, under the circumstances, the Maury Artillerists managed to fire a round every three minutes. In all, they managed to fire twenty-eight rounds in the engagement.[48] Private Jim Hughes, serving the columbiad was described as "a boy" who completely unaided "picked up one of the 128-pound shot … lifted it to the muzzle of the cannon, the shell weighing more than himself."[49]

While Beaumont's and Bidwell's 32-pounder sections fired round after round, Corporal Dan Lyle of Company A, 50th Tennessee, in charge of the powder magazine, efficiently kept the guns supplied with powder and ammunition. After the battle, Captain Beaumont recognized Lyle's critical support role as he said, "by his efficiency aided materially in the victory achieved over the gunboats."[50]

In addition to the incoming 42-pounder rifled shells, rounds of grapeshot[51] fired from the 8-inch naval guns slammed into the earthworks, knocking dirt from the parapet in every direction but somehow injured no one. Bidwell commented, "The boats fired steadily, but with little effect, except to the earthworks, which were damaged considerably."[52]

Captain Beaumont reported that "two large shots penetrated the battery without doing any harm, and some few men were slightly bruised by lumps of earth thrown up by the balls of the enemy and one by the rebound of a cannister shot which struck one of the guns."[53]

Soon, another Federal shell penetrated the parapet and landed at the feet of a stunned Private John William Trotter. Gaining his wits, Trotter picked up the hissing unexploded shell and threw it over the battlement before it detonated. Trotter's quick action doubtless saved many lives of his nearby comrades.[54]

Aside from Trotter, Elisha Downs, Poston Couts, Nelson Davis, Isaac Christie, Thomas Pearce, and R.M. Crumpler, part of the crew of Beaumont's section of 32-pounders were mentioned as acting with "conspicuous courage and coolness" as well as non-commissioned officers, Sergeant J.S. Martin and Corporal W.H. Proctor.[55]

As the battle raged with unabated fury, General Pillow observing from the heights above, pointed out that Lieutenant George S. Martin, commanding Beaumont's Number 1 32-pounder by the river, "particularly captured my attention by his energy and the judgement with which he fought his gun."[56] Aside from the fact that Martin was Pillow's nephew, Martin apparently did distinguish himself, gaining honorable mention not only in Pillow's report but also in Captain Beaumont's report.[57] Instead of using tow[58] to stabilize the round in his gun's bore, Martin cut part of the skirt from his frock coat to "patch" the cannonball. Martin was pleased with the results and cut off the remaining skirt for the same purpose.[59]

As Foote's gunboats approached the river batteries, anxiety mounted in the Confederate line as the ironclads, now only 900 to 1,000 yards out, passed the obstruction placed in the river below the guns. Bedford later explained, "in ordinary stages of water this might have offered some impediment but at the time of the attack the river was very high, and the boats passed over without the least halt or break in their line of approach."[60] An animated Lieutenant Colonel Nathan Bedford Forrest, watching from the heights above the batteries, turned to his second in command, Major David Campbell Kelley, a Methodist minister before the war, and exclaimed, "Parson! For God's sake, pray; nothing but God almighty can save that fort!"[61]

The Federal gunboats continued moving forward, and as they did, the "plunging shot" of the Confederate guns became more effective. On the *St. Louis,* a round from a 32-pounder struck the pilothouse, penetrating "the inch and a half iron and the fifteen-inch oak."[62]

Back in the river batteries, Private John G. Fuqua of Company A, 30th Tennessee, was serving as gunner on the Number 5 gun. Fuqua was enjoying himself despite the volcanic cacophony of battle erupting around him. Disregarding the danger of the incoming 42-pounder and eight-inch shells bursting indiscriminately in their midst, Fuqua carefully and deliberately aimed his 32-pounder. Captain Bidwell noticed Fuqua and described him as standing "perfectly straight, calm, cool, and collected."[63] As Fuqua adjusted windage and elevation, he exclaimed, "Now boys see me take a chimney."[64] With some of the most accurate artillery shooting or unbelievable luck, at the discharge of the gun, both the chimney and flagstaff of the ironclad were seen to fall. The jubilant Fuqua then threw his cap into the air, and with a shout of defiance and unbridled confidence, yelled, "Come on you cowardly scoundrels, you are not at Fort Henry."[65] One of the Federal sailors described,

> ...a thirty-two pound ball struck the flagstaff of the *St. Louis*, carrying it away close to the ship's deck. It had no sooner fallen than one of our brave men jumped before the mouth of a cannon just about to be fired, and seizing the spar placed it in an upright position, and coolly remained a mark for the enemy while he secured it to the ship's deck with a rope. A few moments after this the flagstaff of the *Louisville* was carried off; that of the *Carondelet* went next, and that of the *Pittsburg* followed soon after.[66]

At 4:00 p.m., as "the battle raged with all its horrors," the flotilla closed to within 600 yards, and the Confederate fire began striking with "deadly effect."[67] A round shattered the pilothouse of the *Carondelet*, mortally wounding her pilot. Things soon became far more serious for the *Carondelet* as her left 42-pounder rifle burst. Nevertheless, the intrepid *Carondelet* fought on with her two remaining bow guns.[68] Additional damage was done to the gunboat as an 8-inch shell fired from one of the timber-clads exploded above her, sending shell fragments through her casemate.[69] Signal Quartermaster Matthew Arther was the chief of the *Carondelet's* starboard bow gun. The Scottish-born sailor, who had enlisted at Boston, was awarded the medal of honor for his actions. Arther's citation reads that he was "conspicuous for valor and devotion, serving most faithfully, effectively and valiantly."[70]

Soon Lieutenant Bedford noticed the *Carondelet* a little in advance of the other boats and "hugging the eastern shore."[71] In this position, the Yankee gunboat "offered her side" to the columbiad, of which the Rebel gunners took full advantage. Bedford stated, "Several well-directed shots raked the side and tore away her armor, according to the report of Lieut Sparkman, who was on the lookout. Just as the other boats began to drift back, the *Carondelet* forged ahead for about a half length, as though she intended making the attempt to pass the battery, and it is presumable that she then received the combined fire of all the guns."[72]

By this time, the gun deck of the *Carondelet* was a bloody mess. A Federal seaman described,

> The men were at the muzzle of the middle bow-gun, loading it, the warning came just in time for them to jump aside as a 32-pounder struck the lower sill, and glancing up struck the upper sill, then, falling on the inner edge of the lower sill, bounded on deck and spun around like a top, but hurt no one. It was very evident that if the men who were loading had not obeyed the order to drop, several of them would have been killed.[73]

Again, words of warning sounded,

> "Lookout!" "Down!" were again soon heard down went the gunner and his men, as the whizzing shot glanced on the gun, taking off the gunner's cap and the heads of two of the young

men who trusted to luck, and in defiance of the order were standing up or passing behind him. This shot killed another man also, who was at the last gun of the starboard side, and disabled the gun. It came in with a hissing sound; three sharp spats and a heavy bang told the sad fate of three brave comrades. Before the decks were well sanded, there was so much blood on them that our men could not work the guns without slipping.[74]

As the Confederates banged away at the assaulting gunboats, the Rebel gunners, according to their training, skipped their rounds across the water to strike the ironclads below the waterline. Ross describes, "That was a singular feature in our water practices; where a cannonball strikes with the ricochet. Instantly the spray is in a perpendicular column 30 to 50 feet high when it appears to remain stationary for a distinct interval of time before it falls it is almost perfectly white in appearance."[75] The ricochet shots were effective as the *Carondelet* took two rounds in her bow between "wind and water."[76]

With the nearness of the gunboats, the tapered contour of the 10-inch columbiad and 6.4-inch rifle made it very difficult to take precise aim at such close range. The gunners could see the rounds as they left their guns and made adjustments accordingly. One shot from the rifle was seen to go over the gunboat, as a result, the next shot was aimed much lower. This next round "appeared to take the boat lengthwise and pass entirely through," stated Ross.[77]

Now only 200 yards out, Captain Bidwell observed, "They came within 200 yards of my guns, when the action grew terrible for about one hour and a half, without any damage to us."[78] Bidwell continued, "Their fire was more destructive to our works at 2 miles than at 200 yards. They overfired us from that distance."[79] Private William E. Maurey of the 49th Tennessee observing from the fort stated, "Our Company being in a direct

The USS *St. Louis* served as Flag Officer Foote's flagship in the February 14, 1862, naval assault against the Fort Donelson River Batteries. The *St. Louis* was commanded by Leonard Paulding. In the battle for the Fort Donelson River Batteries, the *St. Louis* was struck 59 times (Naval History and Heritage Command, NH 108512).

line of the Gun Boats and Battery consequently the Shell came whizzing over our heads constantly."[80]

The gunboats now came so close that Captain Ross feared the sailors would attempt to come ashore and storm the batteries. Ross maintained that "We had determined to sell our batteries as dearly as possible even with staves handspikes and sponge staffs. We had no cutlasses."[81]

As the *St. Louis* continued to be pounded, a seaman described, "a shot entered our deck on the starboard side, and passing through it glanced downward to the shell room, striking the ship's cook, Charles H. Baker, of Philadelphia, in the head, literally tearing the skull off."[82] The sailor continued, "Several heavy balls now glanced over the pilot house, piercing the chimneys, and carrying away the chimney guys. These were followed by a couple of shots which struck our vessel just above water mark."[83]

Flag Officer Foote was in the pilothouse of the *St. Louis* when an incoming round smashed through killing the pilot, F.A. Riley, and wounding Foote. The room was "filled with the pieces of broken wheels, chains, room furniture, and rubbish of every sort; there was no one there to take the helm save the Commodore."[84] Flag Officer Foote, "equal to the emergency, … seized the remaining handles of the wheel, and for a quarter of an hour acted the double part of commander and pilot, and at last, when compelled to fall back, he kept his bow to the foe, and gave his orders as calmly and coolly as when first entering the action."[85]

The flagship *St. Louis* and *Carondelet* were not alone in the pummeling being received. The *Pittsburgh*, commanded by Egbert Thompson, steamed ahead and at 4:15 p.m. had advanced to within 450 yards of the fort. To that point, the gunboat had expended 105 shells and six rounds of grape. Like the *St. Louis* and *Carondelet*, the *Pittsburgh* was getting pounded. A 10-inch shell from Bedford's columbiad went through the pilothouse but somehow missed all four pilots inside. Another round went through the middle bow port, passed through the cabin, penetrated a stack of hammocks, bags of coal, continued through the escape pipe, and passed through the wheelhouse before exiting the stern. More seriously, by this time, the *Pittsburgh* was in dire straits with two holes in her bow. To keep the boat afloat long enough to get out of the range of the Rebel guns, Thompson had all the ship's guns ran to the boat's stern to lighten the bow.[86]

The Confederates also played havoc on the *Louisville*. A bystander recalled the horror that was unleashed on her deck as Captain Dove complimented one of the gun crews on a well-placed shot. About that time, a 32-pounder on its deadly errand came through a gunport completely severing the gunner "in twain, scattering the blood and brain and mangled flesh over Captain Dove's person in sickening profusion; but the Captain never blanched; he only wiped the human gore from his face, and in an instant was superintending the replacement of another gun as if nothing had happened."[87]

Undaunted, the *Louisville* remained on station with the other gunboats when a "huge solid shot struck our boat just at the angle of the upper deck and pilot house."[88] The shot "perforated the iron plating, passed through the heavy timbers and buried itself in a pile of hammocks just in front and in a direct line with the boilers."[89] Within minutes, another shell "racked us from bow to stern, passed through the wheel-house, emerged, dropped and exploded in the river just at our stern."[90] Without cessation, "a ten-inch solid shot entered our starboard bow port, demolished a gun carriage, killed three men and wounded four others, traversed the entire length of the boat, and sank into the river in our wake."[91] Another shell "came shrieking through the air, striking fair into our forward

The USS *Pittsburgh* was commanded by Egbert Thompson (Naval History and Heritage Command, NH 45557).

starboard ports, killing another man and wounding two more, passed aft, sundering our rudder chains, and rendering the boat unmanageable."[92] After this beating "we were compelled to drop astern, and leave the scene of action; but our gunners sent their respects to the rebels as long as their fire could be the least effective; and, so far as we were concerned, the battle was over."[93]

Trailing fifteen-hundred yards behind the gunboats were the two timber-clads, the *Tyler* and *Conestoga*. During the engagement, the *Conestoga* fired thirty-six eight-inch shells during the action; the *Tyler* sixty-one.[94]

Captain Culbertson stated, "The fire of the 32-pounder became so destructive when the enemy had advanced to within 300 yards that they were compelled to retire."[95] Commander Walke added,

> At this point of the action, when the "Louisville" backed down, Flag-Officer Foote had been slightly wounded; the pilots of the "St. Louis," "Louisville" and "Carondelet," were wounded mortally; and the port bow-gun of the latter had just exploded, prostrating and blinding the captain, officers and crew. Pilot-houses also, were battered in, and wheels broken, each vessel having been struck about fifty times with 128-pound and 32-pound shot; and forty-five of our men and officers were killed or wounded.[96]

When the battered gunboats drifted out of range, a cheer rang out from the Confederate artillerists that was echoed around the Confederate line. A member of the 30th Tennessee in the fort stated, "The news flew through our entire line and we could here the shouts of triumph reverbiate through the hills and vallies."[97] Lieutenant Bedford commanding the columbiad described, "the gun-boats were seen drifting helplessly down the stream, and a shout of exultation leaped from the lips of every soldier in the fort. It was taken up by the men in the trenches, and for awhile a shout of victory, the sweetest strain

Sketches by Alexander Simplot appearing in the March 15, 1862, issue of *Harper's Weekly*.

to the ears of those who win, reverberated over the hills and hollows around the little village of Dover."[98]

The gunboats had taken a pounding. A Federal sailor expressed his feelings following the attack. "My curiosity is satiated. I have no particular desire to be on board a man-of-war when another battery is to be attacked, but, on the contrary, think I should prefer a land view. The fact is, our boats, are proof against ordinary shot, even as large as a sixty-four; but this trial has demonstrated the fact that rifled thirty-pounders, even, will penetrate our iron sides, while one hundred and twenty pounders nearly laughed at the obstruction."[99]

In the Valentine's Day fight for the river batteries, the flagship *St. Louis* took sixty-one hits. The *Louisville* next in line was hit about forty times. Forty-seven rounds struck the *Pittsburgh*, and the *Carondelet* was hit fifty-four times. A Federal sailor claimed that the Confederates fired about five hundred rounds, while the gunboats fired slightly over three hundred shots with about seventy-five of those being 8-inch shells.[100]

As soon as the gunboats were beaten back, and while the exhausted artillerymen were still panting from the physical exertion of the repeated and fatiguing loading of the heavy guns, Lieutenant Colonel Alfred Robb of the 49th Tennessee Infantry supporting the batteries, sent a "grateful stimulant along the line of guns."[101] Soon dinner which had been prepared by members of the 49th Tennessee was brought down to the gunners, but a parting shot from one of the gunboats covered it with dirt.[102]

All considered, the inexperienced Rebel infantrymen turned artillerists did remarkably well. Commander Walke had hailed that the gunners of the batteries were "manned

INTERIOR OF FORT DONELSON.

INTERIOR OF THE LOWER WATER BATTERY AT FORT DONELSON.—Sketched by Mr. Alexander Simplot.—[See Page 183.]

Additional sketches by Alexander Simplot appeared in the March 22, 1862, issue of *Harper's Weekly*.

and officered by the best men of the Southern army."[103] Nothing could be further from the truth. The men of the Fort Donelson river batteries, for the most part, were a bunch of plowboys fresh from the farm, who had, in the enthusiasm of the day, recently enlisted in the army, most having never even seen a heavy cannon. At the last minute, in desperation, they were assigned to the guns.

The gunboats were forced to retire down the river after receiving severe damage from the batteries. Afterward, Generals Floyd and Pillow personally visited the artillerists and complimented them on their performance and promising them that if they continued keeping the gunboats back, their infantry would keep the land forces at a safe distance. Lieutenant Bedford who had watched the enemy reinforcements coming ashore all morning down in the river bend, remarked, that "as he stood there before the generals, just thirty-six hours before a surrender, receiving their assurances of protection, wondered if they were able to fulfill their promise, or if they were merely indulging in an idle habit of braggadocio."[104]

By this time, the city-class ironclads had limped back downstream around the safety of the bend out of the range of the river batteries. They had been soundly repulsed and spent the next day burying their dead. Commander Walke of the *Carondelet* stated,

The 15th was employed in the burial of our slain comrades. I read the Episcopal service on board the Carondelet under our flag at half-mast; and the sailors bore their late companions to a lonely field within the shadows of the hills. When they were about to lower the first coffin, a Roman Catholic priest appeared, and his services being accepted, he read the prayers for the dead. As the last service was ended, the sound of the battle being waged by

General Grant, like the rumbling of distant thunder, was the only requiem for our departed shipmates.[105]

Ultimately the Battle of Fort Donelson, contrary to initial beliefs, would not be determined by the river batteries and gunboats. Despite everyone's amazement, the river batteries successfully fought off the feared gunboats. The contest would resume the following morning as the Confederates surprisingly seized the initiative.

Epilogue

"One of the bravest acts recorded in warfare"

That night (February 14), Floyd, Pillow, Buckner, and Johnson held a conference of war. With the successful repulse of the gunboats, they devised a plan to break Grant's investment and open a route of escape where they proposed to march the army out of Fort Donelson and link up with Albert Sidney Johnston.

In the meantime, Grant's reinforcements continued maneuvering into position, extending their lines to envelop the Rebel works. The Confederate commanders were quick to realize that with these reinforcements, Grant would soon have them encircled. They also realized that a successful investment would also eventually force their surrender. In addition to McClernand and Smith, a new division commanded by Lew Wallace had arrived on the field. Wallace was positioned between McClernand and Smith, allowing McClernand to continue to move to the right, further enveloping the Confederate flank. With Wallace on the field, Grant had achieved numerical superiority with 26,000 men to the Confederate's 16,000.

Early on the morning of February 15, Grant traveled 6 miles over rough frozen ground to the landing to confer with Flag Officer Foote. As Grant left, he issued orders for his generals not to bring on an engagement, apparently underestimating Floyd and Pillow or giving little thought to the possibility that they might attack him. However, while Grant was several miles away meeting with Foote, the Confederates rolled out of their entrenchments and launched a series of vicious attacks against McClernand ensconced on Dudley's Hill. The Confederate objective was to roll up the Federal right and push them back well beyond the Forge Road, which, if successful, would serve as their avenue of escape.

To make the attack, the Confederates weakened their right flank as they transferred Simon B. Buckner's troops to the left to support the breakout attack. Left holding the works on the Rebel right were only nine companies (450 men) of the 30th Tennessee under Major J.J. Turner. With the shortage of men, Turner scarcely had a man posted in the works about every ten feet.

By 8:00 a.m., the Confederate attack gained initiative as McArthur's Federal brigade gave way, and Oglesby's brigade, under immense pressure, also broke. Next, as Oglesby's line disintegrated, W.H.L. Wallace came up, followed by Charles Cruft. As Cruft advanced, his men fired into the rear of W.H.L. Wallace, causing chaos in the Federal ranks. The Federals continued falling back well beyond the Forge Road, leaving the Confederate avenue of escape open.

With their objective secured, Pillow made a move that totally reversed everything the Confederates had worked so hard to gain up to that point. With the Federal right shattered, instead of following the plan (if there ever was such a thing), and taking his men out by the Forge Road, Gideon Pillow made one of the most incomprehensible decisions of the entire Civil War. With the avenue of escape open, Pillow turned his men around and marched them back into the fort. When Floyd observed Pillow returning, he rode out to meet him and exclaimed, "In the name of God, General Pillow, what have we been fighting all day for? Certainly not to show our powers but solely to secure the [Forge] Road, and after securing it, you order it given up!"[1] But in the company of the persuasive and strong-willed Pillow, Floyd vacillated and handed Grant a decisive victory.

By this time, Grant had arrived on the field and made a couple of very astute observations. Grant noticed that some of the Confederate dead and wounded were wearing their knapsacks. Grant correctly deduced that the Confederate assault was a breakout attempt. Grant also realized that with the strength of the Confederate attack on his right, the Rebel left must be weak. Based on these observations, Grant ordered McClernand to attack and then sent orders to General Charles Ferguson Smith, commanding his left division, and instructed Smith to "charge upon the left."[2]

Smith formed two of his three brigades—Cook's and Lauman's. Smith led Lauman's brigade forward in person. As the insensitive old warrior astride his white horse looked around, he told his anxious Iowans, "you volunteered to be killed for love of country, now you can be."[3] With that, Smith started forward over the snow-covered ground moving against the lightly held outer works of Major J.J. Turner and nine companies of the 30th Tennessee. After a stubborn resistance, the 30th Tennessee gave way, and Smith's men captured the outer works overlooking the Eddyville Road. Here, Color Corporal Voltaire P. Twombly of the 2nd Iowa Infantry, by his heroic actions, was awarded the Medal of Honor. This was the second Medal of Honor given for bravery at the Battle of Fort Donelson.

Now victorious, Smith reformed his men and continued forward. On the next ridge, the 30th Tennessee had formed a new line and was reinforced by the 49th Tennessee and a battalion of the 50th Tennessee. As Smith assaulted this new line, the Confederates stubbornly held, and Smith's men, unable to break this line, withdrew back to the outer line they had just recently captured.

Darkness soon covered the field. That night, the Confederate commanders met for a decisive meeting, the outcome of which would seal the fate of Fort Donelson and its brave defenders, as well as Nashville, Sidney Johnston, and the State of Tennessee.

In this meeting, the Confederate commanders decided to surrender Fort Donelson. As the commanders discussed their options, a report arrived that the Federals had closed the route of escape. This information was based on an erroneous report that Federal pickets were in the area. Nathan Bedford Forrest balked at the news and went out to check for himself. Forrest quickly discovered what the scouts had mistaken as Federal pickets was only a fence row.

Nevertheless, back at the Rice House, the most unbelievable course of events began unfolding. While the bodies of hundreds of dead Confederate soldiers lay frozen to the earth needlessly sacrificed in the break-out attempt earlier in the day, John B. Floyd, spoke up and said, that he feared he was a wanted man by the Federals. Floyd conveyed that when he was Secretary of War, that the North had accused him of overstocking arsenals in the South. Floyd admitted he was afraid of what the Federals might do to him if he was captured. Putting his interests before the concern of his men, Floyd refused to surrender, and he proposed to take his 2 brigades of Virginians out with him. Gideon Pillow, next in command, spoke next. With Pillow, the succession of events became even more absurd. Pillow was the man, who on multiple occasions, had pompously and bombastically announced: "I will never surrender."[4] While many of Pillow's wounded men suffered untold agony lying on the frozen field of battle, Pillow then made good on his claim, as he, like Floyd, abdicated command and passed it to Simon Bolivar Buckner.

By this time, Forrest had returned from reconnoitering the lines. Forrest emphatically stated that he did not come there to surrender. As he left, he pledged to cut his way out with his men. Wasting little time, Forrest gathered his men, crossed Lick Creek, and never even saw an enemy. Pillow and Floyd lost little time in making their escape. Pillow was ferried across the river on a flatboat. Soon, a steamboat arrived at the Dover landing bringing in a regiment of Mississippians as reinforcements. As the Mississippians offloaded, John B. Floyd and his two Virginia regiments boarded, shamelessly abandoning the newly arrived Mississippians sealing their fate with the rest of the garrison.

The Dover Hotel where the Fort Donelson garrison was unconditionally surrendered on the morning of February 16, 1862. Approximately 13,000 Confederate defenders were taken to prisoner of war camps like Camp Douglas, Illinois, while their commanding generals Floyd and Pillow escaped (authors' photograph).

Buckner now attempted to do the honorable thing and sent a message to his old friend, Ulysses S. Grant, asking that commissioners be appointed to discuss terms of surrender. When Grant received the note, he read it, and the surly Charles F. Smith growled, "No terms to the damned Rebels."[5] Grant replied that the only terms he will accept are an immediate and unconditional surrender, "for I propose to move on your works."[6] A runner returned Grant's reply to the Confederate commander. Buckner was appalled as he read it. Buckner, who believed he had no other alternative, accepted what he thought to be very ungracious terms.

Meanwhile, back in the fort, General Buckner sent a courier to Colonel Sugg of the 50th Tennessee with instructions to raise the white flag over the fort. This order proved to be somewhat problematic as no one had a white flag. Third Lieutenant Charles Tyler sarcastically stated, "nobody expecting to need one."[7] Second Lieutenant R.L. Cobb had a white sheet that was raised at daybreak.[8]

Down in the river batteries, word of the impending surrender arrived. Private Joseph Hinkle of Bidwell's company stated, "My company, that had been fighting with the river batteries, had orders to get with the regiment, and we marched up to the village of Dover nearby, where we found everything in a commotion."[9] Captain Bidwell stated, "I was ordered by Colonel Head to leave my battery at 2 o'clock Sunday morning and rejoin the regiment, which I did, and never returned to the guns again."[10] Bidwell continued, "I escaped from Fort Donelson early Sunday morning by crossing the Cumberland River in a skiff with Captain Frank Duffy, of the Thirty-fifth Tennessee. When we crossed we could have been seen by the Federal troops, but they had not come into Dover."[11]

In the meantime, approximately 36 ($N = 92$–39%) of the boys from Company A, 50th Tennessee, took matters into their own hands and escaped (Figure 2).[12] Private Ed Sears was one of them. After the white flag was raised in the fort, Private Sears went to his lieutenant and asked if he was at liberty to attempt an escape. The lieutenant replied, "Do as you please, but to attempt escape is very dangerous as the Federals have us surrounded."[13] Willing to take his chances attempting an escape rather than endure the hell of a Federal prison camp, Sears made his escape by crossing the Cumberland River. Arriving on the opposite shore, Sears, possibly with other men of his company, traveled across country and made the 70-mile journey safely home near the Narrows of the Harpeth in Cheatham County. Consequently, only one member of the Maury Artillery managed to escape while two other men from Bidwell's company followed the lead of their captain and absconded.

Approximately 13,000 Confederate soldiers and 58 pieces of artillery now passed into Grant's custody. In addition to the Confederate soldiers in confinement, there were many slaves captured as well. "Over seventy-four negroes, mostly slaves, captured at Fort Donelson, were transported to Camp Chase, at Columbus, Ohio," reported one newspaper.[14] Aside from those who were body servants to Confederate troops, there was the issue of what to do with the numerous slaves who had been brought to the twin rivers to work on the fortifications. It appears that the Federals impressed them for their own purposes. Fort Donelson Park Ranger Susan Hawkins explains, "After the surrender of Fort Donelson in February 1862, Grant issued an order that explained how slaves would be 'employed for the Quarter Masters Department for the benefit of the Government' rather than returning them to the enemy."[15]

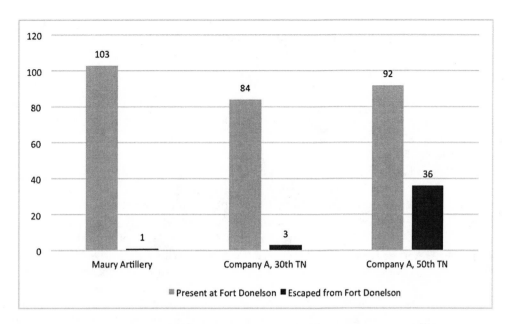

Figure 2. Men Present and Men Escaped from Fort Donelson River Batteries, February 16, 1862

It now became apparent that the dreadful fear of the gunboats at Fort Donelson was misplaced. Given the experience the Confederates had with the gunboats at Fort Henry, everyone from the highest general to the lowest private thought the real threat at Donelson lay not in the thousands of northern troops who had surrounded them but in the dreaded gunboats. Lieutenant Hugh Bedford said as much, "It must be remembered, however, that the great fear was of the gun-boats. It was apprehended that their recent achievements at Fort Henry would be repeated at Donelson."[16] The green infantrymen who were quickly trained on the guns and the Maury Light artillerymen who were hurriedly trained on the big guns gave an excellent account of themselves as they stopped Foote's flotilla dead in its tracks. The primary threat at Fort Donelson as it turned out was Grant's land forces.

The fall of Tennessee's twin river forts was a major catastrophe for the South. Forts Henry and Donelson were the first significant Union victories of the Civil War. The fall of Fort Henry opened the Tennessee River to the Federals to Florence, Alabama. These twin victories served as the initial steps leading to Ulysses S. Grant becoming the General-in-Chief of the Union armies. Grant's victories at Henry and Donelson launched his career forward and earned him the moniker of Unconditional Surrender Grant.

Moreover, after the reduction of Fort Donelson, Federal troops continued their move up the Cumberland River, wreaking havoc on the production facilities of the South. The fall of both forts deprived the South of its richest iron deposits as well as the vast agricultural production of this area known as the Confederate heartland. Specifically, not only were the most extensive iron deposits lost, but also the growing military production facilities in both Clarksville and Nashville along with the loss of the vital iron manufacturing facilities, the Cumberland Iron Works, as well as the significant gunpowder manufacturer, the Cheatham, Watson, and Company, both located just up the Cumberland River from Fort Donelson. Fort Donelson Park Historian Van Riggins stated, "The fall of Fort Donelson stopped nearly all iron production in Middle Tennessee for the duration of the war."[17] The fall of Fort Donelson opened the Cumberland River to Nashville and handed Lincoln the first captured Confederate state capital. The fall of these forts rendered Confederate Department Commander Albert Sidney Johnston's defensive line untenable. It forced him to withdraw out of Kentucky, abandoning critical points like Bowling Green, Hickman, and Columbus.

After their victory at Fort Donelson, the Federals built a new fort closer to Dover (where the National Cemetery is now located). Within a year of the fall of Donelson, the Confederates made two attempts to retake Dover. The first occurred in late August 1862 as Lieutenant Colonel Thomas G. Woodward, who had recently retaken Clarksville, made an ill-fated attempt. Woodward's foray left "the village of Dover mostly destroyed by fire during the attack."[18] Then, on February 3, 1863, the Battle of Dover or the Second Battle of Fort Donelson occurred. Confederate troops under the command of General Joe Wheeler once again tried unsuccessfully to retake Dover.

In March 1867, only five years after the February 1862 Battle of Fort Donelson, a National Cemetery was established. The Federal soldiers who were buried on the field and others who later died from wounds or disease and buried in local cemeteries were disinterred and reburied in a 15.4-acre plot on a bluff overlooking the majestic Cumberland River. Of the 670 Union dead, only 158 are identified. The remaining 512 are unknown.[19] The Confederate dead were left buried in unidentified mass graves across the battlefield, where they remain today known only to God.

As the National Cemetery was established, five heavy guns, original to the Battle of

Nashville, the Tennessee State Capital, was only 76 miles upstream from Fort Donelson. The demise of Fort Donelson brought the fall of Nashville nine days later (DeGolyer Library, Southern Methodist University, Civil War: Photographs, Manuscripts, and Imprints).

Fort Donelson, were returned from the St. Louis Arsenal. One of the handwritten cemetery records states, "There are some 5 (five) heavy cannon and carriages (original trophies captured here) now lying dismounted below ordinary high watermark at the Landing. These were shipped here from St. Louis arsenal to decorate the grounds. They should be at once hauled up near the grounds. If the mule teams are too busy disinterring, perhaps a few yoke of oxen could be hired for this to advantage."[20] These five guns were soon mounted in the National Cemetery. Three of the guns were 63 cwt 32-pounders. The other guns were two crude 12-pounders that had been produced by the Memphis & Charleston Railroad.[21]

In 1916 the Army Corps of Engineers built a lock and dam just to the northeast of the Upper Battery. The workers gained access to the lock by walking "through the center of the parapet."[22] This cut through the parapet was likely the result of a shell crater from the battle, which continued to erode over the years. As it was the lowest point in the parapet, the workers naturally utilized it for their egress to the lock. The presence of the lock increased erosion in the Upper Battery.

Construction on Lock D was at least partially completed by the Foster and Creighton Company. W.F. Foster of this company was the young assistant engineer who helped Adna Anderson choose the site of Fort Donelson in May 1861. As Foster's company dredged the river about ½ to 1 mile below the fort, they pumped up "several 10-inch cannonballs."[23]

Aside from the National Cemetery, it was realized early on that what happened at Fort Donelson should be memorialized. After work by local citizens and Joseph Byrns, a member of the U.S. House of Representatives, the Fort Donelson National Battlefield came into being with the enactment of House Bill #5500.[24]

Fort Donelson became a National Battlefield Park on March 26, 1928, and was dedicated on July 4, 1932. The address was made by Judge John W. DeWitt, who was considered an "outstanding Tennessee historian."[25] In DeWitt's speech, he "impressively

Pictured is a 12-pounder smoothbore, also original to the Battle of Fort Donelson. This gun, like its counterpart, was made by the Memphis and Charleston Railroad in Memphis, Tennessee in 1861 (authors' photograph).

A second 12-pounder, the fifth and final gun known to be original to the Battle of Fort Donelson. It was produced by the Memphis and Charleston Railroad. These five original guns were returned to the park from the St. Louis Arsenal in 1867 with documentation stating that these guns were "original trophies" captured at Fort Donelson (authors' photograph).

described the defense against the gunboats at Fort Donelson as one of the bravest acts recorded in warfare."[26]

Over the years, great care has gone into preserving and interpreting the fort and, in particular, the river batteries. On July 27, 1937, a project to restore the powder magazine of the lower water battery was begun. As the workers excavated the powder magazine, they found burned charcoal, rotten slabs, a hollow cannonball "about six inches in diameter," a second cannonball, and an elongated shell fragment. Instead of rebuilding the powder magazine using wooden timbers for the walls and ceiling, the structure was made permanent by using concrete.[27]

In the 1930s, the Tennessee River was dammed, and Kentucky Dam was completed in 1944. The construction of these dams resulted in the creation of Kentucky Lake and the total submersion of Fort Henry. Around 1965 Lock D was destroyed. A year later, the Cumberland River was dammed near Grand Rivers, Kentucky, forming Lake Barkley. Before this, the narrow strip of land between the twin rivers was called Between the Rivers. Now, this strip is known as the Land Between the Lakes.

Between November 3, 1964, and August 17, 1965, soldiers of the 70th and 326th Airborne Engineer Battalions of the 101st Airborne Division from nearby Fort Campbell were employed to use minesweepers to conduct archaeological salvage operations to search specific locations at Fort Donelson to recover artifacts from sites some of which would be impounded by the creation of Lake Barkley. The soldiers recovered several artifacts. These included many shell fragments, sixty-four 2-inch balls, and two 6-pounders (from stands of 8-inch naval grapeshot). Of additional interest was an unexploded 7-inch

Reconstructed powder magazine of the Lower Battery. The magazine was supervised by Corporal Daniel C. Lyle of Company A, 50th Tennessee (authors' photograph).

Dyer shell found in the area of the Lower Battery and four iron bars recovered from gun position #11, undoubtedly used in the mounting of the 10-inch columbiad.

In the spring of 1968, further archaeological investigations, under the direction of Lee Hanson and the Department of the Interior Division of Archaeology, were conducted in the river batteries. The purpose of the digs was to discover previously unknown construction details of the batteries that could be used in their restoration.[28] The archaeological

Left: Base plate to a 32-pounder grapeshot recovered in the 1968 archaeological excavations of the River Batteries (authors' photograph).
Right: A complete 7-inch Dyer shell. This shell, like many of its kind, failed to explode. Captain Reuben Ross, commanding the 6.4-inch rifled columbiad, counted fourteen unexploded shells of this type within the confines of the Upper Battery (authors' photograph).

A series of 32-pounders of the Lower Battery showing the gun carriages produced by park employee David Nolin in the 1980s. Nolin based the carriages on original 19th century plans of Major Alfred Mordecai as he formed the carriages using concrete (authors' photograph).

investigations uncovered eight heavy artillery positions, which helped to reestablish the line on the northeast end of the heavily eroded Lower Battery. The dig further indicated that the Confederates were "using makeshift materials and working in great haste."[29]

In the early 1980s, the gun emplacements in the Lower Battery were faced with rough lumber, and a log veneer was placed in the lower gun battery magazine. This was the first time that a gun was put into the gun pit, on a painted wood carriage. Later the

Left: 32-pounder grape shot ball recovered in the Lower Battery (authors' photograph). *Right:* 32-pounder solid shot recovered from Fort Donelson (authors' photograph).

Image showing the interior of Fort Donelson which was constructed on the heights above the River Batteries for their protection (authors' photograph).

Large friction primers still wrapped in newspaper recovered from the Lower Battery (authors' photograph).

National Park Service revised the safety rules and requirements for cannon and display carriages. Wood was not permitted if it stayed outdoors. Park employee David Nolin used 19th century Major Alfred Mordecai plans to build forms and re-created the 32-pounder barbette carriages. Mr. Nolin made the forms to construct the concrete carriages for the 32-pounders in the 1990s. Nolin mounted the 32-pounder carronades in the Upper Battery in 2001. In 2003 a cast-iron carriage for the 6.4-inch rifle was obtained from the Paulson Brothers Ordnance Corporation in Clear Lake, Wisconsin. Paulson Brothers also manufactured the carriage for the 10-inch columbiad, which was mounted sometime after 2003.[30]

Pair of 10-inch solid shot for the columbiad. The columbiad was mounted in position #11 in the Lower Battery. These are two of three rounds that were recovered in the vacant adjacent position #10 in the 1968 archaeological excavations (authors' photograph).

Today, Fort Donelson is a beautiful, well-cared-for National Battlefield Park. Markers dot the landscape throughout the park identifying troop positions and explaining the actions that occurred. The premiere display, however, is the Water Battery overlooking the Cumberland River. As the visitor stands in the Water Battery and looks at the majestic Cumberland flowing past the batteries, the river is similar in size to what it was in flood stage at the time of the 1862 battle. In the Lower Battery, the visitor is presented with a refurbished line of works with a powder magazine and six authentic Civil War guns, two of which are original to the battle. If not careful, the visitor will miss the three vacant gun positions (1–3) dropping down the hill to the east toward the river.

Of the five 32-pounders now mounted in the lower battery (and one in the National Cemetery), three (guns in positions 6 and 8 and the one in the cemetery) were originally mounted in the river batteries during the battle. The other three 32-pounders are original Civil War guns, just not present at the 1862 Battle of Fort Donelson. Gun positions 1 through 3 are vacant. The gun in position number 4 is a 32-pounder Seacoast Gun Model 1845. The gun bearing 1846 on the left trunnion was produced in 1846 by the Tredegar Iron Works, Richmond, Virginia (registry number 26). The right trunnion is marked "JRA" over "TF," indicating its Tredegar origination. The gun weight (7,159 pounds) is stamped on the breech and was inspected by Alfred Mordecai (Figure 3).[31]

Current Location	Pattern	Year Produced	Maker	Description	Weight	Original to Water Battery
National Cemetery	63 cwt Gun	?	?	32-pdr		Yes
Lower Battery						
Gun Position 4	M1845	1846	Tredegar	32-pdr	7159	No
Gun Position 5	63 cwt Gun	1833	Bellona	32-pdr	?	No

Current Location	Pattern	Year Produced	Maker	Description	Weight	Original to Water Battery
Gun Position 6	63 cwt Gun	1821	Bellona	32-pdr	60-2-24	Yes
Gun Position 7	M1845	1846	Tredegar	32-pdr	7,185	No
Gun Position 8	63 cwt Gun	1820	West Point	32 pdr	60-1-26	Yes
Gun Position 11	Columbiad	13 January 1863	Tredegar	10-inch	13,365	No
Upper Battery						
Gun Position 1	Ship Carronade	Reproduction	-	-	-	No
Gun Position 2	Columbiad Rifle	Reproduction	-	-	-	No
Gun Position 3	Ship Carronade	Reproduction	-	-	-	No
Details of Other Original Guns						
LB Gun Position 11	Columbiad	1861	Tredegar	10-inch	?	Yes
UB Gun Position 2	Rifled Columbiad	4 November 1861	Tredegar	6.4-inch	?	Yes
LB = Lower Battery						
UB = Upper Battery						

Figure 3. Guns Associated with the Fort Donelson River Batteries

Olmstead, Stark, and Tucker identified the gun in position number 5, as manufactured at the West Point Foundry, West Point, New York, in 1820 (registry number 159). This gun was originally part of the armament of the USS *Congress*. The frigate, *Congress*, was part of the Union blockading squadron and was sunk on March 8, 1862, in the famous Battle of Hampton Roads, Virginia, by the *CSS Virginia*.[32] However, the markings on the gun seem to indicate otherwise. The left trunnion is marked "1833," and the right trunnion is marked "BF," indicating Bellona Foundry not West Point.

Position number 6 is the location of Captain Joseph Dixon's death. The gun in position number 6 is a 32-pounder 60 cwt[33] Navy Gun. Known as a "Gradual Increase Gun." The gun mounted here is one of two guns originally installed in the river batteries. The right trunnion is marked "1821," and the left trunnion is marked "32 pd." The top of the breech near the vent appears to be marked "IG&C BF" It was produced in 1821 at the Bellona Foundry, Midlothian, Virginia (registry #112).[34]

A 32-pounder Model 1845 Seacoast Gun occupies position number 7. The gun was manufactured in 1846 at Tredegar Iron Works, Richmond, Virginia (registry #21). Like the gun in position number 4, this gun's weight (7,185 pounds) is stamped on the breech. It was inspected by Alfred Mordecai.[35] The left trunnion is marked "1846," and the right trunnion is marked "JRA" "TF."

Position number 8 contains another gun original to the river batteries. This gun is a 32-pounder 63 cwt gun produced at the West Point Foundry in 1820 (registry #82). This gun comprised part of the armament of the USS *Ohio* circa 1845.[36] The left trunnion of this gun is marked "32." The right trunnion is marked "1820," and the breech near the vent is marked "WPF" "A" "60-1-26" "P."

The 10-inch columbiad occupies position number 11. This gun, also an original Civil War gun, began as part of the armament of Vicksburg, Mississippi. It was cast at Tredegar Iron Works on January 13, 1863 (foundry number 1735). The gun weighs 13,365 pounds.[37] According to former park historian Jimmy Jobe, the columbiad was buried and later unearthed at Vicksburg and was eventually sent to Fort Donelson. Mr. Jobe indicated that when the gun was discovered, it had a note in a bottle that had been placed in the tube identifying the gun as the one which sunk the USS *Cincinnati*.[38]

Three guns are mounted in the Upper Battery, two 32-pounder carronades, and the 6.4-inch rifle.[39] These are all reproductions.

Today, the guns are silent, but they remain a lasting memorial to the bravery of the men of the Maury Light Artillery, commanded by Captain Reuben Ross; Company A, 30th Tennessee Infantry, commanded by Captain Bell Bidwell; and Company A, 50th Tennessee Infantry, commanded by Captain Thomas Beaumont; and under the overall command of Lieutenant Colonel Milton Haynes (evacuated due to leg injury), Captain Joseph Dixon (killed) and Captain Jacob Culbertson. These men, who at the last minute with as little as a few hours training on the big guns were thrown into hastily constructed positions, and at the time, it was considered their death sentence. Nevertheless, they stood against the newest technology of the U.S. Navy, fighting against what was considered to be tremendous odds and won, losing only one man.

Biographies of Key
People Associated with
the Fort Donelson River Batteries

Allen, 2nd Lieutenant W.C.—William Carney Allen, born March 19, 1838, was the son of William L. Allen and wife Maria. He was raised in the Shiloh Community of Southwestern Montgomery County, Tennessee. In 1860 William was living with his parents, with farming being his occupation.[1]

On August 12, 1861, William enlisted in Thomas W. Beaumont's company in Clarksville, Tennessee. At the organization of the 50th Tennessee Infantry Regiment in December 1861 at Fort Donelson, Allen was elected 2nd Lieutenant of Company A. During the battles with the gunboats, he was the commander of gun #3 in the lower river battery, a 32-pounder smoothbore in Captain Beaumont's four-gun battery on the right nearest the Cumberland River.[2]

Allen was sent to Camp Chase after the surrender of Fort Donelson and was admitted to the post-hospital March 6, 1862, he was noted as being 24 years old, height 5' 9", with blue eyes, and light hair. He was transferred to Johnson's Island, April 24. In September, he was sent to Vicksburg, Mississippi, for exchange. At the regimental reorganization, September 23, 1862, he was promoted to 1st lieutenant of Company A, 50th Regiment, to fill the vacancy left by the promotion of 1st Lieutenant Christopher W. Robertson to major.[3]

On the company roll after the reorganization, he was absent from the regiment on recruiting service back in Tennessee. Receiving a promotion to captain of Company A, 50th Tennessee, on February 1, 1863, he continued in command of the company until the consolidation of the 50th with Colm's 1st Tennessee Infantry Battalion, resulting in some officers being without a command because of being outranked by others. In a letter dated December 27, 1863, written from camp in Tilton, Georgia, William resigned his commission on January 15, 1864. The 50th Regiment consolidation was complete on February 24, 1864. Nothing further of his war service was found.[4]

W.C. Allen married Miss Sarah Alice Dickson on January 1, 1867. She was the daughter of Hugh J. Dickson and Frances Turner Dickson of neighboring Dickson County, Tennessee.[5]

Together they had five children who survived into adulthood, sadly losing three sons who died very early. William and Sarah continued living and raising their children in the Shiloh Community, with William farming. In 1900, he was a merchant in dry goods.[6]

William C. Allen died shortly before his 70th birthday on January 24, 1908. His wife,

The 32-pounder smoothbore in position #6 is one of five guns original to the Fort Donelson River Batteries. This gun was manufactured in 1821 by the Bellona Foundry (authors' photograph).

Sarah Alice Allen, passed away on September 30, 1927. They are buried in the Allen family cemetery in the Shiloh Community, Montgomery County, Tennessee.[7]

Anderson, Adna—Adna Anderson was born on July 25, 1827, in Ridgeway, New York. By age 20, Anderson began his association with the railroad and started his career as a chainman on the New York and New Haven Railroad. By October that year, Anderson was employed as an assistant engineer on the Connecticut Railroad. Anderson successively served as Assistant Engineer on the Mobile and Ohio Railroad (November 1848 to September 1849), Assistant Engineer on the Ashuelot Railroad (September 1849 to March 1850), Resident Engineer of the Michigan Southern and Northern Indiana Railroad, Locating Engineer of the Mobile and Ohio Railroad, Chief Engineer of the Tennessee and Alabama Railroad, Chief Engineer and Superintendent of the Edgefield and Kentucky Railroad, Chief Engineer of the Henderson and Nashville Railroad, and receiver of the Edgefield and Kentucky Railroad.[8]

While Anderson quickly advanced in a successful railroad career, he married Juliet Van Wyck in Washington, D.C., on October 15, 1856.[9] In 1860, the couple was living in Ward 5 of Nashville, Tennessee, with two small children, Sally (age 3) and Van Wyck (age 1). By this time, Anderson had already amassed quite a bit of wealth ($10,000.00 in real estate and $7,000.00 in personal property).[10]

By 1861, the thirty-four-year-old engineer had attained an impressive record of accomplishments. One of his most significant endeavors was engineering the construction of the first railroad bridge over the Cumberland River in Nashville for the Edgefield and Kentucky Railroad. At the time, the bridge represented a tremendous engineering achievement as it spanned over 700 feet and had the "two longest draw spans in the nation."[11] Additionally, Anderson engineered trestle bridges over both Richland Creek and the Elk River, as well as the 1,230-foot tunnel through Madry Hill near Pulaski, Tennessee.[12]

In April 1861, Anderson, the highly esteemed and well-known civil engineer, was commissioned by Tennessee Governor Isham G. Harris "to locate and construct defensive works on the northward flowing Cumberland and Tennessee rivers."[13] The Tennessee Military and Financial Board, concerned about these potential avenues of invasion, stressed the urgency of Anderson's work. In an April 27, telegram, the board urged Anderson to "immediately" assess suitable defensive sites along the likely invasion routes of the twin rivers.[14]

Anderson's first selection was on the Cumberland River, approximately one mile west of Dover, Tennessee. This selection would come to be known as Fort Donelson. Anderson proposed two possible locations on the Tennessee River, but these sites were disapproved by Colonel Bushrod Johnson, Chief Engineer of the Provisional Army of Tennessee, in place of the site, which would become Fort Henry, located in a flood zone.[15]

Once his duties of locating suitable defensive positions on the Tennessee and Cumberland rivers were complete, Anderson offered his services to the Federal government. He was made Assistant Engineer and Chief of the Construction Corps for the Army of the Potomac. By December 1862, Anderson was stationed at Aquia Creek, Virginia.[16] In correspondence from Hermann Haupt, Chief of Construction and Transportation of U.S. Military Railroads to Major General Joseph Hooker, Anderson was listed as the Chief Engineer of the Military Roads of Virginia.[17]

Following the war, Anderson was the Chief Engineer of the Illinois and St. Louis bridge, followed by employment as the General Superintendent of the Kansas Pacific Railroad. After a stint as the Vice President and General Manager of the Toledo, Wabash, and Western Railroad, in 1873 Anderson became the President of the Lafayette and Bloomington Railroad, followed by a job as receiver of the Chicago, Danville, and Vincennes Railroad in May 1875, and Chief Engineer of the Northern Pacific Railroad in 1880.[18]

Continuing his employment with the Northern Pacific Railroad, Anderson was elected Second Vice President. With this position and that of Chief Engineer, Anderson worked in this capacity until January 1888. In May 1889, Anderson became self-employed as he opened a Steel Car Company and organized the Gordon Fire Alarm Company.[19]

Sadly, Anderson's life came to an end on May 14, 1889, by a self-inflicted gunshot at the Lafayette Hotel, in Philadelphia.[20] According to accounts, John Anderson, son of the deceased, indicated that his father had contracted "mountain fever" and had been unable to sleep well for some time.[21] Survived by a wife and six children, Anderson was buried in the Oak Hill Cemetery, Chapel Valley plot, lot 443, in Washington, D.C.[22]

Beaumont, Captain Thomas W.—Thomas Beaumont, born in 1830, was a native of Clarksville, Tennessee, the son of Henry F. Beaumont, a prominent tobacco merchant and his wife, Sara Anderson Beaumont.[23] Honorable Gustavus A. Henry, lawyer, Confederate Senator, and neighbor to the Beaumont family, listed Thomas with other attorneys as a member of the bar in Montgomery County.[24] Having studied law, he made journalism his profession. For two years, 1858–60, he was an associate editor with the Nashville *Banner*, described as "an earnest and forcible writer, courteous and polite to opponents, but strictly tenacious of his own, and his party's rights."[25]

Following his withdrawal as editor in March 1860, Beaumont and G.A. Henry traveled with other well-known citizens in 1860–61, making speeches at barbeques and events in small communities in Montgomery, Dickson, Benton, and Humphreys Counties. Several of the speakers afterward became Confederate officers, including Alfred Robb, James E. Bailey, and William A. Quarles.[26]

In 1861, Brigadier General W.H. Carroll authorized Beaumont to raise a company and swear in the individuals as recruited before a magistrate. The organization began on August 12, and the enrollment was complete on September 16, 1861. The men were from Cheatham, Dickson, and Montgomery Counties in the Western Highland Rim of Middle Tennessee. They would become Company A, 50th Tennessee Infantry.[27]

Beaumont's men were some of the first troops arriving at Fort Donelson to remain at the river batteries until the battles with the gunboats. In early October, they were constructing gun emplacements and training on the heavy guns since there were no artillerists there. Company A manned the four thirty-two pounders on the right of the lower battery.

After the surrender of the fort on February 16, Captain Beaumont was taken prisoner, being sent to Camp Chase at Columbus, Ohio. He was later transferred to Johnson's Island, where he remained until September 1, 1862, where he was sent to Vicksburg, Mississippi, for exchange. At the reorganization of the 50th Tennessee Regiment September 24, he was elected Lieutenant Colonel.[28]

Colonel Beaumont served in that capacity as the regiment participated in actions in Mississippi, including Grenada, Vicksburg, Raymond, and Jackson. They were also at Port Hudson, Louisiana, where, "On the night of March 14 occurred a most terrific bombardment that shook the earth and illuminated the heavens. No grander or more awful spectacle could well be imagined."[29]

In September, the 50th was sent to Georgia to reinforce General Bragg where on the way the train they were on collided with another at Big Shanty, Georgia, killing thirteen men and injuring seventy-five. They reached Bragg's army on September 18 on the eve of the Battle of Chickamauga. Beaumont was in command of the regiment, Colonel C.A. Sugg being in command of the brigade. Colonel Beaumont was killed early in the action on the first day, September 19, 1863. He was one of four brothers who entered the Confederate service, three of whom were killed in battle. One of his comrades later wrote, "He was a man of high intelligence and courage, and never faltered upon what he thought to be the path of duty for fear of consequences."[30]

He was wrapped in a blanket and buried on the battlefield. Afterward, some of his friends found his grave and exhumed his body and placing it in a coffin he was buried near the banks of Chickamauga Creek. In 1868 his family located the grave and had his body brought back to Clarksville for burial in the family plot at the City Cemetery (Riverview Cemetery).[31]

Bedford, 1st Lieutenant Hugh Lawson—Hugh Lawson Bedford, born June 11, 1836, was the son of Benjamin Watkins Bedford and wife, Martha Ann Whyte. His paternal grandfather was Captain Thomas Bedford, Revolutionary War veteran and for whom Bedford County, Tennessee, was named. His maternal grandfather Honorable Robert Whyte, served as a Judge on the Tennessee Supreme Court for many years. Being born in Fayette County, Tennessee, Hugh was raised in Panola County, Mississippi. Entering the University of Mississippi and taking the classical course, he then attended Kentucky

Military Institute studying civil engineering under Colonel E.W. Morgan, graduating in 1855. He read law under Judge J.P. Caruthers and took the full law course at Cumberland University in Lebanon, Tennessee, graduating in 1858.[32] Hugh and his older brother Harry Hill Bedford, also a graduate of Cumberland University, opened a law office in Memphis, Tennessee, but his brother soon became ill and passed away on July 10, 1858. Hugh continued to practice law until the war began.[33]

In October 1861, Lieutenant Bedford was ordered to Fort Donelson as Instructor of Artillery by General Albert S. Johnston. Bedford recalled, "Colonel E.W. Munford aide to General Johnston, informed me that he was instructed by his chief to impress upon me that the Cumberland River cut his rear, and the occupation of Bowling Green was dependent on the proper guarding of that stream."[34]

When Lieutenant Bedford arrived at Fort Donelson, he found that the defenses were unfinished and that Lieutenant Joseph Dixon, the engineer in charge, was often called away to Fort Henry, where he was also supervising the works. The 32-pounder smoothbore guns that had been mounted at Donelson were soon found to be too high on the hill to engage gunboats effectually, and new emplacements were constructed farther down below the crest.

Bedford volunteered to supervise mounting the guns during Dixon's absence and continued assisting Lieutenant Dixon in strengthening the works. When the batteries were pronounced ready to receive the enemy on February 12, 1862, Bedford was assigned command of the 10-inch columbiad at the lower battery assisted by Lieutenant James M. Sparkman and twenty men of the Maury Light Artillery.[35] In Lieutenant Colonel Milton A. Haynes's statement of March 24, 1862, and Captain Jacob Culbertson's October 3, 1862,

Another 32-pounder original to the battle of Fort Donelson is found in position #8. This gun was manufactured in 1820 at the West Point Foundry (authors' photograph).

The 32-pounder displayed in the Fort Donelson National Cemetery is a third gun original to the 1862 battle (authors' photograph).

report of the action of the batteries with the gunboats, Bedford is erroneously listed as Lieutenant H.S. Bedford. This mistake is still often repeated in descriptions of the battle.[36]

After the surrender of Fort Donelson, Bedford was first sent to Camp Chase and then transferred to Johnson's Island. He was sent to Vicksburg, Mississippi, for exchange in September 1862. In October, he was placed in temporary command of a battalion of Colonel B.M. Browder's 51st Tennessee Infantry that had become detached from the regiment.[37]

In 1863 Bedford traveled to Richmond, Virginia, to receive an appointment as 2nd lieutenant in artillery or ordnance in the Confederate States Army. His record states the date of appointment as October 6, the date to take rank May 2, 1863. At Meridian, Mississippi, October 19, Bedford was to report to Captain John Clark for assignment to duty. He was made ordnance officer in General Wirt Adams Brigade of cavalry. In a letter dated January 8, 1864, to Lieutenant Colonel James M. Kennard, Chief Ordnance Officer, Captain Clark said that for some reason, General Adams had virtually refused to recognize Bedford as ordnance officer and ordered him back to the headquarters of General W.H. Jackson. Bedford's next assignment was with General H.P. Mabry's Brigade of cavalry as ordnance officer. He served until Lieutenant General Richard Taylor surrendered his forces in Citronelle, Alabama, on May 4, 1865.[38]

On May 23, 1867, in Grenada, Mississippi, Hugh Bedford was married to Miss Marie Louisa McLean, daughter of Judge Robert D. McLean.[39] By August 1870, they were living with Hugh's father, Benjamin, in Shelby County, Tennessee, with Hugh's occupation listed as a farmer.[40] Hugh and Louisa had two sons, Benjamin Watkins Lee, born in 1872, and Hugh Lawson, born in 1883.[41]

Hugh continued farming and living in Shelby County until his death on December

22, 1915, from pulmonary tuberculosis. Louisa lived until 1933, sadly surviving both of her sons. Benjamin W.L. having passed in 1921 and Hugh L. in 1931. All are buried in Elmwood Cemetery, Memphis, Tennessee.[42]

Bidwell, Captain Bell G.—Bell Girard Bidwell was a native of Robertson County, Tennessee, born February 19, 1837. He was the son of Charles F. Bidwell and Martha Binkley. Charles Bidwell was a 2nd lieutenant in the West Tennessee Militia in the War of 1812 under Colonel William Metcalf.[43]

Bell Bidwell studied medicine at the University of Nashville but decided upon a career in law. In 1860 he graduated from the Cumberland University Law School, Lebanon, Tennessee.[44]

In 1861, he was elected captain of Company A, 30th Tennessee Infantry. The men in Company A were from Robertson County. The regiment was organized on October 22, at Red Springs, Macon County, Tennessee. Being ordered to Fort Donelson, the regiment arrived there on November 27, 1861.[45]

In January 1862, Captain Bidwell's company was detached from the 30th and assigned to the heavy guns in the lower river battery by General Tilghman. They manned the four 32-pounders to the left of Captain Beaumont's guns. It was at Bidwell's gun # 2 that Captain Joseph Dixon was killed when a rifle shell from the USS *Carondelet* struck the carriage dismounting the gun. Bidwell was called to headquarters at 2 a.m. Sunday, February 16, by Colonel Head before the surrender and stated that he had no chance to return to the battery, thus making his escape.[46]

Bidwell made his way to Nashville, where he joined up with General A.S. Johnston's command making their way south. When the 30th regiment was reorganized after being exchanged, Bidwell was elected major on October 4, 1862. By August 28, 1863, he was in command of the military post at Enterprise, Mississippi, by authorization of General Joseph E. Johnston. In June 1864, he was commanding a post in Macon, Mississippi. Major Bidwell surrendered May 17, 1865, at Columbus, Mississippi. He was described as having a dark complexion with dark hair and hazel eyes and being 5'8".[47]

In 1870, Bidwell was living in Paducah, Kentucky, practicing law.[48] He married Miss Ellen P. Flournoy in Paducah on February 2, 1871.[49]

Bell Bidwell served in the Kentucky State Legislature 1873–1877. In 1879 he moved to Weatherford, Texas, where he worked for twenty years in the law department of the Texas and Pacific Railroad.[50] Bell and Eleanor raised their two children, Harry L. and Nellie G., in Weatherford. Bell G. Bidwell died at age 67 and was buried in the City Greenwood Cemetery in Weatherford, Texas.[51]

Culbertson, Captain Jacob—Jacob Culbertson was born November 26, 1828, and was raised on a farm on the Licking River seven miles from the town of Covington in Kenton County, Kentucky.[52] He was the son of James and Elizabeth Youtsey Culbertson. His father died when Jacob was about six years old.[53] He was nominated for an appointment to the U.S. Military Academy on December 8, 1845, by Honorable John W. Tibbatts of the 10th Congressional District, Kentucky, and was accepted. Jacob and his guardian, William H. Pye, both signed the acceptance letter on March 26, 1846.[54]

Culbertson graduated from the Academy in 1850, with the rank of seventh in his class of forty-four cadets. Entering the service with the 4th Artillery. He was appointed 2nd lieutenant on December 11, 1850, he was promoted to 1st lieutenant on February 14, 1856, and served in that capacity until he resigned from the U.S. Army on January 10,

1857.[55] During his time with the 4th Artillery, he was stationed at Fort Columbus, New York Harbor, and Fort Mackinac, Michigan. His name also appears on returns from Fort Brown, Texas, and Fort McRae, Florida.[56]

On July 10, 1850, Jacob married Caroline Biggs in Campbell County, Kentucky.[57] After he resigned from the army in 1857, the couple moved to Kenton County, Kentucky, and Jacob began teaching school, by 1860, they were raising three sons, Charles, Frank, and William.[58]

Culbertson was appointed a 1st lieutenant in the Artillery Corps on October 16, 1861, and reported to General Albert Sidney Johnston. At Fort Donelson on January 13, 1862, General Lloyd Tilghman reported to Headquarters at Bowling Green, Kentucky, that Lieutenant Culbertson was there and acting as Chief of Artillery and that "His ability is unquestionable and his services invaluable and indispensable." Tilghman said that as a Lieutenant in the regular army, Culbertson is ranked by all of the Captains forming the artillery battalion, and the situation "is not as conducive to the best interests of the service as I would desire." Tilghman recommended Culbertson to be promoted to Captain in the Provisional Army.[59] On January 29, Culbertson was promoted to the rank of temporary major for service with volunteer troops. It's possible this communication did not reach him, as he was known as Captain Culbertson and signed as Captain of Artillery, Commanding Batteries.[60]

After the fall of Fort Donelson, Major Culbertson was sent to Johnson's Island, Sandusky, Ohio, and then transferred to Camp Chase on March 1, 1862. On April 5, he was paroled to Columbus, Ohio, until September 1, when he was sent to Vicksburg, Mississippi, for exchange.[61]

Culbertson served as Chief of Artillery in General Tilghman's Brigade in Mississippi.[62] At the Battle of Champion Hill, May 16, 1863, Tilghman's Brigade formed the rear guard as the Confederate Army retreated on the Raymond Road. Facing superior numbers, General Tilghman was killed late in the day by a shell from the enemy's guns. The guns of Cowan's and Culbertson's batteries were ordered to be abandoned by Major General Loring because of the impossibility of moving them over the terrain in the retreat. Culbertson brought off his horses, harness, and men.[63]

Culbertson's problems with the uncertainty of his rank were voiced in a letter written at Meridian, Mississippi, dated October 6, 1863, addressed to General Samuel Cooper, Adjutant and Inspector General, "I beg to be informed whether I am an officer in the Confederate States Army or not." He states that he received the commission of 1st lieutenant from the Provisional President but had not received any other notice of rank after repeated requests. "If I have any rank in the army I desire to know what it is." His record notes that his commission as major expired in December 1863. Nothing of his service record can be found for the remainder of the war.[64]

In 1870, Jacob, age 41, his wife Caroline 39, and children, Charles 19, Frank 17, William 14, May 6, Maude 4, and Calbert 1, were living in Rankin County, Mississippi, with Jacob's occupation being listed as a farmer.[65] Jacob Culbertson continued farming and teaching and passed away just twelve days before his 56th birthday on November 14, 1884, and was buried on his farm near Jackson, Mississippi.[66]

Dixon, Captain Joseph—Joseph Dixon was born near Athens in McMinn County, Tennessee, on December 6, 1836, the son of Eli and Charity Jones Dixon.[67] At age 17, Joseph was nominated by Honorable S.A. Smith, Third Congressional District of

Tennessee, as an applicant to the U.S. Military Academy, in a letter to Jefferson Davis, Secretary of War. On March 18, 1854, Joseph and his father signed an acceptance letter to the Academy.[68]

Graduating third out of twenty-seven cadets in the Class of 1858, as brevet 2nd lieutenant of Topographical Engineers, he was assigned duty in the Northwest Territories.[69] In 1860, he was stationed at the garrison of Fort Vancouver, Washington.[70]

When his home state of Tennessee seceded, he resigned his commission in the U.S. Army on June 28, 1861.[71] Traveling to Richmond, Virginia, with other officers to offer his services to the Confederacy, he received a commission to 1st lieutenant, on September 9, and was listed as Engineer on the staff of General Albert Sidney Johnston.[72]

On October 8, 1861, General Johnston instructed General Leonidas Polk at Columbus, Kentucky, to send Lieutenant Dixon to Fort Donelson to mount the guns there.[73] On a trip back to headquarters at Columbus, he participated in the Battle of Belmont, Missouri, on November 7, 1861. As part of the forces that crossed the Mississippi River, he won for himself "an enviable character for gallantry and soldierly bearing."[74]

Being promoted to captain, the rest of his time at Fort Donelson was spent strengthening the works and armament and according to Major Christopher W. Robertson, "Dixon could get more work out of volunteer troops than any man who was ever at the place," and "was the truest type of soldier that I have ever seen."[75]

Dixon was placed in command of the river batteries by General Gideon J. Pillow. On February 13, 1862, a rifle shell from the USS *Carondelet* entered the embrasure of Captain B.G. Bidwell's gun # 2, striking the right cheek of the carriage and a piece of a bolt struck him in the left side of the head killing him instantly. General Pillow remarked, "His death was a serious loss to the service and was a source of no little embarrassment in our after operations."[76]

Captain Joseph Dixon's body was returned to his home in Athens, Tennessee, for burial, and on February 16, 1862, followed by a large crowd of citizens of the town and county, he was laid to rest.[77]

Fitzgerald, Lieutenant P.L.—Patrick Leonard "Len" Fitzgerald was born in April 1825 in Maury County, Tennessee. He married Miss Delila Pigg on October 8, 1844, in Maury County. She was the daughter of Henderson and Nancy Pigg. In 1850, Len and Delila were living in the household of her parents with their children, Nancy J., age 3, and Rebecca A., age 1. His occupation was farming.[78] In 1860, Patrick and Delila were the parents of four children, three daughters, and a son, and he was doing well as a farmer in the Santa Fe community of Northwestern Maury County.[79]

In September 1861, when the Maury Light Artillery was being formed, Patrick, age 36, joined and was mustered into service by Captain G.H. Monsarrat, on October 16, 1861. At Camp Weakley near Nashville, he was elected 3rd lieutenant. A pay voucher for October 16, to November 16, 1861, lists him as 2nd lieutenant.[80] In December 1861, sickness had depleted the ranks of the Maury Artillery, and Lieutenant J.M. Sparkman went back to Maury County on recruiting service, and while there, he was sick with the measles.[81] During Sparkman's absence, Lieutenant Fitzgerald signed as commanding the Maury Artillery at Hopkinsville, Kentucky, on requisitions for thirty horses for the company and for clothing in late December.[82]

At Fort Donelson, Lieutenant Fitzgerald was assigned command of the 32-pounder howitzer to the right of the 6.4-inch columbiad rifle in the upper river battery by Captain

Reuben R. Ross.[83] During the battle with the ironclads on February 14, 1862, Captain Ross stated, "Two men were struck dead apparently, one on each side of me. We took only time to place them in the magazine. Lieutenant Fitzgerald and Private Mays" (Private F. Augustus "Gus" Mays).[84] In a local history of the Maury Artillery by Frank Smith in 1908, it was said that Fitzgerald and Mays were standing too near the 6.4-inch rifle when it was fired, and the concussion shocked them so severely they were carried from the battery and that Fitzgerald never fully recovered and suffered from hearing loss from then on.[85]

Sent to Camp Chase after the fall of Fort Donelson, Fitzgerald was transferred to Johnson's Island on April 24, 1862. He was sent to Vicksburg, Mississippi, on September 1, 1862, for exchange. His record doesn't show whether he was not reelected at the reorganization or if he resigned, but his service with the Maury Light Artillery appears to have ended at that time. He was not reported as being with the company at Port Hudson, Louisiana.[86]

On October 10, 1862, P.L. Fitzgerald enlisted as a private in Colonel Jacob B. Biffle's Company E, 19th Tennessee Cavalry at Columbia, Tennessee.[87] Colonel Biffle's cavalry was with General Nathan Bedford Forrest on his West Tennessee raid in December and participated in the Battle of Parker's Crossroads on December 31, 1862. The regiment fought at Thompson's Station and Brentwood, Tennessee, with Forrest in March 1863. In September, Biffle's Cavalry was in the Battle of Chickamauga as part of Colonel George G. Dibrell's command under Forrest. After Chickamauga, the regiment went into East Tennessee with General Joseph Wheeler. There, near Sweetwater in Monroe County, Tennessee, Private Fitzgerald was captured on October 26. Sent once again to Camp Chase, Ohio, November 14, 1863, Fitzgerald's name appeared later in June 1864 on a roll of prisoners who desired to take the oath of allegiance. He remained in prison until the end of the war and was paroled at Nashville, Tennessee April 10, 1865, where he was noted as being 5' 10", with a fair complexion, blue eyes, and dark hair.[88]

After the war, Fitzgerald returned to his family and farming. In 1870, he was living in Hickman County, Tennessee.[89] Sometime before 1880, he had relocated to Montague County, Texas, with his wife and son James J. age 23, and daughter Margaret age 13.[90] In 1900, in Jackson County, Texas, P.L. Fitzgerald was listed as a widower, age 75, with his daughter Sallie, a widow age 41, and several grandchildren.[91]

Fitzgerald had his will drawn up on September 13, 1904. He named his two surviving daughters as executors, Mrs. Sallie D. Johns, and Mrs. Margaret "Maggie" Elizabeth Belschner. Patrick Leonard Fitzgerald, age 79, died seventeen days later, September 30, 1904.[92]

A place of burial for Fitzgerald was not found, although his daughter Maggie E. Fitzgerald Belschner was buried in the Memory Gardens section of Edna Cemetery, Jackson County, Texas. His grave may be unmarked.[93]

Foster, 1st Lieutenant Wilbur Fisk—Born on April 18, 1834, in Springfield, Massachusetts, he was the third of six children of Dexter and Euphrasia Allin Foster. Dexter Foster was a civil engineer on the Western Railroad of Massachusetts. When Wilbur was only ten years old, his father died.[94]

Growing up, Foster attended public school in Northampton and Springfield, Massachusetts, graduating in 1851. He planned to attend Yale University, but this dream did not materialize due to a lack of finances.[95]

Captain John Childe, who was the Chief Engineer of the Mobile and Ohio Railroad and a close associate of Wilbur's father, gave him employment as a rodman. Foster left Springfield, Massachusetts, on December 29, 1851, and headed south to Hamburg, Tennessee, where he joined the locating party of Adna Anderson. Foster and Anderson became close associates and worked together throughout the next ten years. Under the watchful eye of Adna Anderson, Foster gained great aptitude as an engineer in his own right and was given increasing levels of responsibility. Paired with Anderson, the duo worked together on various projects.[96]

In September 1856, Anderson and Foster undertook the construction of the first railroad bridge across the Cumberland River, reaching from Nashville to Edgefield. Anderson was assigned as Chief Engineer, and Foster served as Engineer in Charge. The project was completed on August 1, 1858. Next, the two accomplished several other major engineering feats, including bridges over Richland Creek and the Elk River, as well as the 1,230-foot tunnel through Madry Hill near Pulaski, Tennessee.[97]

From December 1860 to April 1861, Foster was engaged in surveying on the Hopkinsville and Nashville Railroad. With the coming of the Civil War, and while Foster was working in Nashville, on April 25, 1861, he enlisted in Captain R.C. Foster's infantry company. This would become Company C, 1st (Feild's) Tennessee Infantry.[98]

Soon, Adna Anderson was charged by Governor Harris with selecting defensive positions along the likely invasion routes of the Tennessee and Cumberland rivers. To accomplish the assignment, he immediately asked for his pre-war associate, Wilbur F. Foster, to assist. As Foster was transferred from the 1st Tennessee to fulfill Harris's assignment, the young engineer was promoted to 2nd lieutenant and was reassigned to the Tennessee Engineer Corps.[99]

Following orders, Foster left Camp Cheatham in nearby Robertson County, where his regiment was in training and proceeded to Nashville. On his arrival at the state capital, he was instructed by Anderson to assemble a team that would be able to fulfill the governor's wishes.[100]

By the beginning of May, not quite a month before Tennessee's secession, Foster was with Anderson's team, surveying the Cumberland River near the town of Dover in Stewart County, Tennessee. The party located a water battery about a mile below Dover "on the western bluffs of the Cumberland River" at the mouth of Hickman Creek.[101]

The party next traversed the twelve miles between the Cumberland and Tennessee rivers, where surveys for a defensive position along the Tennessee were completed. The party found two suitable sites, but these were not accepted by Colonel Bushrod Johnson, who chose the site of what would become Fort Henry at Kirkman's Landing. Foster disagreed with the Kirkman Landing site due to its susceptibility of flooding, but when reported to the Governor, Foster was told he was too young to criticize the work of older engineers. Foster was charged with the responsibility of laying off the works for the ill-fated Fort Henry.[102]

After completing his work at Fort Henry, Lieutenant Foster was sent to Cumberland Gap, where he served under the command of General Edmund Kirby Smith. By December 1862, Foster had been promoted to captain, and by January 1863, he was the Chief Engineer of the Department of East Tennessee. On March 17, 1863, Foster was promoted to major. From May 27, 1864, to July 18, 1864, Foster was assigned to General W.E. Jones at Dublin Depot, Virginia. Following that assignment, in July 1864, Major Foster was transferred back to the Army of Tennessee as an engineer in Major General Alexander P. Stewart's Corps. The following month (August), he was listed as the Chief Engineer of

Stewart's Corps, a position he held until the surrender of the Army of Tennessee on April 26, 1865.[103]

After the war, Foster returned to Nashville, where he was tasked with rebuilding the suspension bridge across the Cumberland River. The bridge was completed in 1866.[104]

Foster married Elizabeth Nichol in 1866, but the honeymoon was delayed until the bridge construction was completed. The couple had two daughters, Martha, who was born in 1867, and Gertrude, born in 1869.[105]

Gilmer, Major Jeremy Francis—Gilmer was born in Guilford County, North Carolina, on February 23, 1818, to Robert and Ann Forbes Gilmer.[106] Jeremy Gilmer entered the United States Military Academy at West Point in 1835 and was graduated in 1839, ranking fourth in his class of 31 cadets.[107] A close classmate of Gilmer's was future Civil War General Henry W. Halleck, who ranked third, just ahead of Gilmer. Upon graduation, 2nd Lieutenant Gilmer served at the Academy as Assistant Professor of Engineering until June 1840. As Assistant Engineer, he assisted with the construction of Fort Schuyler in New York Harbor until 1844. For the next two years, he served in Washington, D.C., as assistant to the chief engineer and received a promotion to 1st lieutenant in 1845.[108]

Gilmer gained additional experience in the Mexican War as he was Chief Engineer of the Army of the West in New Mexico. After serving a stint in Washington, he was transferred to Georgia, where he was the superintending engineer for the repairs to forts Jackson and Pulaski and served in improvements to the Savannah River. Gilmer was promoted to captain on July 1, 1853. Gilmer worked on various fortifications and river improvements until he resigned his commission on June 29, 1861, and offered his services to the Confederacy.[109]

With the rank of major, Gilmer was assigned as Chief Engineer to Department Number 2, commanded by General Albert Sidney Johnston, where he superseded Lieutenant Joseph Dixon. Specifically, Gilmer was in charge of the defenses of Forts Henry and Donelson, Clarksville, and Nashville.

Gilmer was severely wounded at the Battle of Shiloh, Tennessee, on April 7, 1862, and was promoted to brigadier general on August 4, 1862, and assumed duties as the chief engineer of the Department of Virginia. The following year, he was promoted to major general and took his place in the Department of South Carolina, Georgia, and Florida.[110]

On December 17, 1850, Gilmer married Louisa Frederica Alexander (sister of future Confederate Brigadier General Edward Porter Alexander) in Chatham County, Georgia.[111] The Gilmer's had two children, Louisa born on September 3, 1852, and Henry born on November 7, 1854.[112]

From 1867 to 1883, Gilmer served as the president of the Savannah Gas Light Company. Gilmer died on December 1, 1883, of heart disease and is buried in the Laurel Grove Cemetery (North) in Savannah, Georgia.[113]

Haynes, Lieutenant Colonel Milton A.—Milton Andrews Haynes was born in 1814 to James Sloan Haynes and Asenath Wilson Haynes in Cornersville, Marshall County, Tennessee.[114]

By the time of the Civil War, Haynes was an experienced soldier. He was graduated eighteenth in the West Point Class of 1838.[115] Upon graduation, he was commissioned a brevet 2nd lieutenant and assigned to the U.S. 3rd Artillery. Haynes was promoted to 2nd lieutenant on July 7, 1838.[116] Next, 2nd Lieutenant Haynes served in the Florida War (1838–39).[117] Haynes resigned from the army on September 30, 1839.[118] With the coming of the Mexican War, Haynes again entered military service, enlisting on May 28, 1846, and serving as captain of Company E, 1st Tennessee Mounted Infantry. He was mustered out of use at New Orleans, Louisiana May 31, 1847.[119]

After resigning from the army, Haynes returned to Tennessee and pursued a law career, with a six-year stint as a lawyer in Nashville (1840–46), part of the time serving as the Assistant Adjutant General of the Tennessee Militia (1844–46).[120] In 1858, he married Penelope Brabson, and the couple had one daughter.[121]

At the outbreak of the Civil War, Haynes once again answered the call to arms. In May 1861, Haynes was commissioned lieutenant colonel of the Tennessee Artillery Corps.[122] As Haynes set to his duties, he wrote a military manual for Tennessee troops, *Instructions in Field Artillery, Horse, and Foot.*[123] On January 15, 1862, Lieutenant Colonel Haynes received orders from Major General Leonidas Polk to leave Columbus, Kentucky, and to report to Brigadier General Lloyd Tilghman at Fort Henry.[124] Upon arrival, Tilghman sent Haynes to Fort Donelson to take command of the artillery there.

At Fort Donelson, Lieutenant Colonel Haynes organized Maney's Light Artillery Battery and two companies of infantry (Captain Bell Bidwell's Company A, 30th Tennessee, and Captain Thomas W. Beaumont's Company A, 50th Tennessee) into an artillery battalion. Maney's battery was soon assigned a position on the left of the Confederate line and was replaced by Captain Reuben Ross's company, the Maury Light Artillery. Under Haynes's watchful eye, Lieutenants J.J. McDaniel and George S. Martin, artillery instructors sent from Columbus, drilled the infantry companies on the heavy artillery of the Fort Donelson river batteries.[125]

With Federal troops converging on Fort Henry, Haynes arrived at that fort on the morning of February 6. After examining the works, Haynes offered his opinion that Fort Henry should be abandoned because of the rising water, which had cut off support from the infantry. With the impending Federal attack, this was an impossibility, and within a few hours, Fort Henry and its brave defenders surrendered. Haynes was not present in the fort at the time of the surrender and therefore was at liberty to escape with the troops then headed to Fort Donelson. Haynes quickly found a horse, and even though unbridled and without a saddle, mounted the horse and climbing the riverbank and swimming the backwater, soon caught up with the escaping troops, including Major Jeremy Gilmer, who was on foot.[126]

After a twenty-two mile journey, Haynes made it back, with the other escaping troops, to Fort Donelson. At some point, whether in the escape from Fort Henry or at some other point, Haynes sustained some type of injury requiring him to be confined to crutches. Still on crutches, the Federal gunboat flotilla descended on Fort Donelson on February 13. In the fierce bombardment which ensued, one of the 32-pounder guns of the lower battery was dismounted, and Captain Joseph Dixon was killed. At General Floyd's instruction, Haynes commanded twelve artificers and carpenters to remount the gun, which they were unsuccessful in doing. Haynes's wound continued to worsen, and at the orders of Surgeon Williams, Haynes was evacuated by steamer with the other wounded.[127]

On June 29, 1862, under Special Order 98/1, Haynes was assigned to duty under General Bragg. Other records show that Lieutenant Colonel Haynes was assigned to duty on May 15, with General Edmund Kirby Smith at Knoxville, Tennessee, and subsequently on October 10, 1863, to Dublin Depot, Virginia.[128]

After the war, Haynes returned to Tennessee and continued his law career. Haynes passed away on September 27, 1867, at age 53 in Memphis, Shelby County, Tennessee. He is buried in the Elmwood Cemetery, Memphis, Tennessee.[129]

Martin, Lieutenant George S.—George Saunders Martin, born January 3, 1840, was the son of George W. Martin and Narcissa Pillow, daughter of Gideon Pillow and Anne Payne, and younger sister of General Gideon J. Pillow, prominent citizens of Maury County, Tennessee.[130]

George was admitted to the Western Military Institute in Nashville, Tennessee, on January 27, 1856, and listed in the Register of Cadets 1856–57 as a sergeant in the Sophomore class from Columbia, Tennessee.[131]

His father died in 1854, and in 1860 George was living with his mother and grandmother Anne Pillow, age 84, in Maury County, along with his younger siblings. His mother was the head of the household, her occupation listed as a farmer with a real estate value of $225,000 and personal estate valued $128,000.[132]

In May 1861, George volunteered for service in Columbia, Tennessee, and was elected 2nd corporal in Captain William R. Johnston's Company H, 1st Tennessee Infantry Regiment. By July, he had transferred to the artillery service, and at Fort Pillow on the Mississippi River, he was appointed 2nd lieutenant on July 18 and was promoted to 1st lieutenant on August 12, 1861. On the muster roll of Captain Stewart's Company, Tennessee Artillery dated August 21, he is noted as "absent on detached service with General Pillow."[133]

On January 15, 1862, Lieutenant Colonel Milton A. Haynes was sent from Columbus, Kentucky, by Major General Leonidas Polk to report to Brigadier General Lloyd Tilghman, who, in turn, made Colonel Haynes Chief of Artillery and directed him to Fort Donelson. Haynes organized an artillery battalion and finding the soldiers only slightly trained on the heavy guns of the river batteries, telegraphed General Polk asking for artillery officers to act as instructors. Lieutenant George S. Martin and Lieutenant J.J. McDaniel were sent and started drilling the men on the guns. Haynes said, "they were, under my own eye, taught to fire their guns at targets 1,000, 1,500, and 2,000 yards, and the elevation for particular range explained and taught to them."[134]

In February, during the engagements with the gunboats, Lieutenant Martin was placed in command of the 32-pounder on the right closest to the Cumberland River in the lower river battery. Known as gun #1 of Captain Beaumont's four guns, he was assisted by members of Company A, 50th Tennessee.[135] General Gideon Pillow mentioned his nephew in his February 18, report of the battle with the gunboats. "Lieutenant George S. Martin, whose company is at Columbus, Kentucky, but who was ordered to that post by Major General Polk, commanded one of the guns, particularly attracted my attention by his energy and the judgement with which he fought his gun. The wadding of his gun having given out, he pulled off his coat and rammed it down his gun as wadding, and thus kept up the fire until the enemy were finally repulsed."[136]

In the early morning hours of February 16, 1862, at the famous council of war held at the Rice House in Dover, Tennessee, headquarters of General Pillow, George Martin, was in attendance. In the sworn statement of Major W.H. Haynes, given at Decatur, Alabama, on March 14, 1862, Haynes says he was awakened at 1 a.m. on February 16, and ordered to report to General Pillow immediately, "I instantly proceeded to headquarters, where I saw Brigadier Generals Floyd, Pillow, and Buckner, Colonel Forrest, Majors Henry (assistant adjutant-general), Gilmer, and Jones, and Lieutenants Nicholson and Martin; the two latter volunteer aides to General Pillow."[137]

Although not named by General Pillow as being with him when he crossed the Cumberland River to escape surrender, Lieutenant Martin and Lieutenant Hunter Nicholson probably accompanied him along with others of his staff. George S. Martin was later taken prisoner at Island Number 10 on the Mississippi River on April 7, 1862. He was sent to Johnson's Island on April 26. Released at Vicksburg, Mississippi, for exchange September 20, 1862, he was present at the muster roll dated October 3, of Captain Winston's Company Light Artillery. A remark on his record states that he declined to run for re-election and resigned.[138]

George S. Martin married Miss Mary Gordon Nicholson in Columbia, Tennessee, on November 13, 1862. She was the daughter of U.S. Senator A.O.P. Nicholson Sr. (1808–1876), and sister of Lieutenant Hunter Nicholson previously mentioned of Pillow's staff.[139] At Columbia on December 13, 1862, George had his last will and testament drawn up, it states, "If I should die or be killed at any time or in any way, I give my whole interest in my father's estate to my wife Mary Gordon to be her own." Witnesses Narcissa Martin and J.A. Martin.[140]

George S. Martin was shot by a "bushwhacker" near Leighton, Alabama, on August 20, 1863, according to an undated newspaper clipping from the Columbia *Journal*. It's unclear as to the duty he was performing, but it was reported that he was serving on the staff of General Nathan Bedford Forrest and was "carrying dispatches to his chief." Records have not been found to confirm that, but the account says that he died in a cabin near where he was wounded on September 23, 1863. His body was brought back to Maury County, Tennessee, and buried in the churchyard of St. John's Church at Ashwood, near his father.[141]

McDaniel, First Lieutenant J.J.—James J. McDaniel was born in Nashville in 1821.[142] He enlisted in Nashville on May 28, 1846, in Company L, 1st Tennessee Infantry, to serve in the Mexican War. McDaniel was promoted in rank from fourth sergeant to first sergeant. He was mustered out of service at New Orleans, Louisiana, on May 23, 1847.[143] The following year, he married Rowena C. Shivers on October 22, 1848.[144]

At the beginning of the Civil War, he once again answered the call to arms and enlisted in Nashville and was elected 1st lieutenant in the Nelson Artillery. In January 1862, McDaniel, along with 1st Lieutenant George S. Martin, was sent from Columbus, Kentucky, to Fort Donelson to act as artillery instructors for the infantrymen (Company A, 30th Tennessee and Company A, 50th Tennessee) who had been assigned to the heavy guns in the river batteries.[145] During the battle with the Federal gunboats, McDaniel commanded one of the 32-pounders in the lower battery. When Fort Donelson fell on February 16, 1862, McDaniel escaped his captors but was captured soon after that at the failed defense of Island Number 10 in the Mississippi River. Upon capture, McDaniel was imprisoned at Johnson's Island. McDaniel was exchanged in September 1862 but, due to failing health, was unable to continue his military duties.[146] After the war, McDaniel engaged in printing with the Nashville papers, *Union and American,* and the *Republican Banner*. McDaniel died in Nashville on October 13, 1871, at age fifty and is buried in the Mount Olivet Cemetery.[147]

Raimey, Third Lieutenant J.K.—James K. Raimey, a native of Montgomery County, Tennessee, the son of Solomon D. Raimey and Eliza Ann McAlister Raimey, was born on August 19, 1841. Solomon Raimey was a prosperous farmer who lived close to the Louisa Iron Furnace, south of Clarksville, near the Montgomery County and Dickson County line.[148]

In August 1861, just a few days before his twentieth birthday, James enlisted at Old Antioch, in Thomas W. Beaumont's company. The Old Antioch Campground served as a rendezvous area for many of the men from the Montgomery County area south and west of the Cumberland River. Being a well-known citizen, Raimey was instrumental in the recruiting effort.[149]

At the organization of the 50th Tennessee Infantry Regiment at Fort Donelson, Beaumont's company became Company A, and Raimey said that at the fort, they helped build the fortifications. James was elected 3rd lieutenant of Company A and during the battles with the gunboats, commanded gun # 4, a 32-pounder smoothbore in the lower river battery, under Captain Beaumont.[150]

After the surrender at Fort Donelson, Lieutenant Raimey was sent to Camp Chase, Ohio, and then transferred to Johnson's Island. In September, he was exchanged at Vicksburg, Mississippi. At the reorganization of the 50th, he was not reelected and was discharged on September 23, 1862.[151] His older brother John, and Elisha Downs, both privates in Company A, were sick after their release from prison, and James stayed with them at the hospital in Brandon, Mississippi, attending to their needs. Elisha Downs died in November 1862. He had been named along with six other privates, "who acted with conspicuous courage and coolness" in Captain Beaumont's report of the action with the gunboats. James' brother John A. Raimey, age 24, died in December 1862.[152]

Leaving Mississippi after his brother's death, James stated that he joined the 2nd Kentucky Cavalry under Colonel Thomas G. Woodward near Spring Hill, Tennessee, and was in command of Company C at the end of the war. In a letter included with his Confederate Pension Application in 1910, he described his service after joining the cavalry. Raimey was in the battles of Chickamauga, Tunnel Hill, Dalton, Dug Gap, Resaca, and was wounded in the left hip at Peachtree Creek near Atlanta. Spending six weeks recovering from his wound, he rejoined his company near Macon, Georgia. He was in "the battle in front of Columbia, South Carolina, Fayetteville, and through the battle of Smithfield, or Bentonville, North Carolina. Was National Guard to Mr. Davis and train from Greensboro to Savannah River, where he left us. We then surrendered about fifteen miles from Washington, Wilkes County, Georgia, the 9th day of May 1865. Was paroled by Captain Lot Abraham, U.S. Officer." Raimey concluded by saying, "I reckon I came as near being in every fight from start to finish as anybody."[153]

After the war, James married Miss Luella H. Black ca. 1875, and they had four children, Eliza A., Laura K., Robina A., and William Woodward Raimey.[154] At home in the 16th Civil District of Montgomery County, James served as the Justice of the Peace for twelve years, and as a Notary for sixteen years.[155] James K. Raimey died on January 22, 1918, at the age of 76 years, five months, and three days and was buried in the Raimey Cemetery near his home in the Louise Community of Montgomery County, Tennessee.[156]

Robertson, Major Christopher W.—Christopher Wills Robertson, a native of Dickson County, Tennessee, was the son of Benjamin C. Robertson, wealthy businessman and farmer and his wife Ann G. Napier Robertson. Their large family home, "Harpeth Hall," was located on the Harpeth River northeast of Charlotte, the county seat. His family was related to General James Robertson, known as the Father of Tennessee, and were some of the first to settle in the area. Christopher studied law and graduated with high honors in the 1859 class of Cumberland University in Lebanon, Tennessee.[157]

Putting his plans for law practice aside in 1861 when war was inevitable, at age twenty-two, he became instrumental in helping recruit men from the Harpeth River area of Cheatham and Dickson Counties for the company being raised by his friend Thomas W. Beaumont from neighboring Montgomery County. He enrolled on September 9, and was elected 1st lieutenant when the men in the company selected their officers.[158]

The company reported to Lieutenant Colonel Randal W. MacGavock at Fort Donelson in early October. It was put to work on the construction of the gun emplacements at the lower river battery. During November and December, when they were not improving the works, the men were trained on the thirty-two pounder guns that they would eventually use to defend the batteries against the ironclad gunboats. When the 50th Tennessee Infantry Regiment was organized on December 25, 1861, Beaumont's company became Company A. Christopher Robertson was elected major of the regiment January 26, 1862.[159] When Foote's gunboats threatened the fort in February, Robertson volunteered his services to fight along-side his companions in Company A and commanded gun # 2 at the lower battery.[160]

Taken prisoner after the surrender, Robertson was first sent to Camp Chase, Ohio, and in March 1862, was transferred to Fort Warren, Massachusetts. He was noted as being 5'10", with blue eyes, and brown hair. He was released for exchange on July 31, 1863. At Jackson, Mississippi, at the reorganization of the 50th Tennessee, on September 23, he was reelected major.[161]

During the campaigns of Mississippi and East Louisiana, the regiment took part in the action on Chickasaw Bayou near Vicksburg in late December. They were at Port Hudson, Louisiana, from January 7 to May 2, 1863. As part of Gregg's Brigade, they marched back to Jackson, Mississippi, and took an active role in the engagement at Raymond, on May 12, 1863. Leaving Mississippi in September to reinforce the Army of Tennessee, the regiment reached General Bragg's command on the eve of the Battle of Chickamauga.[162]

On the first day's fighting (September 19), Colonel T.W. Beaumont was killed while commanding the regiment. Colonel Cyrus Sugg had taken command of the brigade when General John Gregg was wounded. After Beaumont's death, command of the 50th fell upon Major Robertson.[163] The next day while leading his men against the Federal line Major Robertson was mortally wounded. While he lay helpless on the battlefield, his watch and money were stolen. Taken to a hospital, he died from his wounds on September 30 and was buried in Atlanta, Georgia.[164]

Robertson was remembered in a history of the regiment written by C.W. Tyler, a former member, "To my mind he was the noblest Roman of them all. When he stepped to the front and gave the word of command, all obeyed him, for he was a born leader of men; and yet he was a brother to the humblest soldier in the ranks. In his twenty-third year in front of his regiment, and leading his men to victory, he fell to rise no more."[165]

In a touching tribute penned by a close friend of Robertson, Miss Eleanora Willauer at Cumberland Furnace, Tennessee, after a visit to Harpeth Hall on May 1, 1864, she described her feelings. "Poor Mrs. Robertson seems crushed by the loss of her husband and best beloved child. Dear old lady, poor dear Chris, they have a picture of him, rather good, hanging in the parlor just over the piano, it almost broke my heart at first when I would chance to glance at it. The thought, what a dreary thought, would come that this was all that was on earth of him, so fitted to make this world brighter and better, and how much need it has of such, alas that goodness and genius should have been linked so tightly in the chain of life!"[166]

Ross, Captain Reuben R.—Reuben Reddick Ross, born April 17, 1830, was the son of Professor James H. Ross and Mary D. Barker Ross, of Montgomery County, Tennessee. He was named after his grandfather, Elder Reuben Ross, an early Baptist minister in Montgomery County. His education in early life was under his father at the Masonic College in Clarksville, Tennessee.[167]

In July 1849, young Ross was accepted to the U.S. Military Academy at West Point. He was graduated in 1853 ranking 51 out of 52 cadets. Several of his classmates would become well known during the war, John Bell Hood, James McAllister Schofield, James B. McPherson, and Phillip H. Sheridan, among them. Ross was assigned as brevet 2nd lieutenant in the 1st Infantry and served until his resignation on January 24, 1854.[168]

Shortly after leaving the army, Reuben married Miss Mary E. Herman in Christian County, Kentucky, on February 15, 1854.[169] By 1861 they had three children, Caroline "Carrie" H., Charles R., and Mary R. Ross. In the years before the war, Reuben was teaching school in Clarksville.[170]

When the war began, Ross was made a Captain in the Tennessee Artillery Corps by Governor Isham G. Harris, on May 17, 1861.[171] Writing in his journal in March 1862, as he describes the batteries at Fort Donelson, he states, "the upper battery, so called because higher up the river, had been erected ten months before by the State Government of Tennessee. It contained two 32-pounder Sea Coast howitzers which I myself had mounted eight months before."[172] The two howitzers were the first heavy guns mounted in the fort.

In the late summer of 1861, Ross was authorized by the War Department to raise a regiment of infantry. Ross raised three companies that were joined by others in Hopkinsville, Kentucky, to form the regiment that would become the 8th Kentucky Infantry. Ross was elected lieutenant colonel, and Senator Henry C. Burnett of Kentucky was elected colonel. Ross failed to receive the commission because of remarks made by a competitor to the War Department. The accusations were later proven false, and Ross was acquitted. He then continued in the training of artillery. He was elected captain of the Maury Light Artillery, a company of men mostly from the small town of Santa Fe, and the Duck River area of northwestern Maury County, Tennessee.[173]

On February 11, 1862, the Maury Light Artillery reported to General Gideon Pillow at Fort Donelson. Pillow informed Ross that he needed men for the heavy guns at the river batteries, Ross accepted the position. During the battles in the next three days with the gunboats, Ross personally took charge of the 6.4-inch columbiad rifle in the upper battery, and his men worked the 32 pounder carronades. 1st Lieutenant James M. Sparkman, with twenty men of the Maury Artillery, served the 10-inch columbiad in the lower river battery commanded by Lieutenant Hugh L. Bedford.[174]

At the surrender of Fort Donelson, Ross was made a prisoner, and at St. Louis, he saw his old friend and classmate General John M. Schofield. As the story goes, Schofield took his gloves off and gave them to Ross. He later secured for Captain Ross a parole to his home near Clarksville, Tennessee. There at "Rossview," with the events still fresh in his mind, Ross wrote of the engagements between the river batteries and the ironclads. In a letter to Reuben's younger brother Dr. John W. Ross, dated August 18, 1896, General Schofield remembered his old friend and classmate as one of the best-hearted fellows he ever knew and added, "I was very fond of him."[175]

Trouble arose for Captain Ross in Louisville, Kentucky, in August 1862 as he traveled to be exchanged. While reporting to the Federal authorities there, a provost guard saw his sidearms and found some papers in his valise and reported the items as contraband, thus violating Ross' parole.[176] Ross was arrested and was kept a prisoner finally being exchanged in October. After his exchange, he found that the Maury Light Artillery had already been exchanged and reorganized with 1st Lieutenant James M. Sparkman being elected captain. Rather than call for another reorganization, Ross applied for several positions in the next few months.[177]

In a letter to President Jefferson Davis, on February 2, 1864, applying for a commission as Captain or 1st Lieutenant of Cavalry in the "regular army." Ross explains his service after Fort Donelson, "I entered the cavalry service. I first acted under General Pillow, was then ordered by General Bragg to General Forrest, and finally passed from him to Brigadier General Davidson's Cavalry Brigade as Assistant Inspector General."[178]

On May 30, 1863, Ross signed as Captain Commanding Battalion of Cavalry, on receiving money for expenses used by men scouting in areas of Middle Tennessee. A document dated June 23, at Columbia, Tennessee, regarding money spent for lodging and food at various places by the men, states that "the services were rendered, money expended in the Secret Service CSA under orders from Brigadier General Forrest. R.R. Ross Captain Commanding Cavalry."[179]

In a letter written from Villanow, Georgia, dated November 21, 1863, to Richmond, Ross asked for promotion to colonel of cavalry and to be placed in command of a brigade in Major General Wheeler's Cavalry Corps. Writing of his actions since being exchanged, he says, "I have since fought in six different engagements, doing my duty therein completely, receiving wounds."[180]

Ross was once again captured near Columbia, Tennessee, on September 5, 1864. On the records as a prisoner, he is listed as Lieutenant Colonel and Inspector General on the staff of General William Y.C. Humes. A remark states, "Colonel Ross has the reputation of being a very humane man and has, on several occasions, rendered aid to Federal prisoners of war."[181] While being transported to Johnson's Island, Colonel Ross took a risk by jumping from a moving train near Cincinnati, Ohio, and, although badly hurt, made his escape.[182] Making his way back south, he was later seen at Cumberland Furnace, an iron furnace north of the town of Charlotte in Dickson County, Tennessee, by Miss Eleanora Willauer, on December 2, 1864. In her diary, she entered, "A party of Confederate Cavalry under Colonel Rube Ross passed here yesterday, some of them escaped prisoners. Colonel Ross himself was one."[183]

Colonel Reuben R. Ross accompanied Brigadier General Hylan B. Lyon on a cavalry raid into Kentucky, where on December 16, at Hopkinsville, Federals of General E.M. McCook's Brigade attacked Lyon's troops in a running battle.[184] In a hand-to-hand fight with several soldiers, one clubbed Ross in the head with his musket. Mortally wounded, he died at age thirty-four on December 21, 1864. Colonel Ross was buried near his mother and other family members in the Meriwether Cemetery near Guthrie, Todd County, Kentucky. His family believed he had been promoted to Brigadier General, and on his tombstone, he is listed as such, but official records have not been found to confirm his promotion to that rank.[185]

Shuster, Captain J.P.—Jacob Powhatan Shuster, born ca. 1824, was the son of John and Abigail Bartee Shuster. In 1850, Jacob, age 26, and his wife Miranda, age 20, were listed as living with his parents in the city of Norfolk, Virginia.[186]

Shuster entered the service early in the war. A date of commission as captain is not recorded. Lieutenant Colonel Milton A. Haynes mentioned him as "formerly of the

U.S. Navy," but the position in which he served is not known.[187] In a statement given at Richmond, Virginia, March 24, 1862, concerning the action at Fort Donelson, Colonel Haynes says, "Captain J.P. Shuster, who had reported to me for duty by order of General A.S. Johnston was appointed chief of the battalion, and under his direction, the ammunition and stores necessary for ten guns were arranged in the magazine, with matches, port-fires, lanterns, etc."[188] Captain Shuster was injured on February 13, 1862, during the engagement with the gunboat USS *Carondelet*.

In Colonel James E. Bailey's report (October 9, 1862), he states that "Captain Shuster, a volunteer in the batteries, being injured by the blast of one of the guns, the command of the batteries, after Captain Dixon's death, devolved upon Captain Culbertson."[189] Captain Jacob Culbertson says in his report, "In the first day's fight, Captain Shuster was disabled by the blast from one of the 32 pounders, near which he was standing when it was fired."[190] Captain B.G. Bidwell, commander of four of the 32 pounders in the lower battery, stated on September 30, 1862, that "Captain Shuster was also slightly injured by negligently standing too near the muzzle of one of my guns."[191]

The truth of the matter of Captain Jacob P. Shuster's injury is that he was more than "slightly injured," as Captain Bidwell remarked. He suffered a "compound comminuted fracture," a severe injury where the bones are broken in more than one place, and the end of a bone is sticking through the skin. Judging from his service record entries from then until 1865, it is highly doubtful that he ever fully recovered. On December 9, 1862, after examinations by several army doctors in Atlanta, Georgia, it was reported, "It is the opinion of all army surgeons who have examined Colonel Shuster that he will have to be subjected to the operation before his recovery." Shuster, writing from Athens, Georgia, on May 13, 1863, to Colonel William Preston Johnston, son of his old friend General Albert Sidney Johnston, reminds Johnston, "You know the condition of my leg, I must have it operated on or I will lose it."[192]

Captain Shuster also had problems regarding his rank. As he understood it, he had been informed by General Albert S. Johnston while at Corinth, Mississippi, in early 1862, that he was promoted to lieutenant colonel. Writing to General P.G.T. Beauregard, on February 7, 1863, while seeking a position as commander of a post at Atlanta because of his condition he says, "I was severely wounded at the Battle of Fort Donelson where I had the honor of commanding the heavy batteries in a protracted contest with the gunboats of the enemy. While at Jackson, Mississippi last June, I was tendered the command of the heavy batteries at Vicksburg by yourself, but was compelled to resign on account of my health." In another correspondence with G.A. Henry at Richmond, April 24, 1863, he says "I was surprised to hear today that there is no record of my promotion as Lieutenant Colonel in the War Department," he continues, "You will notice in my letter to General Beauregard (which he so strongly endorsed) that I alluded to his offering me command of all the heavy batteries at Vicksburg last summer. When he offered this command, he addressed me as Lieutenant Colonel, and General Johnston informed him that I had been appointed to that rank."[193] His financial situation at this time was bleak as well, "I am only drawing at this time captain's pay," it was not enough to cover his expenses or to take care of his family, "before the war I was independent, but now I have not one dollar's income." He continues saying that his property had been stolen or destroyed by the enemy, and the little remaining was in their hands in Norfolk, Virginia, and North Carolina.[194]

Things continued to get worse for Captain Shuster on May 13, 1863, he received word that his wife is extremely ill in Athens, Georgia. He sends word to Colonel William

Preston Johnston that he is leaving immediately for Athens and says that his disability is out on May 18. Asking again to be placed at a post in Atlanta, and that if not sent there, he requests an extension of disability for at least two months more.[195]

The incomplete state of Shuster's service record does not show if the commission ever came through, or if he ever recovered from his wound. Pay records for September 30, 1864, and April 19, 1865, show that he was still receiving pay for the rate of captain. In Athens, Georgia, May 8, 1865, his name appears on a roll of prisoners as Colonel and Chief of Artillery, CSA.[196]

Nothing further could be found regarding his time after the war, but in a city directory of Augusta, Georgia, in 1877, his wife Miranda is listed as the widow of J.P. Shuster. The date of his death or place of burial has not been found.[197]

Sparkman, Lieutenant James Madison—James Madison Sparkman, born January 25, 1833, was the son of Williams Sparkman and Elizabeth Vestal Sparkman. By 1850, his father had passed away, and James, called Matt, and his older brother John and siblings were still living with their mother in the 10th Civil District of Maury County, Tennessee. The Sparkman brothers were listed as farmers.[198] James married Miss Minerva A. Hill in Maury County on October 19, 1854,[199] and by 1860 he and brother John had become prosperous merchants in Santa Fe, Civil District 18, Maury County. Santa Fe, pronounced locally as "Santa Fee," is a small crossroads village near Snow Creek on the original Charlotte/Columbia Road, northwest of Columbia, the county seat of Maury County.[200] Situated in the fertile farming region of the Duck River Valley, Santa Fe was naturally a popular place for locals to congregate, learn the latest news, and buy goods that they were unable to produce on the farm.

When in 1861, as Maury Countians were joining infantry and cavalry units headed to war, Sparkman saw the need for an artillery company to be raised. He set about recruiting men from the area of northwestern Maury County. Even though his popularity helped in raising the company, neither Sparkman, nor any of the other men, knew anything of artillery. When the men wanted to make him captain, James insisted that since he had no military experience, he could not in good conscience serve as captain. Such modesty and lack of experience did not stop Robert P. Griffith, a 32-year-old teacher from Mt. Pleasant in Maury County, from accepting a commission as captain. Griffith was said to have been elected with the influential help from his brother James O. Griffith, a Nashville newspaper editor. The farm boys accepted Griffith as captain, unaware of the fact that he knew nothing more of the artillery drill than they did. It became apparent, though, soon enough. James Sparkman was made 1st lieutenant.[201]

The company, now called the Maury Light Artillery, marched away from Santa Fe, on October 3, 1861, to the Duck River Station near Columbia where they boarded the rail cars, for many their first trip, and headed to Nashville where upon arriving, crossed the Cumberland River and entered into Camp Weakley, a camp of instruction situated "just east of Edgefield in a beautiful grove, having extensive parade and drill grounds." There the company was mustered into service by Captain G.H. Monsarrat, October 16. After a few weeks, they were sent to Clarksville, Tennessee. From there, they traveled to Hopkinsville, Kentucky, arriving in December.[202]

At Hopkinsville, they were first drilled by Lieutenant William Dunlap of Kentucky. Dunlap was described as having some artillery experience and was a competent drillmaster, but personal habits made him unpopular with the men. Captain Reuben R. Ross was also a drillmaster and was educated at West Point. Being a very competent officer, he made progress with the new artillerymen and became a candidate for captain of the company running against Lieutenant Dunlap after Captain R.P. Griffith was asked to resign. Ross received every vote but one and took command of the Maury Light Artillery, on January 7, 1862.[203]

The Maury Light Artillery arrived at Fort Donelson on February 11, 1862, with their six-gun field battery. General Gideon Pillow asked for artillerymen at the river batteries, and Ross accepted the position. The men left their guns in Dover and marched to the river batteries, where they saw the heavy guns for the first time. When the gunboat USS *Carondelet* appeared, the next morning interrupting their drill, Ross assigned Lieutenant Sparkman with twenty men to assist Lieutenant Hugh L. Bedford at the 10-inch columbiad smoothbore in the lower battery. Ross and the rest of the men served the 6.4-inch columbiad rifle and two 32 pounder howitzers in the upper battery.[204]

After the surrender, Lieutenant Sparkman was first sent to Camp Chase and then transferred to Johnson's Island. Being exchanged in September 1862, Sparkman was elected captain of the Maury Artillery at the reorganization. Captain Reuben Ross had been arrested at Louisville, Kentucky, because of a violation of his parole and was still in a northern prison.[205]

In March 1863, Captain Sparkman and company were in the 1st Tennessee Battalion of Heavy Artillery, attached to the 12th Louisiana Heavy Artillery under Lieutenant Colonel P.F. DeGournay.[206] Sparkman was listed as commander of Battery Number 7, at Port Hudson, Louisiana. His battery was a "hot shot" battery with two 24 pounder smoothbore cannons, one #74, weight 5,550 pounds made in 1828, the other #11, weight 5,515, cast in 1835.[207]

On the night of March 14, 1863, the men from Maury County witnessed the burning of the USS *Mississippi*, a side-wheel steamer of Admiral David G. Farragut's fleet. The boats of the fleet attempted passing the batteries at Port Hudson, with several being successful, but the *Mississippi* was grounded and attempts to free her were unsuccessful. In a local history of the Maury Light Artillery written by historian Frank H. Smith of Columbia in 1908, Smith said it was probable that a hotshot entered a porthole, causing damage and setting her afire. That was not the case.[208] While the boat was grounded, artillery fire was indeed causing damage, but in his report after the action, Captain Melancton Smith of the *Mississippi* gave details of having the fire started in the forward storeroom to destroy the boat rather than have it captured by the Confederates. When a yeoman was sent to check on the progress of the fire, three cannonballs had entered the storeroom letting water in, extinguishing the blaze. Captain Smith then had four more fires set in different locations between the decks and accompanied by executive 1st Lieutenant George Dewey (Later Admiral Dewey), who abandoned the ship, which eventually freed herself by being lightened by burning, and floated downstream with guns firing from the fires in every direction. The *Mississippi's* magazine exploded at 5:30 A.M., causing a tremendous concussion felt for miles around.[209]

At Port Hudson on Wednesday, May 27, 1863, Captain Sparkman received a deep wound in the groin caused by a shell fragment. He was taken to a hospital tent where he suffered for nine days. With gangrene setting in, Sparkman died on Friday, June 5, 1863. Sparkman was buried underneath a tree just east of a big brick house, according to soldiers interviewed by Frank Smith in his history of the company. In 1908, several Maury Countians made the trip to Port Hudson in search of the location. Once there, they found the tree gone, the house destroyed, and the area in cultivation. All traces of Captain Sparkman's grave were obliterated.[210]

Thompson, Lieutenant Elijah B.—Elijah B. Thompson, born ca. 1838, was the son of Captain Absalom Thompson and wife Mary B. Sandford Thompson, of Spring Hill, Tennessee.[211] He attended Cumberland University in Lebanon, Tennessee, and was a member of the graduating class of 1858.[212]

After school, Thompson practiced law in nearby Columbia until the beginning of the war. Enlisting in the Maury Light Artillery in September at Santa Fe, Tennessee, he was elected 4th lieutenant at the organization. A note on his record shows that he was acting as junior 1st lieutenant by the appointment of Captain Robert P. Griffith, September 23, 1861.[213] In a local history of the company written in 1908, he was described as a very handsome, wealthy young lawyer from Columbia.[214]

Lieutenant Thompson traveled with the Maury Artillery to Camp Weakley in Nashville.[215] From there, the company went to Clarksville, Tennessee, and Hopkinsville, Kentucky, before arriving at Fort Donelson, on February 11, 1862. At Fort Donelson, the Maury Light Artillery under Captain Reuben R. Ross served in the heavy batteries at the Cumberland River. In the upper battery, Ross assigned command of the 32-pounder howitzer carronade on the left of the 6.4-inch rifle to Lieutenant Thompson. During the battles with the gunboats, the howitzers of the upper battery were fired very few times, their range being insufficient to do any damage to the ironclads.[216]

At the surrender, Thompson was sent to Camp Chase, Ohio, where he was paroled to Columbus, Ohio. Sent to Vicksburg, Mississippi, on September 1, 1862, for exchange, he was elected 1st Lieutenant at the reorganization of the company. At Port Hudson, Louisiana, the Maury Artillery was part of the 1st Tennessee Artillery Battalion and was attached to the 12th Louisiana Heavy Artillery under Lieutenant Colonel P.F. DeGournay.[217]

When Port Hudson was surrendered in July 1863, Lieutenant Thompson, with other members of the Tennessee Artillery Battalion, was sent to New Orleans on the Steamer *Zephyr*. At New Orleans, Thompson was confined to the Custom House on July 15. A note on his record mentions that he escaped on August 3.[218] Historian Frank Smith of Columbia, Tennessee, writing a history of soldiers from Maury County in the early 1900s, notes that Thompson escaped on the way to prison and later went to Canada.[219]

A historic event happened at his boyhood home in Spring Hill, Tennessee, on November 29, 1864. Elijah Thompson's brother, Dr. James T.S. Thompson, was serving on the staff of General John Bell Hood. On the flanking movement from Columbia to block General John M. Schofield's army from reaching Franklin, Dr. Thompson invited General Hood to stay at his father, Captain Absalom Thompson's home, "Oaklawn."[220]

Hood used the Thompson house as his headquarters, and during the night as Hood slept, the Federals slipped past the Confederates and reached Franklin, where the tragic battle took place the next afternoon. The events of that night have been debated ever since.[221]

After the war, very little is found of Thompson. In 1870 he was living in Little Rock, Arkansas, listed as a planter. His real estate value was $100,000 and personal estate valued at $5,000.[222] Elijah died soon after, purportedly of tuberculosis that he contracted during the war. The date of his death is unknown.[223]

His place of burial is not listed, but his parents and brothers are buried in the Old

Brick Church Cemetery, also known as the Jackson College Cemetery near the Thompson house in Spring Hill, Tennessee.[224] The cemetery has been overgrown over the years with many of the stones knocked down, it is possible that Elijah's body could be there in an unmarked grave.

Watts, Lieutenant William Ormsby—William Ormsby Watts was a native of Maysville, Mason County, Kentucky. His birth date is not known but was ca. 1814–17. In December 1844, he married Miss Amelia Lewis Thomson in Hamilton County, Ohio.[225] Amelia was a native of Louisiana. In 1850, they were living in Cincinnati, Ohio, where he was working as a merchant.[226]

By 1860, Ormsby and Amelia had relocated and were living in Nashville, Tennessee, with three children, Minnie 10, Evalina 8, and Miles age 2. His occupation was listed as a clerk.[227]

In May 1861, at Nashville, W.O. Watts enlisted in the Tennessee Artillery Corps and was commissioned a 4th lieutenant. He was a member of Captain Jesse Taylor's Artillery Company at Fort Henry on the Tennessee River. In the fall of 1861, Colonel Adolphus Heiman sent Brevet 1st Lieutenant Watts to Fort Donelson as ordnance officer and to train the soldiers there at that time as artillerymen. Returning later to his duties as ordnance officer at Fort Henry, he was present during the gunboat battle and was taken prisoner at the surrender on February 6, 1862. In his report of the battle, General Tilghman mentioned Lieutenant Watts as acting ordnance officer and complimented him on the admirable condition of the ordnance department at the post and added, "Lieutenant Watts is the coolest officer under fire I ever met with."[228]

Being sent to Alton, Illinois, he was listed as 45 years old with black hair, dark complexion, and height of 5'9". He was transferred to Johnson's Island on April 10, 1862.[229]

After being exchanged at Vicksburg, Mississippi, in September 1862, he was made chief of ordnance under General Lloyd Tilghman and served in that capacity until Tilghman's death on May 16, 1863, at the Battle of Champion Hill. He was then ordnance officer under General William W. Loring. During this time, he was referred to as Major Watts and was announced as chief of ordnance to General Leonidas Polk in May 1864. After Polk's death on June 14, 1864, Watts was again under General Loring as ordnance officer and served with the Army of Tennessee until the surrender at Durham Station, North Carolina, on April 26, 1865.[230]

After the war, Ormsby Watts and his wife were living at 377 Magazine Street in New Orleans, Louisiana. On September 6, 1867, Watts died of yellow fever and was buried at the Girod Street Cemetery, a cemetery that is no longer in existence, if he was disinterred and moved to another cemetery, it is not listed. His age was given as 53 years old.[231]

After Watts' death, his widow Amelia returned to Cincinnati with her children and lived there the remainder of her life, passing in 1917 at age 90. She was buried in the Spring Grove Cemetery in Cincinnati.[232]

Casualties in the Fight for the River Batteries

February 6–12, 1862

CONFEDERATE CASUALTIES

TENNESSEE ARTILLERY CORPS
Lieutenant Colonel Milton A. Haynes
(wounded or injured)

February 13, 1862

CONFEDERATE CASUALTIES

TENNESSEE ARTILLERY CORPS
Captain Joseph Dixon (k)

50TH TENNESSEE INFANTRY
James Beard, Company D (k)

FEDERAL CASUALTIES

USS *CARONDELET*

John Flaherty
Dennis Relay
Michael Riley
John Conner
Thomas Foley
Arthur Blackburn
Maurice Phillips
J.J. Kinney
W.L. Reid

February 14, 1862

CONFEDERATE CASUALTIES

TENNESSEE ARTILLERY CORPS
Captain J.P. Shuster (w)

MAURY LIGHT ARTILLERY
2nd Lieutenant P.L. "Len" Fitzgerald (w)
Gus Mayes (w)

FEDERAL CASUALTIES

USS *ST. LOUIS*
Charles H. Baker, ship's cook (mw)
F.A. Riley (k)
Flag Officer Andrew H. Foote (later died)
R.J. Baldwin, pilot (w)
Charles Smith, boatswain's mate (w)
Antonio Caldwin, seaman (w)
Thomas Kirkman, seaman (w)
R.H. Medill, carpenter (w)
W.S. Coon, seaman (w)
John Thompson, seaman (w)

USS *CARONDELET*
Albert Richardson, seaman (k)
Joseph Laycock, seaman (k)
Albert Markham, seaman (k)
Wm. Duff, seaman (k)
Wm. Hinton, of USS *Cincinnati*, pilot (since dead)
Samuel Brooks, Second Assistant Engineer (w)
Owen Carty, seaman (w)
James Plant, seaman (w)
James Brown, seaman (w)
Patrick Laughlin, seaman (w)
Edward Green, seaman (w)
Owen Curley, seaman (w)
Henry Smith, seaman (w)
Pat Sullivan, seaman (w)
John Owen, seaman (w)

Wm. B. Rooney, seaman (w)
Thomas Burns, seaman (w)
James McFadden, seaman (w)
John Diamond, seaman (w)
Amos Dutch, seaman (w)
Richard Mahoney, seaman (w)
Richard O'Brien, seaman (w)
Wm. Johnson, seaman (w)
Patrick O'Brien, seaman (w)
William Thielman, seaman (w)
Benjamin Edger, seaman (w)
Henry Anderson, seaman (w)
Daniel F. Charles, seaman (w)
John Doughty, seaman (w)
John Murphy, seaman (w)
John McConnell, seaman (w)
John Doherty, Second Master (w)
John McBride, cook (w)

USS *Pittsburgh*

Charles Merwin, seaman (w)
George Smith, seaman (w)

USS *Louisville*

James Curtis (k)
E.W. Avilla (k)
Charles Billips (k)
John Williams (k)
Michael Kelly (w)
Wm. Higgins (w)
E.S. Collins (w)
Charles Might (w)

APPENDIX 3

Ordnance Received for the River Batteries at Fort Donelson, Tennessee[1]

January 1, 1862–February 15, 1862

Date	Received By	Items	Book and Page
January 1	Lt. J. Culbertson	96 32-pdr blank cartridges (6 lb); 343 32-pdr Solid Shot	Vol. 108, 1
January 2	Lt. J. Culbertson	1 10-in Columbiad; 1 Iron Carriage; 1 Sponge and Rammer; 8 Traverse Segments; 1 Center Ring; 1 Pintle Plate; 2 Priming Wires; 2 Gunners Gimlets; 1 Pintle Pin; 1 Elevating Screw; 28 Bolts; 2 Maneuvering Handspikes; 2 Rollers; 8 Tie Plates	Vol. 108, 3; Vol. 104, 24, 44, 48, 72, 80, 82
January 6	Lt. J. Culbertson	154 32-pdr Shell Strapped	Vol. 108, 5
January 13	Lt. J. Culbertson	48 10-in Solid Shot; 52 10-in Shell	Vol. 108, 10
January 15	Lt. J. Culbertson	100 32-pdr Blank Cartridges (6 lb); 254 32 pdr Fuze; 500 Large Friction Primers; 37 Stand 32-pdr Grape	Vol. 108, 12
January 15	Lt. J. Culbertson	37 Stands 32-pdr Grape	Vol. 104, 154
January 15	Lt. J. Culbertson	500 Large Friction Primers	Vol. 104, 340
January 16	Lt. J. Culbertson	90 Blank Cartridges 10-in (16 lb); 10 Blank Cartridges 10-in (20 lb)	Vol. 108, 13
January 17	Lt. J. Culbertson	50 Fuze Plugs 10-in Columbiad; 130 Paper Fuzes (50 20 Sec; 50 28 Sec; 30 36 Sec)	Vol. 108, 14
January 18	Lt. J. Culbertson	50 8-in Shell; 50 8-in Fuze Plugs; 80 8-in Paper Fuzes; 40 8-in Cannister Fixed	Vol. 108, 15
January 22	Lt. J. Culbertson	12 Thumbstalls	Vol. 108, 18
January 23	Capt. J. Culbertson	50 Stands 32-pdr Grape	Vol. 104, 154
January 23	Capt. J. Culbertson	6.4 Rifled Columbiad; 6.4-in Gun Carriage; 6.4-in Iron Chassis; 2 6.4-in Handspikes; 1 6.4-in Lindstock, 2 6.4-in Priming Wires; 1 6.4-in Rammer; 1 6.4-in Sponge; 6.4-in Gun Sight; 6.4-in Elevating Screw	Vol. 104. 25, 42, 46, 98, 112, 120; 138, 242

Appendix 3.

Date	Received By	Items	Book and Page
January 25	Lt. R.L. Cobb	25 Rifle Shell 6.4-in Columbiad; 36 Rifle Shell 6.4-in Columbiad; 100 32-pdr Blank Cartridge (8 lb); 100 32-pdr Blank Cartridges (6 lb)	Vol. 108, 21
January 28	Lt. R.L. Cobb	19 Gunners Haversacks; 19 Tube Punches; 18 32-pdr Priming Wires; 18 Lanyards; 1 Rifle Shell Fuze Wrench	Vol. 108, 23
January 28	Lt. R.L. Cobb	4 Gunner's Levels	Vol. 104, 76
February 1	Lt. R.L. Cobb	1500 Large Friction Primers	Vol. 104, 340
February 6	Lt. R.L. Cobb	100 32-pdr Blank Cartridges (8 lb); 49 6.4 Blank Cartridges (10 lb); 20 6.4-in Rifled Shell	Vol. 108, 31
February 6	Lt. R.L. Cobb	1 Barrel Cannon Powder (100 lbs)	Vol. 104, 266
February 6	Lt. R.L. Cobb	49 10 lb Charges for 6.4 Rifled Gun	Vol. 104, 282
February 7	Lt. R.L. Cobb	100 Stands 32-pdr Grape	Vol. 104, 154
February 8	Lt. R.L. Cobb	100 Stands 32-pdr Grape; 100 32-pdr Shell	Vol. 104, 154, 162
February 8	Lt. R.L. Cobb	75 10-in Sabots	Vol. 104, 378
February 9	Lt. R.L. Cobb	12 32-pdr Vent Covers; 4 32-pdr Vent Punches; 8 32-pdr Rammers; 8 32-pdr Sponges; 1 Budge Barrel; 51 6.4-in Rifled Shell	Vol. 108, 34
February 13	Lt. R.L. Cobb	50 Blank Cartridges 6.4-in Rifle (10 lb); 50 32-pdr Shell	Vol. 108, 39
February 13	Lt. R.L. Cobb	75 10-in Balls; 50 32-pdr Rifled Shell	Vol. 104, 158, 164
February 13	Lt. R.L. Cobb	50 10 lb Charges for 6.4 Rifled Gun	Vol. 104, 282
February 15	Lt. R.L. Cobb	500 32-pdr Balls, 100 10-in Balls	Vol. 104, 156, 158
February 15	Lt. R.L. Cobb	1200 Large Friction Primers	Vol. 104, 340

Chapter Notes

Preface

1. Hugh L. Bedford, "H.L. Bedford Memoirs," University of Tennessee, Knoxville, Special Collections, Manuscript 2176, 1.
2. *Ibid.*, 10.
3. Reuben R. Ross, "Reuben R. Ross Journal," *Ross Family Journals 1851–1871* (Tennessee State Library and Archives, 1862), 57.
4. Bedford, "H.L. Bedford Memoirs," 3.

Chapter 1

1. *War of the Rebellion: Official Records of the Union and Confederate Armies*, Series 3 vol. 5 (Harrisburg, PA: National Historical Society, 1985), 885.
2. Thomas Lawrence Connelly, *Army of the Heartland: The Army of Tennessee, 1861–1862* (Baton Rouge, LA: Louisiana State University Press, 1967), 35; Larry H. Whiteaker, *Tennessee Encyclopedia,* "Civil War," https://tennesseeencyclopedia.net/entries/civil-war/.
3. Benjamin Franklin Cooling, *Forts Henry and Donelson—The Key to the Confederate Heartland* (Knoxville, TN: University of Tennessee Press, 1987), 12.
4. Edwin C. Bearss, "The Fort Donelson Water Batteries, Fort Donelson National Military Park, Historic Structures Report Part 2" (Fort Donelson National Battlefield Archives, 1968), 2.
5. J.L. Nichols, *Confederate Engineers* (Tuscaloosa, AL: The Confederate Publishing Company, 1957), 42.
6. Military and Financial Board, "Military and Financial Board Nashville, Tenn., Records, 1861," M623 R1, Tennessee State Library and Archives.
7. Wilbur F. Creighton, Jr., "Wilbur Fisk Foster: Soldier and Engineer," *Tennessee Historical Quarterly* 31/3 (Fall 1972): 262.
8. *Ibid.*, 263.
9. *Ibid.*, 261.
10. W.F. Foster, *Compiled Service Records of Confederate Soldiers Who Served in Organizations from the State of Tennessee, 1st (Feild's) Tennessee Infantry*, M268 R102, Washington, D.C.: National Archives Records Administration, 1960.
11. Creighton, "Wilbur Fisk Foster: Soldier and Engineer," 261–62.

12. Bromfield Lewis Ridley, *Battles and Sketches of the Army of Tennessee* (Mexico, MO: Missouri Print. & Pub. Co., 1906), 65.
13. Van L. Riggins, "A History of Fort Donelson National Military Park Tennessee," *Park Histories* (1958), https://www.nps.gov/parkhistory/online_books/fodo/fodo_history.pdf (3 January 2019), 1; "Letter from Donelson," *Union and American*, January 1, 1862.
14. The Dover site was being referred to by Randal W. MacGavock as "Camp Donelson" as early as May 26, 1861, only sixteen days after the surveying crew identified the position. Randal W. MacGavock, "The Randal W. MacGavock Diary, October 5, 1860—February 5, 1862," *Randall W. MacGavock Papers 1848–1898* (Tennessee State Library and Archives, 1860), May 26, 1861.
15. W.C. Jones, "Gun Boats on th Cumberland River," *Republican Banner*, November 15, 1861. This is likely an insinuation regarding the political pull of John Bell, 1860 presidential candidate and partner in the Cumberland Iron Works, just above Dover.
16. Wilbur F. Foster, "The Building of Forts Henry and Donelson," in *Battles and Sketches of the Army of Tennessee*, ed. Bromfield L. Ridley (Mexico, MO: Missouri Printing and Publishing, 1906), 65.
17. Foster, "The Building of Forts Henry and Donelson," 65.
18. *Ibid.*
19. *Ibid.*
20. Bushrod Johnson to Isham Harris, June 11, 1861, *Governor Isham G. Harris Papers 1857 to 1862*, GP 19, Box 3, No. 2, War Correspondence May 1861—February 19, 1863 (Tennessee State Library and Archives).
21. *Ibid.*
22. *Ibid.*
23. *Ibid.*
24. *Ibid.*
25. *Ibid.*
26. Isham Harris to Bushrod Johnson, June 14, 1861, *Governor Isham G. Harris Papers 1857–1862*, GP 19, Box 3, No. 2, War Correspondence May 1861—February 19, 1863 (Tennessee State Library and Archives).
27. Cooling, *Henry and Donelson*, 48.
28. Creighton, "Wilbur Fisk Foster: Soldier and Engineer," 265.

29. *Ibid.* Despite objections, Fort Henry, as it would come to be known, was built on the site chosen by Bushrod Johnson. Foster would be vindicated, as at the fort's surrender, the Confederate gunners were serving their guns in rising knee-deep water. Foster was later promoted to major and was chief engineer to General Alexander P. Stewart.

30. Foster, "The Building of Forts Henry and Donelson."; Wilbur F. Foster, *Compiled Service Records of Confederate Soldiers Who Served in Organizations Raised Directly by the Confederate Government, Engineers,* M258 R105. Washington, D.C.: National Archives Records Administration, 1960.

31. Jesse Taylor, "The Defense of Fort Henry," in *Battles and Leaders of the Civil War* (Edison, NJ: Castle, n.d.), 368.

32. *Ibid.*, 369.

33. *Ibid.*

34. *Ibid.*

35. Actually, this was Lieutenant Joseph Dixon who was sent there.

36. Taylor, "The Defense of Fort Henry," 369.

37. *War of the Rebellion: Official Records of the Union and Confederate Armies.*, Series I vol. 7 (Harrisburg, PA: National Historical Society, 1971), 139.

38. Several notable contemporary historians have credited General Daniel S. Donelson as the person who approved the Dover site and have recognized Donelson with the selection of the Kirkman Landing site for Fort Henry. In our research, we could find but one primary source reference to Donelson's involvement. This reference is in William Preston Johnston's biography of his father, General Albert Sidney Johnston. Johnston wrote, "The same consideration governed the selection of points for the defense of the Tennessee and Cumberland Rivers. Governor Harris wished to locate the forts as near the Kentucky line as he could find suitable sites for them, and sent General Daniel S. Donelson, a West Point graduate, and a man of influence and standing, to select proper situations. He reported Donelson as the strongest position on the Cumberland near the State line, and that there was no good position on the Tennessee River within the jurisdiction of the State. General Donelson wished to build a fort in Kentucky, on better ground; but under the Governor's orders, adopted the site at Fort Henry as the best near the Kentucky line, and because of the convenience of mutual support between it and Fort Donelson. These locations are to have been approved by General Bushrod R. Johnson also." Johnston, William Preston, *The Life of General Albert Sidney Johnston* (New York, NY: D. Appleton, 1879), 407. In other primary sources, such as the accounts by Engineer Wilbur F. Foster, Captain Jesse Taylor, and most importantly, in the letters exchanged between Governor Harris and Bushrod Johnson in June 1861, there is not one mention of General Donelson's involvement. Moreover, Chief Engineer, Colonel Bushrod Johnson, in his letter of June 11, 1861 to Governor Harris states, "I selected Kirkman's Old Landing … as the best place at which to erect defensive works." William P. Johnston never

mentions the involvement of the survey team led by Anderson and Foster which evidence supports selected the Fort Donelson site, and in his passing reference to Johnson, seems to indicate that Bushrod Johnson had very little to do with the selection other than perhaps give a final approval. From the majority of the evidence at hand, it appears that Anderson and Foster selected the Fort Donelson location, not General Donelson, and that Colonel Bushrod Johnson, after rejecting the Tennessee River sites selected by Anderson and Foster, is alone responsible for the selection of the Kirkman Landing site that would become Fort Henry.

39. "Donelson," *St. Albans Weekly Messenger,* February 27, 1862; MacGavock, "MacGavock Diary," May 28, 1861.

40. "Stewart County Volunteers," Nashville (TN) *Union and American,* June 9, 1861.

41. "Election Returns," Nashville (TN) *Union and American,* June 13, 1861.

42. Samuel D. Smith, Charles P. Stripling, and James M. Brannon, *A Cultural Resource Survey of Tennessee's Western Highland Rim Iron Industry, 1790s-1930s* (Nashville, TN: Tennessee Department of Conservation, Division of Archaeology, 1988), 185.

43. *Ordnance Department—Arsenals at Nashville, Tennessee and Atlanta, Georgia.*

44. "Letter from Donelson."

Chapter 2

1. Ezra J. Warner, *Generals in Blue: Lives of the Union Commanders* (Baton Rouge, LA: Louisiana State University Press, 1964), 429–30.

2. Gary D. Joiner, *Mr. Lincoln's Brown Water Navy* (Plymouth, UK: Rowman & Littlefield Publishers, 2007), 9.

3. *Ibid.*

4. Myron J. Smith, *The USS Carondelet: A Civil War Ironclad on the Western Waters* (Jefferson, NC: McFarland, 2010), 7.

5. *War of the Rebellion: Official Records of the Union and Confederate Navies,* Series 1 vol. 22 (Washington, D.C.: Government Printing Office, 1908), 279.

6. *Ibid.*

7. *Ibid.*, 280.

8. Barbara Brooks Tomblin, *The Civil War on the Mississippi: Union Sailors, Gunboat Captains, and the Campaign to Control the River* (Lexington, KY: University Press of Kentucky, 2016), 6.

9. *O.R.N., I,,* 22, 19.

10. *Ibid.*

11. *Ibid.*, 281.

12. Joiner, *Brown Water Navy,* 21.

13. *Ibid.*

14. Smith, *The USS Carondelet: A Civil War Ironclad on the Western Waters,* 16.

15. Joiner, *Brown Water Navy,* 22.

16. *O.R.N., I,* 22, 284.

17. *Ibid.*, 286.

18. *Ibid.*, 284–85.

19. *Ibid.*, 286.

20. Paul H. Silverstone, *Warships of the Civil War Navies* (Annapolis, MD: Naval Institute Press, 1989), 158–60.

21. *O.R.N.*, I, 22, 295.

22. Joiner, *Brown Water Navy*, 24.

23. *Ibid.*, 25.

24. *O.R.N.*, I, 22, 307–08.

25. *Ibid.*, 307.

26. Tomblin, *Civil War on the Mississippi*, 14.

27. Joiner, *Brown Water Navy*, 27.

28. *O.R.N.*, I, 22, 495.

29. Silverstone, *Warships of the Civil War Navies*, 151–55.

30. H. Allen Gosnell, *Guns on the Western Waters: The Story of River Gunboats in the Civil War* (Baton Rouge, LA: Louisiana State University Press, 1949), 16.

31. Joiner, *Brown Water Navy*, 26.

32. Edwin C. Bearss, "Full Speed Ahead: Yankee Ironclads Unleashed into the Volunteer State," *Tennessee Historical Quarterly* 69/1 (Spring 2010): 20.

33. *O.R.N.*, I, 22, 384–85.

34. *Ibid.*, 451–52.

35. *Ibid.*, 459.

36. *Ibid.*, 464.

37. *Ibid.*, 515.

38. John Milligan, *From the Fresh Water Navy: 1861–1865; The Letters of Acting Master's Mate Henry R. Browne and Acting Ensign Symmes E. Browne* (Annapolis, MD: Naval Institute Press, 1971), 23.

Chapter 3

1. Timothy B. Smith, *Grant Invades Tennessee: The 1862 Battles for Forts Henry and Donelson* (Lawrence, KS: University Press of Kansas, 2016), 4.

2. Isham Harris to Beriah Magoffin, August 30, 1861, *Governor Isham G. Harris Papers 1857 to 1862*, GP 19, Box 3, No. 2, War Correspondence May 1861—February 19, 1863 (Tennessee State Library and Archives).

3. Steven E. Woodworth, *Jefferson Davis and His Generals: The Failure of Confederate Command in the West* (Lawrence, KS: University Press of Kansas, 1990), 156.

4. Joseph Howard Parks, *General Leonidas Polk, C.S.A.: The Fighting Bishop* (Baton Rouge, LA: Louisiana State University Press, 1990), 11–21; Randy Bishop, *Civil War Generals of Tennessee* (Gretna, LA: Pelican, 2013), 154; Ezra J. Warner, *Generals in Gray: Lives of the Confederate Commanders* (Baton Rouge, LA: Louisiana State University, 1987), 242.

5. Francis B. Heitman, *Historical Register and Dictionary of the United States Army, From Its Organization, September 29, 1789 to March 2, 1903*, 2 vols., vol. 1 (Washington, D.C.: Government Printing Office, 1903), 648.

6. Parks, *General Leonidas Polk*, 156–57.

7. Leonidas Polk, "Compiled Service Records of Confederate General and Staff Officers and Nonregimental Enlisted Men," M331 R199, General Services Administration National Archives and Record Service (Washington, D.C.: National Archives Records Administration, 1960).

8. Nathaniel Cheairs Hughes, *The Battle of Belmont: Grant Strikes South* (Chapel Hill, NC: University of North Carolina, 1991), 1.

9. Smith, *Grant Invades Tennessee*, 10.

10. *ibid.*

11. Stanley F. Horn, *The Army of Tennessee* (Wilmington, NC: Broadfoot, 1987), 51.

12. Isham Harris to Jefferson Davis, September 4, 1861, *Governor Isham G. Harris Papers 1857 to 1862*, GP 19, Box 3, No. 2, War Correspondence May 1861—February 19, 1863 (Tennessee State Library and Archives).

13. Isham Harris to General Leonidas Polk, September 4, 1861, *Governor Isham G. Harris Papers 1857 to 1862*, GP 19, Box 3, No. 2, War Correspondence May 1861—February 19, 1863 (Tennessee State Library and Archives).

14. Isham Harris to Beriah Magoffin, September 4, 1861, *Governor Isham G. Harris Papers 1857 to 1862*, GP 19, Box 3, No. 2, War Correspondence May 1861—February 19, 1863 (Tennessee State Library and Archives).

15. *War of the Rebellion: Official Records of the Union and Confederate Armies*, Series I vol. 4 (Harrisburg, PA: National Historical Society, 1971), 185.

16. *Ibid.*, 175.

17. Smith, *Grant Invades Tennessee*, 11.

18. *Ibid.*, 9.

19. William Preston Johnston, *The Life of Gen. Albert Sidney Johnston: Embracing His Services in the Armies of the United States, the Republic of Texas, and the Confederate States* (New York, NY: Da Capo Press, 1997), 496.

20. Gary D. Joiner, *Mr. Lincoln's Brown Water Navy* (Plymouth, UK: Rowman & Littlefield Publishers, 2007), 34.

21. Thomas Lawrence Connelly, *Army of the Heartland: The Army of Tennessee, 1861–1862* (Baton Rouge, LA: Louisiana State University Press, 1967), 62.

22. Johnston, *Albert Sidney Johnston*, 411.

23. Heitman, *Historical Register*, 1, 375.

24. Joseph Dixon, "Population Schedules of the Eigth Census of the United States, 1860, Garrison, Clarke, Washington Territory," M653 R1398, General Services Administration National Archives and Record Service (Washington, D.C.: National Archives Records Administration, 1965).

25. Heitman, *Historical Register*, 1, 375.

26. "Accessions from U.S. Army," *Athens Post* (Athens, TN) August 30, 1861; "General Johnston's Staff," *Athens Post* (Athens, TN) October 25, 1861.

27. Johnston, *Albert Sidney Johnston*, 410.

28. *Ibid.*

29. *Ibid.*

Chapter 4

1. "Proclamation," *Union and American* (Nashville, TN) September 27, 1861.

2. Isham G. Harris, "Proclamation!," *Daily Patriot* (Nashville, TN) October 3, 1861.

3. *Ibid.*

4. *Ibid.*

5. "Proposals for Contracts," *ibid.*, September 19.

6. This is a biblical reference to Joel 3:10. During this time, the firm of Sharp and Hamilton or Nashville Plow Works, laid aside the making of farm implements and began manufacturing military equipment, including their Nashville Plow Works swords.

7. John Berrien Lindsley, *Military Annals of Tennessee: Confederate* (Nashville, TN: J.M. Lindsley & Co., 1886; repr., Facsimile of the first edition, Wilmington NC: Broadfoot Publishing, 1995), 282.

8. Bromfield Lewis Ridley, *Battles and Sketches of the Army of Tennessee* (Mexico, MO: Missouri Print. & Pub. Co., 1906), 65–66.

9. *Ibid.*

10. *War of the Rebellion: Official Records of the Union and Confederate Armies*, Series I vol. 4 (Harrisburg, PA: National Historical Society, 1985), 461.

11. Writing in March 1862 Ross stated, "It contained two 32 pdrs. Seacoast howitzers which I myself had mounted eight months before." Ross, "Reuben R. Ross Journal," 54–55. Later in July, Ross received authority by the War Department to raise a regiment of infantry. Ross was unsuccessful in the attempt and would in December 1861 be elected as captain of the Maury Light Artillery and as he returned to the River Batteries with his artillery company in February 1862, he would go down in history for his action with the batteries in the Battle of Fort Donelson.

12. *Ibid.*

13. W. Ormsby Watts, "Compiled Service Records of Confederate Soldiers Who Served in Organizations from the State of Tennessee, Capt. Weller's Co., Light Artillery," M268 R99, General Services Administration National Archives and Record Service (Washington, D.C.: National Archives Records Administration, 1960). Both Lieutenant Watts and later Captain Reuben Ross refer to the carronades as being mounted on casemate carriages.

14. Reuben R. Ross, "Reuben R. Ross Journal," *Ross Family Journals 1851–1871* (Tennessee State Library and Archives, 1862), 2.

15. *War of the Rebellion: Official Records of the Union and Confederate Navies*, Series 1 vol. 4 (Washington, D.C.: Government Printing Office, 1908), 306.

16. Dave Page, *Ships Versus Shore: Civil War Engagements along Southern Shores and Rivers* (Nashville, TN: Rutledge Hill Press, 1994), 30.

17. *O.R.*, I, 4, 461.

18. "Seventh Census of the United States, 1850 Montgomery County, Tennessee," M432 R891, General Services Administration National Archives and Record Service (Washington, D.C.: National Archives Records Administration).

19. Ursula S. Beech, *Along the Warioto; or, A history of Montgomery County, Tennessee. In cooperation with the Clarksville Kiwanis Club and the Tennessee Historical Commission*. (Clarksville, TN: Tennessee Historical Commission, 1964), 138–39.

20. "Beaumont Withdraws," *Clarksville Chronicle* (Clarksville, TN) March 23, 1860, 3.

21. "Public Speaking in Montgomery County," *Clarksville Chronicle* (Clarksville, TN) May 31, 1861, 3.

22. "Nearly Full," *Clarksville Chronicle* (Clarksville, TN) August 30, 1861; J.K. Raimey, "Tennessee Confederate Pension Applications, Soldiers, 1891–1965," *Tennessee Board of Pension Examiners* (Nashville, TN: Tennessee State Library and Archives, 1910).

23. *Catalogue of the Officers and Students of Cumberland University, at Lebanon, Tenn. for the Academic Year 1858–59* (Lebanon, TN: Neal & Spillers, Printers, 1859), 4.

24. "A Big Treat," *Clarksville Chronicle* (Clarksville, TN) October 4, 1861.

25. *O.R.*, I, 4, 461.

26. *Ibid.*

27. *O.R.N.*, I, 4, 371.

28. Watts, "Service Records."

29. *War of the Rebellion: Official Records of the Union and Confederate Navies*, Series 1 vol. 22 (Washington, D.C.: Government Printing Office, 1908), 561.

30. Watts, "Service Records."

31. *O.R.*, I, 4, 440.

32. H.L. Bedford, "Fight Between the Batteries and Gunboats at Fort Donelson," *Southern Historical Society Papers* 13, no. January—December (1885): 165.

33. Hugh L. Bedford, "H.L. Bedford Memoirs," University of Tennessee, Knoxville, Special Collections, Manuscript 2176, 2.

34. *Catalogue of the Officers and Students of the Law Department of Cumberland University at Lebanon, TN for the Academic Year 1857–8* (Lebanon, TN: Neal & Spillers, Printers, 1858), 7.

35. J. Harvey Mathes, *The Old Guard in Gray* (Memphis, TN: S.C. Toof, 1897), 39.

36. Bedford, "H.L. Bedford Memoirs," 5.

37. A "mess" in Civil War times was when a group of approximately three or more soldiers grouped together to share rations, cooking chores, and sleeping arrangements.

38. J.H. M'Neily, "A Queer Order," *Confederate Veteran* 1/10 (1893): 308.

39. J.H. McNeilly, "Some Reminiscences of Civil War," *Banner* (Nashville, TN) January 27, 1911.

40. Randal W. McGavock, "Compiled Service Records of Confederate Soldiers Who Served in Organizations from the State of Tennessee, 10th Tennessee Infantry," M268 R157, General Services Administration National Archives and Record Service (Washington, D.C.: National Archives Records Administration, 1960).

41. MacGavock's name has been variously spelled McGavock and MacGavock. However, in his own handwriting in his 1860–62 journal, he spells his name MacGavock. That spelling will be used

throughout this work except in instances of quotations where the variant spelling is employed.

42. Herschel Gower, and Jack Allen, *Pen and Sword: The Life and Journals of Randal W. McGavock* (Nashville, TN: Tennessee Historical Commission, 1959), 29, 32, 48, 65–67, 77–79.

43. Tennessee Civil War Centennial Commission, *Tennesseans in the Civil War: A Military History of Confederate and Union Units with Available Rosters of Personnel*, 2 vols., vol. 1 (Nashville, TN: Civil War Centennial Commission, 1964), 285.

44. Johnston, *Albert Sidney Johnston*, 412.

45. *War of the Rebellion: Official Records of the Union and Confederate Armies*, Series I vol. 7 (Harrisburg, PA: National Historical Society, 1985), 462.

46. "In Anticipation," *Clarksville Chronicle* (Clarksville, TN) October 18, 1861.

47. *O.R.*, I, 4, 458.

48. *Ibid.*, 453–54.

49. *Ibid.*, 459.

50. *Ibid.*, 456.

51. *Ibid.*, 458.

52. *Ibid.*

53. *Ibid.*

54. *Ibid.*, 460; Adolphus Heiman to Governor Isham G. Harris," 18 October 1861, *Governor Isham G. Harris Papers 1857 to 1862*, GP 19, Box 3, No. 2, War Correspondence May 1861—February 19, 1863 (Tennessee State Library and Archives).

55. *O.R.*, I, 4, 461.

56. *Ibid.*; *O.R.*, I, 7, 394.

57. *O.R.* I, 7, 461.

58. Lee H. Hanson, Jr., *Archaeological Excavations in the Water Batteries At Fort Donelson National Military Park* (N.P.: National Park Service; U.S. Department of the Interior, 1968), 40.

59. This front-pintle design kept the front of the gun pinioned while wheels on the rear of the chassis, moving in a semi-circular direction on a wooden platform called a traverse arc, allowed the rear of the gun to be swiveled right or left, thus changing the direction of the cannon's muzzle. In barbette means that the guns were mounted to fire over the parapet instead of through an embrasure.

60. *Tennessee Civil War Correspondence, vol. 3 Middle Tennessee*, ed. Mrs. John Trotwood Moore, Tennessee Historical Records Survey (Nashville, TN: N.P., 1939), 282.

61. *Ibid.*

62. *O.R.*, I, 4, 463–64.

63. Jeremy F. Gilmer, "Find a Grave, Laurel Grove Cemetery, Savannah, Georgia," https://search.ancestry.com/cgi-bin/sse.dll?indiv=1&dbid=60525&h=1427011&tid=&pid=&usePUB=true&_phsrc=igT197&_phstart=successSource.

64. Francis B. Heitman, *Historical Register and Dictionary of the United States Army, From Its Organization September 29, 1789 to March 2, 1903*, vol. 1 (Washington, D.C.: Government Printing Office, 1903), 458.

65. Johnston, *Albert Sidney Johnston*, 412.

66. Heitman, *Historical Register*, 458; Johnston, *Albert Sidney Johnston*, 412; Jeremy F. Gilmer,

"Compiled Service Records of Confederate General and Staff Officers and Nonregimental Enlisted Men," M331 R106, General Services Administration National Archives and Record Service (Washington, D.C.: National Archives Records Administration, 1960).

67. *O.R.*, I, 4, 481.

68. J.L. Nichols, *Confederate Engineers* (Tuscaloosa, AL: The Confederate Publishing Company, 1957), 44.

69. *O.R.* I, 7, 698.

70. *O.R.*, I, 4, 476.

71. *Ibid.*, 480.

72. *Ibid.*, 481.

73. *Ibid.*, 491.

Chapter 5

1. *War of the Rebellion: Official Records of the Union and Confederate Armies*, Series I vol. 4 (Harrisburg, PA: National Historical Society, 1971), 496.

2. *Ibid.*, 496–97.

3. *Ibid.*, 497.

4. *Ibid.*, 495.

5. *Ibid.*, 501.

6. *Ibid.*

7. *Ibid.*, 500–01.

8. *Ibid.*, 496.

9. *War of the Rebellion: Official Records of the Union and Confederate Navies*, Series 1 vol. 22 (Washington, D.C.: Government Printing Office, 1908), 396–97.

10. *Ibid.*

11. *Ibid.*, 394.

12. *O.R.*, I, 4, 506.

13. Lineport no longer exists. The original site was approximately 13 miles below Fort Donelson on the east side of the Cumberland River and just downstream from Tobacco Port.

14. *Ibid.*, 506.

15. *Ibid.*, 507.

16. *Ibid.*, 544–45.

17. *War of the Rebellion: Official Records of the Union and Confederate Armies*, Series I vol. 7 (Harrisburg, PA: National Historical Society, 1985), 735.

18. *O.R.*, I, 4, 514.

19. *Ibid.*

20. *Ibid.*

21. It is interesting that during this time, Dixon is often referred to as captain. However, as late as December 4, Gilmer is still referring to him as Lieutenant and in a November 21, message to Gilmer, Dixon signs it as 1st lieutenant. Dixon's service record is incomplete and does not show any promotion beyond 1st lieutenant.

22. *Ibid.*, 519.

23. *Ibid.*

24. *Ibid.*, 522.

25. *Ibid.*

26. Parks, *General Leonidas Polk*, 192.

27. Nathaniel Cheairs Hughes, *The Battle of*

Belmont: Grant Strikes South (Chapel Hill, NC: University of North Carolina, 1991), 35.

28. *O.R.,* I, 4, 539.

29. *Ibid.,* 526.

30. *Ibid.*

31. *Ibid.*

32. *Ibid.,* 528.

33. *Ibid.,* 557.

34. *Ibid.,* 491.

35. Lloyd Tilghman, "Compiled Service Records of Confederate General and Staff Officers and Non-regimental Enlisted Men," M331 R249, General Services Administration National Archives and Record Service (Washington, D.C.: National Archives Records Administration, 1960).

36. Ezra J. Warner, *Generals in Gray: Lives of the Confederate Commanders* (Baton Rouge, LA: Louisiana State University, 1987), 306.

37. *O.R.,* I, 4, 472.

38. *O.R.* I, 7, 560.

39. *Ibid.*

40. *O.R.* I, 4, 560.

41. *O.R.* I, 7, 698.

42. *Ibid.*

43. Jill Knight Garrett, *A History of Humphreys County, Tennessee* (Columbia, TN: Jill Knight Garrett, 1963), 354.

44. John Berrien Lindsley, *Military Annals of Tennessee: Confederate* (Nashville, TN: J.M. Lindsley & Co., 1886; repr., Facsimile of the first edition, Wilmington NC: Broadfoot Publishing, 1995), 558.

45. *Ibid.*

46. *O.R.* I, 7, 699.

47. *Ibid.,* 698–99.

48. *Ibid.,* 698.

49. *Ibid.*

50. Hugh L. Bedford, "H.L. Bedford Memoirs," University of Tennessee, Knoxville, Special Collections, Manuscript 2176, 5.

51. *O.R.* I, 7, 685.

52. *Ibid.,* 132. The 27th Alabama Infantry was organized at Fort Heiman in December 1861.

53. Randal W. MacGavock, "The Randal W. MacGavock Diary, October 5, 1860—February 5, 1862," *Randall W. MacGavock Papers 1848–1898* (Tennessee State Library and Archives, 1860), November 23, 1861.

54. *O.R.* I, 7, 719.

55. MacGavock, "MacGavock Diary," November 23, 1862.

56. *Ibid.*

57. *O.R.* I, 7, 735.

58. Nashville Ordnance Department records only show gun powder purchases from Cheatham, Watson, and Company. Thomas L. Connelly states that the powder mills were established by Tennessee's Military and Financial Board and was the only source of gunpowder for Johnston's army. Thomas Lawrence Connelly, *Army of the Heartland: The Army of Tennessee, 1861–1862* (Baton Rouge, LA: Louisiana State University Press, 1967), 6–7.

59. *Ordnance Department: Record of Stores Purchased, Received and Issued, Nashville, Tennessee and Atlanta Arsenal, Georgia, 1861–1862,* Record Group 109, Chapter IV, Volume 19, National Archives Records Administration, Washington, D.C., 4, 18, 25.

60. *Ibid.,* 17, 29.

61. Joseph A. Hinkle, "J.A. Hinkle Reminiscences," in *Southern Historical Collection,* University of North Carolina Chapel Hill (1911), 5.

62. Wesley Smith Dorris, "Wesley Smith Dorris Diary," *Special Collections Online,* University of Tennessee, 26 November 1861.

63. Hinkle, "J.A. Hinkle Reminiscences," 2.

64. Randal W. MacGavock, "The Randal W. MacGavock Diary, October 5, 1860—February 5, 1862," *Randall W. MacGavock Papers 1848–1898* (Tennessee State Library and Archives, 1860), November 27, 1861.

65. "Attention Volunteers," *Union and American* (Nashville, TN) November 28, 1861.

Chapter 6

1. Russell Dickenson, Joseph Bryan, and Ahnna Reyes, ed., "Diary of First Sergeant William E. Maurey, 49th Tennessee Infantry," (Battle of Franklin Trust), December 10, 1861.

2. This company would become Company C, 49th Tennessee Infantry. The 49th Tennessee was organized on December 24, 1861 at Fort Donelson. James E. Bailey was elected colonel. The 49th was assigned to John W. Head's Brigade and with other members of the brigade (30th Tennessee and 50th Tennessee), served as the fort's garrison. The 49th Tennessee would play a supporting role to the River Batteries during the engagements with the Federal ironclads.

3. *War of the Rebellion: Official Records of the Union and Confederate Armies,* Series I vol. 7 (Harrisburg, PA: National Historical Society, 1985), 731–32.

4. *Ibid.,* 700.

5. *Ibid.,* 709.

6. The arrival of these guns account for six of the eight 32-pounders mounted at the lower battery of Fort Donelson. Apparently two additional 32-pounders were received at Donelson between the December 4, shipment from Clarksville and the beginning of January 1862. Ordnance records of January and February 1862 for Fort Donelson seem to be very complete, and while there is record of ammunition for the guns and the arrival of the 10-inch columbiad and the 6.4-inch rifled columbiad, there is no mention of the other two 32-pounders. This provides evidence that all eight of the 32-pounders of the lower battery were in place by the end of December 1861.

7. On December 4, Major Gilmer instructed Lieutenant Dixon to extend the parapet of the lower battery as one to two additional 32-pounders were being sent there. There is a gap in piecing together the existing records. We have fairly detailed records from the Nashville Ordnance Department regarding

ordnance sent to Fort Donelson in the months of January and February 1862. We also know that on December 4, Major Gilmer informed Lieutenant Dixon that four guns were being sent from Clarksville (two for Fort Henry and two for Fort Donelson). It is likely that two 32-pounder guns were sent to Fort Donelson from Clarksville around December 4, and two additional 32-pounders were sent from the Nashville Ordnance Department as a result of Gilmer's requisition to Captain Wright.

8. Lee H. Hanson, Jr., *Archaeological Excavations in the Water Batteries at Fort Donelson National Military Park* (N.P.: National Park Service; U.S. Department of the Interior, 1968), 3.

9. *Ibid.*, 7.

10. Wesley Smith Dorris, "Wesley Smith Dorris Diary," *Special Collections Online*, University of Tennessee, December 2, 1861.

11. *Ibid.*, December 9, 1862.

12. Jeremy F. Gilmer, "To Loulie Gilmer," in *Southern Historical Collection, Jeremy Francis Gilmer Papers, 1839-1894, Series 3, Civil War Papers 1861-1865, Folder 40-1861*, University of North Carolina Louis Round Wilson Special Collections Library, Chapel Hill.

13. John Bell, "Confederate Papers Relating to Citizens or Business Firms, compiled 1874-1899, documenting the period 1861-1865," M346 R56, General Services Administration National Archives and Record Service (Washington, D.C.: National Archives Records Administration).

14. Josiah Gorgas, "Compiled Service Records of Confederate General and Staff Officers, and Non-Regimental Enlisted Men," M331 R109, General Services Administration National Archives and Record Service (Washington, D.C.: National Archives and Records Administration, 1960).

15. Dorris, "Dorris Diary," December 24, 1861.

16. *Ibid.*

17. "Letter from Donelson," *Union and American* (Nashville, TN), January 1, 1862; MacGavock, "MacGavock Diary," November 27, 1861.

18. MacGavock, "MacGavock Diary," November 27, 1861.

19. *Ibid.*

20. *Ibid.*, 96.

21. *Ibid.*

22. *Ibid.*

23. *O.R.* I, 7, 817.

24. Record of Events, "Compiled Service Records of Confederate Soldiers Who Served in Organizations from the State of Tennessee, 30th Tennessee Infantry," M268 R242, General Services Administration National Archives and Record Service (Washington, D.C.: National Archives Records Administration, 1960).

25. Hugh L. Bedford, "H.L. Bedford Memoirs," University of Tennessee, Knoxville, Special Collections, Manuscript 2176, 6.

26. Jacob Culbertson, "Compiled Service Records of Confederate General and Staff Officers, and Non-Regimental Enlisted Men," M331 R68, General Services Administration National Archives

and Record Service (Washington, D.C.: National Archives Records Administration, 1960).

27. "Returns from U.S. Military Posts, 1800–1916," M617 R694, General Services Administration National Archives and Record Service (Washington, D.C.: National Archives Records Administration).

28. Culbertson, "Compiled Service Records."

29. *Ibid.*

30. *Ibid.*

31. *Ibid.*

32. Dorris, "Dorris Diary," January 3, 1862.

33. Dickenson, "William E. Maurey Diary," December 25, 1861.

Chapter 7

1. *Ordnance Department—Invoices of Supplies Sent to Various Stations, December 1861—August 1862*, vol. Record Group 109, Chapter IV, Volume 108, National Archives Records Administration, Washington, D.C., 1, 5.

2. *War of the Rebellion: Official Records of the Union and Confederate Armies*, Series I vol. 7 (Harrisburg, PA: National Historical Society, 1985), 817.

3. *Ibid.*

4. *Ibid.*

5. *Ibid.*

6. *Ordnance Department—Record of Ordnance and Ordnance Stores Received and Issued, Arsenals at Nashville, Tennessee and Atlanta, Georgia, 1861-1862*, Record Group 109, Chapter IV, Volume 104, National Archives Records Administration, Washington, D.C., 158–59; *ibid.*, 24–25.

7. *Ordnance Department—Invoices of Supplies Sent*, 3. The 10-inch columbiad currently emplaced in the lower battery at Fort Donelson, is an original though not the gun actually at the battle of Fort Donelson. The current 10-inch columbiad at Fort Donelson was cast at Tredegar Iron Works on January 13, 1863. Edwin Olmstead, Wayne E. Stark, and Spencer C. Tucker, *The Big Guns: Civil War Siege, Seacoast, and Naval Cannon* (Alexandria Bay, NY: Museum Restoration Service, 1997), 250.

8. Josiah Gorgas, "Compiled Service Records of Confederate General and Staff Officers, and Non-Regimental Enlisted Men," M331 R109, General Services Administration National Archives and Record Service (Washington, D.C.: National Archives and Records Administration, 1960).

9. *War of the Rebellion: Official Records of the Union and Confederate Navies*, Series 1 vol. 22 (Washington, D.C.: Government Printing Office, 1908), 485.

10. *Ordnance Department—Record of Ordnance and Ordnance Stores Received and Issued*, 160–61; *Ordnance Department—Invoices of Supplies Sent*, 10.

11. Randal W. MacGavock, "The Randal W. MacGavock Diary, October 5, 1860–February 5, 1862," *Randall W. MacGavock Papers 1848-1898* (Tennessee State Library and Archives, 1860), January 7, 1862.

12. *Ibid.*, January 9, 1862.

13. *Ibid.*

14. *Ordnance Department—Invoices of Supplies Sent*, 12–15.

15. *O.R.* I, 7, 388.

16. Hugh L. Bedford, "H.L. Bedford Memoirs," University of Tennessee, Knoxville, Special Collections, Manuscript 2176, 8.

17. Army Service Schools, *Fort Henry and Fort Donelson Campaigns, February 1862. Sourcebook* (Fort Levenworth, KS: The General Service Schools Press, 1923), 1398.

18. Francis B. Heitman, *Historical Register and Dictionary of the United States Army, From Its Organization, September 29, 1789 to March 2, 1903*, 2 vols., vol. 1 (Washington, D.C.: Government Printing Office, 1903), 516.

19. Army Service Schools, *Source Book*, 1398; Heitman, *Historical Register*, 1, 516.

20. Army Service Schools, *Source Book*, 1398.

21. Milton A. Haynes, "Compiled Service Records of Volunteer Soldiers Who Served During the Mexican War in Organizations from the State of Tennessee," M638 R4, General Services Administration National Archives and Record Service (Washington, D.C.: National Archives Records Administration).

22. "Proclamation by Governor," *Union and American* (Nashville, TN) May 19, 1861.

23. "Instructions in Field Artillery, Horse, and Foot," *Republican Banner* (Nashville, TN) December 1, 1861, 3.

24. Hugh L. Bedford, "H.L. Bedford Memoirs," University of Tennessee, Knoxville, Special Collections, Manuscript 2176, 8.

25. *O.R.* I, 7, 409.

26. *Catalogue of the Officers and Students of Cumberland University at Lebanon, Tenn., for the Academic Year 1859-60* (Lebanon, TN: Neal & Spillers, 1860), 19.

27. Tennessee Civil War Centennial Commission, *Tennesseans in the Civil War: A Military History of Confederate and Union Units with Available Rosters of Personnel*, 2 vols., vol. 1 (Nashville, TN: Civil War Centennial Commission, 1964), 237–38.

28. *O.R.* I, 7, 388.

29. J.J. McDaniel, "Compiled Service Records of Volunteer Soldiers Who Served During the Mexican War in Organizations From the State of Tennessee," M638 R2, General Services Administration National Archives and Record Service (Washngton, DC: National Archives Records Administration, 1960).

30. "Compiled Service Records of Confederate Soldiers Who Served in Organizations from the State of Tennessee, Capt. Burrough's Co., Light Artillery (Rhett Artillery); Caruther's Battery, Heavy Artillery; Capt. Fisher's Co., Artillery (Nelson Artillery)," M268 R92, General Services Administration National Archives and Record Service (Washinton, DC: National Archives Records Administration, 1960).

31. George S. Martin, "Find a Grave, St. John's Church Cemetery, Ashwood, TN," https://www.findagrave.com/memorial/9337007.

32. *University of Nashville, Collegiate Department, Western Military Institute, Regiser of Cadets for the Collegiate Year 1856-7* (Nashville, TN: Cameron & Fall, 1857), 11.

33. George S. Martin, "Compiled Service Records of Confederate Soldiers Who Served in Organizations from the State of Tennessee, 1st (Feild's) Infantry," M268 R103, General Services Administration National Archives and Record Service (Washington, D.C.: National Archives Records Administration, 1960); "Compiled Service Records of Confederate Soldiers Who Served in Organizations from the State of Tennessee, Capt. Sparkman's Co., Light Artillery (Maury Artillery); Capt. Sterling's Co., Heavy Artillery; Capt. Stewart's Co., Artillery; Capt. Tobin's Co., Light Artillery (Memphis Light Battery)," M268 R99, General Services Administration National Archives and Record Service (Washington, D.C.: National Archives Records Administration, 1960).

34. *O.R.* I, 7, 595–96.

35. Wesley Smith Dorris, "Wesley Smith Dorris Diary," in *Special Collections Online*, University of Tennessee, January 16, 1861.

36. *O.R.* I, 7, 409–10.

37. Reuben R. Ross, "Reuben R. Ross Journal," *Ross Family Journals 1851–1871* (Tennessee State Library and Archives, 1862), 20.

38. *O.R.* I, 7, 409–10.

39. G.T. Williams to Cousin, January 18, 1862, 30th Tennessee Infantry Files, National Park Service, Fort Donelson National Battlefield.

40. *Ibid.*

41. MacGavock, "MacGavock Diary," January 19, 1862.

42. *Ibid.*

43. *Ibid.*, 114.

44. *Ibid.*, 110.

45. *Ibid.*

46. *Ordnance Department—Record of Ordnance and Ordnance Stores Received and Issued*, 24; Gorgas, "Compiled Service Records of Confederate General and Staff Officers, and Non-Regimental Enlisted Men." During the summer of 1861 Tredegar Foundry began casting large smoothbore gun blocks of prewar or early war designs and modifying them by boring and rifling to smaller calibers. Eight-inch Confederate columbiads were bored and rifled to 5.82-in. (24-pdr rifle). Ten-inch columbiads were bored and rifled to 6.4-in. (32-pounder rifle). Several of the rifled guns burst when being fired, most notable was the "Lady Polk" at Columbus, Kentucky and the "Belmont" at Island #10. During the same time period that the 6.4-inch rifle was being prepared to be sent to Fort Donelson, on December 23, 1861, Tredegar was sending another 6.4-inch rifled columbiad to General Polk at Columbus, Kentucky (gun #1289). This gun, which some have called the "Belmont," was to replace the initial 6.4-inch rifled columbiad, the "Lady Polk," which burst, killing and wounding

many of her crew. General Polk, who was standing nearby when the "Lady Polk" burst, was evidently concerned about receiving another. Chief of Ordnance, Josiah Gorgas, writing Polk on December 23, 1861 reassured him stating, "both of these guns (also referring to a 5.82-inch rifle being sent to Columbus) have been well proved and are made of different kinds of iron from the 6.4 "Columbiad last sent you." Unfortunately, the "Belmont," like the "Lady Polk," also burst, but after it had been taken from Columbus and mounted in the fortifications of Island No. 10. The 6.4-inch columbiad sent to Fort Donelson (#1295), performed well. The only known 6.4-inch rifled columbiad still in existence (#1285, cast October 17, 1861) is located in Mobile, Alabama, see Edwin Olmstead, Wayne E. Stark, and Spencer C. Tucker, *The Big Guns: Civil War Siege, Seacoast, and Naval* Cannon (Alexandria Bay, NY: Museum Restoration Service, 1997), 66, 219. Olmstead, Stark, and Tucker state that from the 142 10-inch columbiads cast, "at least two were bored and rifled 6.4-inches." *Ibid.*, 66. In the research for this book, at least four 6.4-inch rifled columbiads have been identified: The 6.4-inch rifle named the "Lady Polk," (serial number unknown); the second 6.4-inch rifled columbiad sent to Columbus, the "Belmont," (#1289); the gun presently in Mobile, Alabama (#1285), and the 6.4-inch rifle sent to Fort Donelson (#1295—cast November 4, 1861). The 6.4-inch rifled columbiad currently mounted in the upper battery at Fort Donelson is a reproduction.

47. Larry J. Daniel, Riley W. Gunter, *Confederate Cannon Foundries* (Union City, TN: Pioneer Press, 1977), 95.

48. Ross, "Reuben R. Ross Journal," 30.

49. Olmstead, Stark, and Tucker, *The Big Guns*, 219.

50. Charles B. Dew, *Ironmaker to the Confederacy: Joseph R. Anderson and the Tredegar Iron Works* (Richmond, VA: Virginia State Library, 1999), 95.

51. *Ordnance Department—Record of Ordnance and Ordnance Stores Received and Issued*, 350, 420; ibid., 24–25, 45, 47, 80, 82, 98, 118, 21. Records from the Nashville Ordnance Depot indicate "by account received from Captain L. Gibbon" for the columbiad (January 1) and "64 Rifled Columbiad" (January 20). Captain Lardner Gibbon was an inspector of ordnance at Tredegar. Lardner Gibbon, "Compiled Service Records of Confederate General and Staff Officers and Nonregimental Enlisted Men," M331 R105, General Services Administration National Archives and Record Service (Washington, D.C.: National Archives Records Administration, 1960).

52. *Ordnance Department—Record of Ordnance and Ordnance Stores Received and Issued*, 242, 340; *ibid..*, 154.

53. *O.R. I, 7*, 389, 410; George T. Moorman, "Compiled Service Records of Confederate Soldiers Who Served in Organizations from the State of Tennessee, 1st Heavy Artillery (Jackson's Regiment)," M268 R86, General Services Administration National Archives and Record Service (Washington,

D.C.: National Archives Records Administration, 1960).

54. *O.R. I, 7*, 411.

55. *Ibid.*, 388.

56. *Ibid.*, 410.

57. *Ibid.*

58. MacGavock, "MacGavock Diary," January 24, 1862. During the battle with the gunboats 6 February, the 5.82-in columbiad rifle burst killing three men and wounding others.

59. *Ibid.*, January 25, 1862.

60. *O.R. I, 7*, 842.

61. Milton A. Haynes, "Compiled Service Records of Confederate Soldiers Who Served in Organizations from the State of Tennessee, Capt Winson's Co, Light Artillery (Belmont Battery), D-Y AND First Zouaves AND First Light Artillery (First Battalion, Light Artillery) AND Artillery (McCown's) Corps," M268 R100, General Services Administration National Archives and Record Service (Washington, D.C.: National Archives Records Administration, 1960).

62. Second Lieutenant Robert L. Cobb was a member of Captain Thomas W. Beaumont's Company A 50th Tennessee. Cobb had enlisted on August 12, 1861 in Clarksville. On November 10, he was detached to the Ordnance Department at Fort Donelson. Cobb, R.L., 1960, Compiled Service Records of Confederate Soldiers Who Served in Organizations from the State of Tennessee, 50th Tennessee Infantry, M268 R319, National Archives and Records Service, General Services Administration, Washington, D.C..

63. *Ordnance Department—Invoices of Supplies Sent*, 21.

Chapter 8

1. *War of the Rebellion: Official Records of the Union and Confederate Navies*, Series 1 vol. 22 (Washington, D.C.: Government Printing Office, 1908), 602.

2. *Ibid.*

3. Randal W. MacGavock, "The Randal W. MacGavock Diary, October 5, 1860—February 5, 1862," *Randall W. MacGavock Papers 1848–1898* (Tennessee State Library and Archives, 1860), February 4, 1862.

4. *O.R.N., I, 22*, 538.

5. *War of the Rebellion: Official Records of the Union and Confederate Armies*, Series I vol. 7 (Harrisburg, PA: National Historical Society, 1985), 141; *O.R.N., I, 22*, 603.

6. William David Porter was the brother of Admiral David Dixon Porter and the foster brother of Admiral David Farragut.

7. *O.R.N., I, 22*, 538, 40.

8. *Ibid.*, 495, 538.

9. "Randal McGavock's Missing Civil War Diary Back in Tennessee," *Tennessean* (Nashville, TN), 20 August 2014. Lieutenant Colonel R.W. MacGavock's journal is left behind when his regiment makes

a hurried withdrawal from Fort Henry. The book was found by Captain Mindret Wemple Company H, 4th Illinois Cavalry and taken back home and presented to a family member. It was found in a closet in Cincinnati, Ohio and returned to the State of Tennessee in 2014. There is no entry for February 6, 1862.

10. Russell Dickenson, Joseph Bryan, and Ahnna Reyes, ed., "Diary of First Sergeant William E. Maurey, 49th Tennessee Infantry," (Battle of Franklin Trust), 2.

11. *O.R.* I, 7, 388.

12. Dickenson, "William E. Maurey Diary," 2.

13. *Ibid.*

14. *O.R.* I, 7, 366.

15. Dickenson, "William E. Maurey Diary," 3.

16. Wesley Smith Dorris, "Wesley Smith Dorris Diary," *Special Collections Online*, University of Tennessee, February 7, 1862.

17. *O.R.* I, 7, 388–89; 94.

18. Hugh L. Bedford, "H.L. Bedford Memoirs," University of Tennessee, Knoxville, Special Collections, Manuscript 2176, 7–8.

19. *O.R.* I, 7, 394.

20. Hugh L. Bedford, "H.L. Bedford Memoirs," 9.

21. *O.R.* I, 7, 869.

22. Lieutenant Robert L. Cobb was a member of Captain Tom Beaumont's Company A, 50th Tennessee Infantry. Though details are sketchy, it seems that Cobb was detached from the 50th Tennessee in January 1862 and was appointed Ordnance Officer at Fort Donelson. The supply invoices for Fort Donelson from January 25 to February 15, 1862 are all to the attention of Lieutenant R.L. Cobb.

23. *Ordnance Department—Record of Ordnance and Ordnance Stores Received and Issued, Arsenals at Nashville, Tennessee and Atlanta, Georgia, 1861–1862*, Record Group 109, Chapter IV, Volume 104, National Archives Records Administration, 90, 144, 54, 60, 62, 78, 342, 44, 78.

24. *O.R.* I, 7, 867.

25. Stewart Sifakis, *Who was Who in the Confederacy: A Comprehensive, Illustrated Biographical Reference to more than 1,000 of the Principal Confederacy Participants in the Civil War* (New York, NY: Facts on File, 1988), 227.

26. Nathaniel Cheairs Hughes, and Roy P. Stonesifer, *The Life and Wars of Gideon J. Pillow* (Chapel Hill, NC: University of North Carolina Press, 1993), 49.

27. Campbell commanded the 1st Tennessee Infantry Regiment in the Mexican War. It was known as "The Bloody First."

28. Hughes, *Life and Wars*, 47.

29. *Ibid.*

30. *Ibid.*, 86.

31. Ezra J. Warner, *Generals in Gray: Lives of the Confederate Commanders* (Baton Rouge, LA: Louisiana State University, 1987), 241.

32. Hughes, *The Battle of Belmont: Grant Strikes South*, 33.

33. Benjamin Franklin Cooling, *Forts Henry and Donelson—The Key to the Confederate Heartland*

(Knoxville, TN: University of Tennessee Press, 1987), 127.

34. *Ordnance Department—Record of Ordnance and Ordnance Stores Received and Issued*, 60, 94, 98, 116, 36, 50, 88, 412.

35. Herschel Gower, and Jack Allen, *Pen and Sword: The Life and Journals of Randal W. McGavock* (Nashville, TN: Tennessee Historical Commission, 1959), 589.

36. *O.R.* I, 7, 262.

37. *Ibid.*, 869.

38. Gower, *Pen and Sword: The Life and Journals of Randal W. McGavock*, 589.

39. Bedford, "H.L. Bedford Memoirs," 3.

40. Sifakis, *Who was Who in the Confederacy*, 93.

41. Warner, *Generals*, 90.

42. *Ibid.*

43. This is a reference to the 6.4-inch rifle. In addition to the 6.4-inch designation, this gun was variously referred to as a 6.5-inch rifle, a 32-pounder rifle, and a 68-pounder rifle.

44. *O.R.* I, 7, 870.

45. *Ibid.*, 272.

46. James Jobe, "The Battles for Forts Henry and Donelson," *Blue & Gray* 28/4 (2011): 25.

47. *Ibid.*

48. *O.R.* I, 7, 328.

49. *Ibid.*, 329.

50. *Ibid.*

51. Edward B. Ross, "River Batteries at Fort Donelson," *Confederate Veteran* 4/11 (1896): 393.

52. Francis B. Heitman, *Historical Register and Dictionary of the United States Army, From Its Organization September 29, 1789 to March 2, 1903*, vol. 1 (Washington, D.C.: Government Printing Office, 1903), 1, 847.

53. Jordan Dodd, comp., "Kentucky, Compiled Marriages, 1851–1900," ancestry.com https://search.ancestry.com/cgibin/sse.dll?indiv=1&dbid=4428&h=84658&tid=&pid=&usePUB=true&_phsrc=gfh5551&_phstart=successSource (September 10, 2019).

54. Reuben R. Ross, *Population Schedules of the Ninth Census of the United States, 1870, Tennessee: Montgomery and Morgan Counties* M653 R1266, General Services Administration National Archives and Record Service (Washington, D.C.: National Archives Records Administration, 1965), 168; Mary R. Ross, "1870 Census Montgomery County, Tennessee," M593 R1551, General Services Administration National Archives and Record Service (Washington, D.C.: National Archives Records Aministration, 1965), 8.

55. "Proclamation by Governor," *Union and American* (Nashville, TN) May 19, 1861.

56. R.R. Ross, "Compiled Service Records of Confederate General and Staff Officers and Nonregimental Enlisted Men," M331 R216, General Services Administration National Archives and Record Service (Washington, D.C.: National Archives Records Administration, 1960); Reuben R. Ross, "Compiled Service Records of Confederate Soldiers Who Served in Organizations from the State

of Tennessee, Capt. Sparkman's Co., Light Artillery," M268 R98, General Services Administration National Archives and Record Service (Washington, D.C.: National Archives Records Administration, 1960).

57. Ross, "Compiled Service Records of Confederate General and Staff Officers and Nonregimental Enlisted Men."

58. Frank Smith, "Maury Light Artillery," in *The Civil War in Maury County*, ed. Jill K. Garrett and Marise P. Lightfoot (Columbia, TN: Maury County Public Library, 2014), 51.

59. *Ibid.*; J.W. Robison, to Josephine Robison (October 6, 1861).

60. J.M. Sparkman, "Compiled Service Records of Confederate Soldiers Who Served in Organizations from the State of Tennessee, Capt. Sparkman's Co., Light Artillery (Maury Artillery); Capt. Sterling's Co., Heavy Artillery; Capt. Stewart's Co., Artillery; Capt. Tobin's Co., Light Artillery (Memphis Light Battery)," M268 R98, General Services Administration National Archives and Record Service (Washington, D.C.: National Archives Records Administration, 1960).

61. R.P. Griffith, Compiled Service Records of Confederate Soldiers Who Served in Organizations from the State of Tennessee, Capt. Sparkman's Co., Light Artillery (Maury Artillery); Capt. Sterling's Co., Heavy Artillery; Capt. Stewart's Co., Artillery; Capt. Tobin's Co., Light Artillery (Memphis Light Battery), M268 R98, General Services Administration National Archives and Record Service (Washington, D.C.: National Archives Records Administration, 1960); Sparkman, "Compiled Service Records."

62. J.W. Robison to Father, Mother, and Sisters," (November 22, 1861).

63. J.W. Robison to Father (December 10, 1861).

64. *War of the Rebellion: Official Records of the Union and Confederate Armies*, Series I vol. 4 (Harrisburg, PA: National Historical Society, 1971), 526.

65. J.W. Robison to Josephine Robison (November 13, 1861).

66. Sparkman, "Compiled Service Records."

67. Garrett, *Civil War in Maury County*, 53.

68. Griffith, "Compiled Service Records."

69. J.W. Robison to Josephine Robison," (January 23, 1862).

Chapter 9

1. *War of the Rebellion: Official Records of the Union and Confederate Armies*, Series I vol. 7 (Harrisburg, PA: National Historical Society, 1985), 397.

2. *Ibid.*

3. *Ibid.*

4. Frank Smith, "Maury Light Artillery," in *The Civil War in Maury County*, ed. Jill K. Garrett and Marise P. Lightfoot (Columbia, TN: Maury County Public Library, 2014), 53.

5. Reuben R. Ross, "Reuben R. Ross Journal," *Ross Family Journals 1851–1871* (Tennessee State Library and Archives, 1862), 54.

6. Smith, "Maury Light Artillery," 59.

7. Edward B. Ross, "River Batteries at Fort Donelson," *Confederate Veteran* 4/11 (1896): 393.

8. *O.R.* I, 7, 863.

9. Ross, "River Batteries at Fort Donelson," 393.

10. Ross, "Reuben R. Ross Journal," 16.

11. Ross, "River Batteries at Fort Donelson," 393.

12. Lee H. Hanson, Jr., *Archaeological Excavations in the Water Batteries At Fort Donelson National Military Park* (N.P.: National Park Service; U.S. Department of the Interior, 1968), 3.

13. Ross, "Reuben R. Ross Journal," 1.

14. Hugh L. Bedford, "H.L. Bedford Memoirs," University of Tennessee, Knoxville, Special Collections, Manuscript 2176, 9–10.

15. The numbers present for Company A 50th Tennessee and Company A, 30th Tennessee, and the Maury Artillery are based on the service records of the soldiers who were indicated present at Fort Donelson. In the various officers' reports the numbers differ, the service records were used to attain a consistent number.

16. A 6.4-inch rifled columbiad, known as "The Lady Polk" had been sent as part of the Confederate defenses at Columbus, Kentucky. In a test fire on November 11, 1861, the "Lady Polk" burst killing Captain William Keiter, battery commander, and the gun crew. General Leonidas Polk, who was standing nearby was also wounded. Writing from Richmond on December 23, Josiah Gorgas, Chief of Ordnance for the Confederate States, wrote to General Polk, "The agent leaves with the 6.4" Rifled Columbiad (No. 1289) will also take a 5.82" Rifled Columbiad (#1290) with carriage, chassis, implements, etc. Both of these guns have been well proved and are made of different kinds of iron from the 6.4" Columbiad last sent you." This 6.4-inch columbiad rifle (#1289) that replaced the "Lady Polk" was named the "Belmont." Captain W.Y.C. Humes took command of "The Belmont Battery" as it was then known. Being removed from Columbus, the Belmont gun was mounted in Battery #1 on the extreme upper end of Island Number 10 in the Mississippi River. On March 21, 1862 at the third fire at the enemy the gun burst into fragments, without injury to anyone. Tredegar did not conform to the government insisting that the Rodman process of casting be used. As a result, Tredegar lost the government contracts. Obviously, Ross was keenly aware of the bursting of the "Lady Polk," as he wrote, "The bursting of cannon is not a necessary thing. If artillery are well and coolly encouraged no tolerable good guns need be bursted. The safeguards are to grease every ball or shell. Wet well before every sponging out rifle cannon whenever the balls begin to go down with difficulty wetting well first. The time will be saved in the cooling of the gun. Above all never fire a ball which does not rest against the cartridge and for this purpose there ought to be a log rammer for each different caliber and length in a battery." Nathaniel Cheairs Hughes, *The Battle of Belmont:*

Grant Strikes South (Chapel Hill, NC: University of North Carolina, 1991), 36, 191; Josiah Gorgas, "Compiled Service Records of Confederate General and Staff Officers, and Non-Regimental Enlisted Men," M331 R109, General Services Administration National Archives and Record Service (Washington, D.C.: National Archives and Records Administration, 1960); Larry J. Daniel and Lynn N. Bock, *Island No. 10: Struggle for the Mississippi Valley* (Tuscaloosa, AL: University of Alabama Press, 1996), 31; Ross, "Reuben R. Ross Journal," 28.

17. *O.R.* I, 7, 389.
18. Hanson, *Archaeological Excavations*, 22.
19. *O.R.* I, 7, 397.
20. Hanson, *Archaeological Excavations*, 24.
21. *O.R.* I, 7, 397.
22. Hanson, *Archaeological Excavations*, 25, 28.
23. *O.R.* I, 7, 397.
24. Hanson, *Archaeological Excavations*, 28–34.
25. J.M. Barbee, "Compiled Service Records of Confederate Soldiers Who Served in Organizations from the State of Tennessee, 30th Tennessee Infantry," M268 R242, General Services Administration National Archives and Record Service (Washington DC: National Archives Records Administration, 1960).
26. Hanson, *Archaeological Excavations*, 34–35.
27. *Ibid.*, 35, 39.
28. *Ibid.*, 39.
29. *Ibid.*
30. H.L. Bedford, "Fight Between the Batteries and Gunboats at Fort Donelson," *Southern Historical Society Papers* 13, January—December (1885): 169.
31. Smith, "Maury Light Artillery," 58.
32. Revetted means that the interior was faced, in this case, with sapwood hurdles and planking.
33. Merlons are the upright sections of the earthwork and embrasures are the openings in the earthwork between the merlons. An example would be the battlements on a castle. The merlons are the upright sections and the embrasures are the openings in between. This provides cover for the gun crew and allows an opening for the gun to fire.
34. Hanson, *Archaeological Excavations*, 11; Ross, "Reuben R. Ross Journal"; W. Ormsby Watts, "Compiled Service Records of Confederate Soldiers Who Served in Organizations from the State of Tennessee, Capt. Weller's Co., Light Artillery," M268 R99, General Services Administration National Archives and Record Service (Washington, D.C.: National Archives Records Administration, 1960). There is a discrepancy here between commonly accepted belief and primary source material. The archaeological report written by Hanson in 1968 indicates that the carronades were mounted on front-pintle chassis. Mr. Hanson acknowledges the statement by Captain Reuben Ross that these were mounted on casemate carriages, but then states that Ross must have meant a front-pintle barbette carriage. Part of the issue here is that when the archaeological investigations were done in the upper battery none of the gun platforms were actually found. The only evidence recovered in

this position were eight square wrought iron nails (Hanson, 40). However, Captain Ross, commanding the Upper Battery was a West Point graduate and the remainder of his testimony is credible. Though possible, it is unlikely that Ross was mistaken about the type of carriage. Additionally, a document titled "Ordnance and Ordnance Status at Fort Donelson" found in the service record of Lieutenant W.O. Watts, detached from Taylor's Battery at Fort Henry and serving as an artillery instructor at Fort Donelson, states that the two 32-pounder carronades were "mounted on casemate chassis and carriages in the water battery." Based on these primary sources, there is evidence to substantiate that the carronades were mounted on casemate carriages, not front-pintle barbette carriages as commonly believed.

35. Smith, "Maury Light Artillery," 58.
36. *O.R.* I, 7, 394; Ross, "Reuben R. Ross Journal," 2.
37. *War of the Rebellion: Official Records of the Union and Confederate Navies*, Series 1 vol. 22 (Washington, D.C.: Government Printing Office, 1908), 605.
38. *O.R.* I, 7, 162.
39. U.S. Grant, *Personal Memoirs of U.S. Grant* (New York, NY: Charles L. Webster, 1885; repr., Project Gutenberg EBook), 412.
40. Ross, "Reuben R. Ross Journal," 2.
41. Joseph A. Hinkle, "J.A. Hinkle Reminiscences," in *Southern Historical Collection*, University of North Carolina Chapel Hill (1911), 3.
42. Ross, "Reuben R. Ross Journal," 3.
43. *Ibid.*
44. Henry Walke, "The Western Flotilla at Fort Donelson, Island Number Ten, Fort Pillow, and Memphis," in *Battles and Leaders of the Civil War* (NP: Castle, 1887), 431.
45. Ross, "Reuben R. Ross Journal," 3.
46. *Ibid.*
47. Walke, "The Western Flotilla," 431.
48. Ross, "River Batteries at Fort Donelson," 394.
49. Ross, "Reuben R. Ross Journal," 4.
50. *Ibid.*
51. *Ibid.*, 5.
52. *Ibid.*
53. *Ibid.*, 9.
54. *Ibid.*, 6.
55. Grant, *Memoirs of Grant*, 129.
56. *O.R.N.*, I, 22, 609.
57. Timothy B. Smith, *Grant Invades Tennessee: The 1862 Battles for Forts Henry and Donelson* (Lawrence, KS: University Press of Kansas, 2016), 166.
58. *Ibid.*, 165.

Chapter 10

1. Wesley Smith Dorris, "Wesley Smith Dorris Diary," *Special Collections Online*, University of Tennessee, February 12, 1862.
2. Reuben R. Ross, "Reuben R. Ross Journal," *Ross Family Journals 1851–1871* (Tennessee State Library and Archives, 1862), 7.

3. *Ibid.*

4. *War of the Rebellion: Official Records of the Union and Confederate Armies,* Series I vol. 7 (Harrisburg, PA: National Historical Society, 1985), 267.

5. Benjamin Franklin Cooling, *Forts Henry and Donelson—The Key to the Confederate Heartland* (Knoxville, TN: University of Tennessee Press, 1987), 138.

6. *Ibid.,* 139.

7. *Ordnance Department—Record of Ordnance and Ordnance Stores Received and Issued, Arsenals at Nashville, Tennessee and Atlanta, Georgia, 1861–1862,* Record Group 109, Chapter IV, Volume 104, National Acchives Records Administration, Washington, D.C., 158, 64, 416.

8. Hugh L. Bedford, "H.L. Bedford Memoirs," University of Tennessee, Knoxville, Special Collections, Manuscript 2176, 13.

9. Ross, "Reuben R. Ross Journal," 7.

10. A geometric term where the portion of a cone or pyramid which remains after its upper part has been cut off by a plane parallel to its base, or which is intercepted between two such planes.

11. Ross, "Reuben R. Ross Journal," 7.

12. *War of the Rebellion: Official Records of the Union and Confederate Navies,* Series 1 vol. 22 (Washington, D.C.: Government Printing Office, 1908), 495.

13. *Ibid.,* 588.

14. Ross, "Reuben R. Ross Journal," 9.

15. Bedford, "H.L. Bedford Memoirs," 12–13.

16. Ross, "Reuben R. Ross Journal," 8–9.

17. H. Walke, *Naval Scenes and Reminiscences of the Civil War in the United States, on the Southern and Western Waters During the Years 1861, 1862 and 1863.* (New York, NY: F.R. Reed & Company, 1877), 73.

18. Ross, "Reuben R. Ross Journal," 9; James Calvin Cook, "Diary of James Calvin Cook," 50th Tennessee Infantry File, Fort Donelson National Battlefield, February 13, 1862.

19. Ross, "Reuben R. Ross Journal," 9.

20. J.A. Hinkle, "J.A. Hinkle," *Confederate Veteran* 5, no. 12 (1897): 624.

21. *O.R.* I, 7, 396.

22. *Ibid.,* 393; Ross, "Reuben R. Ross Journal," 17.

23. *O.R.* I, 7, 396.

24. "The Late Captain Jo. Dixon," *Athens Post* (Athens, TN) August 29, 1862.

25. Ross, "Reuben R. Ross Journal," 8.

26. *Ibid.,* 11, 32.

27. "Capt. Jo. Dixon," *Athens, Post,* February 21, 1862.

28. Joseph A. Hinkle, "J.A. Hinkle Reminiscences," in *Southern Historical Collection,* University of North Carolina Chapel Hill (1911), 3.

29. Hinkle, "J.A. Hinkle," 624.

30. *O.R.* I, 7.

31. *Ibid.,* 389.

32. Bedford, "H.L. Bedford Memoirs," 13.

33. Ross, "Reuben R. Ross Journal," 9.

34. *Ibid.*

35. *Ibid.,* 18.

36. Timothy B. Smith, *Grant Invades Tennessee: The 1862 Battles for Forts Henry and Donelson* (Lawrence, KS: University Press of Kansas, 2016), 230.

37. *O.R.N.,* I, 22, 588.

38. Ross, "Reuben R. Ross Journal," 10–11.

39. *Ibid.,* 18–19.

40. *Ibid.,* 19.

41. Dorris, "Dorris Diary," 32–33.

42. Spot F. Terrell, "Spot F. Terrell Diary," *Civil War Collection: Confederate and Federal 1861–1865, Confederate Colletion* (Tennessee State Library and Archives), 5.

43. *O.R.* I, 7, 411.

44. Ross, "Reuben R. Ross Journal," 19.

45. *Ibid.,* 11.

46. *Ibid.,* 19–20.

47. *Ibid.,* 12.

48. *Ibid.*

49. *Ibid.,* 19–20.

50. Army Service Schools, *Fort Henry and Fort Donelson Campaigns, February 1862. Sourcebook* (Fort Levenworth, KS: The General Service Schools Press, 1923), 560.

51. Ross, "Reuben R. Ross Journal," 12–13.

52. *O.R.* I, 7, 396.

Chapter 11

1. Edward B. Ross, "River Batteries at Fort Donelson," *Confederate Veteran* 4/11 (1896): 395.

2. *War of the Rebellion: Official Records of the Union and Confederate Armies,* Series I vol. 7 (Harrisburg, PA: National Historical Society, 1985), 390.

3. Ross, "River Batteries at Fort Donelson," 394.

4. These are most likely a squad of Birge's Western Sharpshooters. Birge's Sharpshooters were part of C.F. Smith's Division operating on the Federal left. These sharpshooters were specially armed with Dimick hunting rifles and on the morning of the 14th were dispersed to operate against Confederate batteries all along the line.

5. Ross, "River Batteries at Fort Donelson," 395; Hinkle, "J.A. Hinkle Reminiscences," 2.

6. Joseph A. Hinkle, "J.A. Hinkle Reminiscences," in *Southern Historical Collection,* University of North Carolina Chapel Hill (1911), 2.

7. J.A. Hinkle, "J.A. Hinkle," *Confederate Veteran* 5, no. 12 (1897): 624.

8. Jack Bell, *Civil War Heavy Explosive Ordnance: A Guide to Large Artillery Projectiles, Torpedoes, and Mines* (Denton, TX: University of North Texas Press, 2003), 106.

9. Hinkle, "J.A. Hinkle Reminiscences," 2.

10. *Ibid.*

11. Reuben R. Ross, "Reuben R. Ross Journal," *Ross Family Journals 1851–1871* (Tennessee State Library and Archives, 1862), 20.

12. *Ibid.,* 20–21.

13. Army Service Schools, *Fort Henry and Fort Donelson Campaigns, February 1862. Sourcebook* (Fort Levenworth, KS: The General Service Schools Press, 1923), 560.

14. H. Walke, *Naval Scenes and Reminiscences of the Civil War in the United States, on the Southern and Western Waters During the Years 1861, 1862 and 1863*. (New York, NY: F.R. Reed & Company, 1877), 433.

15. Hugh L. Bedford, "H.L. Bedford Memoirs," University of Tennessee, Knoxville, Special Collections, Manuscript 2176, 14.

16. *Ibid.*, 14–15.

17. Ross, "Reuben R. Ross Journal," 21.

18. Hugh L. Bedford, "H.L. Bedford Memoirs," 14.

19. Walke, *Naval Scenes*, 77.

20. Walke, "The Western Flotilla," 431.

21. Bedford, "H.L. Bedford Memoirs," 15.

22. Army Service Schools, *Source Book*, 562.

23. *Ibid.*

24. *Ibid.*, 568.

25. *Ibid.*, 562.

26. *Ibid.*, 568.

27. Frank Smith, "Maury Light Artillery," in *The Civil War in Maury County*, ed. Jill K. Garrett and Marise P. Lightfoot (Columbia, TN: Maury County Public Library, 2014), 58.

28. Bedford, "H.L. Bedford Memoirs," 16.

29. Ross, "Reuben R. Ross Journal," 22.

30. *O.R.* I, 7, 393.

31. *Ibid.*, 395.

32. Ross, "Reuben R. Ross Journal," 22.

33. *Ibid.*

34. Wesley Smith Dorris, "Wesley Smith Dorris Diary," *Special Collections Online*, University of Tennessee, 35.

35. Bedford, "H.L. Bedford Memoirs," 15.

36. Ross, "Reuben R. Ross Journal," 22.

37. *Ibid.*

38. *Ibid.*

39. Army Service Schools, *Source Book*, 562.

40. Dorris, "Dorris Diary," 34.

41. Ross, "River Batteries at Fort Donelson," 395.

42. Ross, "Reuben R. Ross Journal," 25.

43. Smith, "Maury Light Artillery," 57.

44. Ross, "River Batteries at Fort Donelson," 396.

45. *Ibid.*

46. *Ibid.*

47. *Ibid.*; Smith, "Maury Light Artillery," 58.

48. "Maury Light Artillery," 58.

49. *Ibid.*

50. *O.R.* I, 7, 397.

51. Archaeological investigations in the River Batteries recovered naval grapeshot balls and end plates from stands of grape scattered indiscriminately throughout the battery.

52. *O.R.* I, 7, 396.

53. *Ibid.*, 397.

54. Carolyn Stier Ferrell, *Occupied: The Story of Clarksville, Tennessee During the Civil War* (Nashville, TN: Westview, Inc., 2012), 99.

55. *O.R.* I, 7, 397.

56. *Ibid.*, 281.

57. *Ibid.*, 397.

58. Tow or flax fiber was used as a packing material for transporting ammunition. In the ordnance records "tow hooks" are often seen. The artillery tow hook was used to remove the flax fibers or "tow" from the ammunition crates. Tow was used by the gunners to help stabilize the rounds in the gun tube in the loading process.

59. *O.R.* I, 7, 281; Smith, "Maury Light Artillery," 58. Martin's mother Narcissa Pillow Martin was General Gideon J. Pillow's sister.

60. Bedford, "H.L. Bedford Memoirs," 10.

61. John A. Wyeth, *That Devil Forrest: Life of General Nathan Bedford* (Baton Rouge, LA: Louisiana State University Press, 1989), 40.

62. Army Service Schools, *Source Book*, 563.

63. *O.R.* I, 7, 395.

64. *Ibid.*

65. *Ibid.*

66. Army Service Schools, *Source Book*, 564.

67. Walke, *Naval Scenes*, 77.

68. *Ibid.*

69. *War of the Rebellion: Official Records of the Union and Confederate Navies*, Series 1 vol. 22 (Washington, D.C.: Government Printing Office, 1908), 591.

70. Matthew Arther, "Medal of Honor, Civil War," https://www.army.mil/medalofhonor/crandall/medal/citations1.htm (October 19, 2019).

71. Bedford, "H.L. Bedford Memoirs," 18.

72. *Ibid.*

73. Walke, "The Western Flotilla at Fort Donelson, Island Number Ten, Fort Pillow, and Memphis," 435.

74. *Ibid.*

75. Ross, "Reuben R. Ross Journal," 9.

76. Walke, *Naval Scenes*, 77; United States War Department, *Instruction for Heavy Artillery* (Washington, D.C.: Gideon and Co., 1851), 93.

77. Ross, "Reuben R. Ross Journal," 25.

78. *O.R.* I, 7, 396.

79. *Ibid.*, 395.

80. Russell Dickenson, Joseph Bryan, and Ahnna Reyes, ed., "Diary of First Sergeant William E. Maurey, 49th Tennessee Infantry," (Battle of Franklin Trust), 4.

81. Ross, "Reuben R. Ross Journal," 25.

82. Army Service Schools, *Source Book*, 563–64.

83. *Ibid.*, 563–64.

84. *Ibid.*, 571.

85. *Ibid.*

86. *O.R.N.*, I,, 22, 592–93.

87. Army Service Schools, *Source Book*, 571.

88. *Ibid.*, 570.

89. *Ibid.*

90. *Ibid.*

91. *Ibid.*, 570.

92. *Ibid.*

93. *Ibid.*, 570.

94. *Ibid.*, 562.

95. *O.R.* I, 7, 393.

96. Walke, *Naval Scenes*, 77–78.

97. Dorris, "Dorris Diary," February 14, 1861.

98. Bedford, "H.L. Bedford Memoirs," 19.

99. Army Service Schools, *Source Book*, 572.

100. *Ibid.*, 565.

101. H.L. Bedford, "Fight Between the Batteries and Gunboats at Fort Donelson," *Southern Historical Society Papers* 13, January—December (1885): 172.

102. *The Civil War in Maury County*, ed. Jill K. Garrett and Marise P. Lightfoot (Columbia, TN: Maury County Public Library, 2014), 53.

103. Walke, *Naval Scenes*, 78.

104. Bedford, "H.L. Bedford Memoirs," 20.

105. Walke, "The Western Flotilla," 436–37.

Epilogue

1. Nathaniel Cheairs Hughes, and Roy P. Stonesifer, *The Life and Wars of Gideon J. Pillow* (Chapel Hill, NC: University of North Carolina Press, 1993), 230.

2. *War of the Rebellion: Official Records of the Union and Confederate Armies*, Series I vol. 7 (Harrisburg, PA: National Historical Society, 1985), 160.

3. Timothy B. Smith, *Grant Invades Tennessee: The 1862 Battles for Forts Henry and Donelson* (Lawrence, KS: University Press of Kansas, 2016), 341.

4. O.R. I, 7, 292.

5. Benjamin Franklin Cooling, *Forts Henry and Donelson—The Key to the Confederate Heartland* (Knoxville, TN: University of Tennessee Press, 1987), 209.

6. Army Service Schools, *Fort Henry and Fort Donelson Campaigns, February 1862. Sourcebook* (Fort Levenworth, KS: The General Service Schools Press, 1923), 1010.

7. John Berrien Lindsley, *Military Annals of Tennessee: Confederate* (Nashville, TN: J.M. Lindsley & Co., 1886; repr., Facsimile of the first edition, Wilmington NC: Broadfoot Publishing, 1995), 560.

8. *Ibid.*

9. Joseph A. Hinkle, "J.A. Hinkle Reminiscences," in *Southern Historical Collection*, University of North Carolina Chapel Hill (1911), 5.

10. O.R. I, 7, 396.

11. John A. Wyeth, *That Devil Forrest: Life of General Nathan Bedford* (Baton Rouge, LA: Louisiana State University Press, 1989), 60.

12. "Compiled Service Records of Confederate Soldiers Who Served in Organizations from the State of Tennessee, 50th Tennessee Infantry," M268 R319–322, General Services Administration National Archives and Record Service (Washington, D.C.: National Archives Records Administration, 1960).

13. E.G. Sears, "Tennessee, Confederate Pension Applications, Soldiers, 1891–1965," *Record Group 3, Tennessee Board of Pension Examiners Records*, Tennessee State Library and Archives (Nashville, TN).

14. "Slavery in Ohio," *Weekly News Democrat* (Emporia, KS) April 26, 1862.

15. Susan Hawkins, "Forts Henry, Heiman, and Donelson: The African American Experience" (Thesis, Murray State University, 2003), 24.

16. Hugh L. Bedford, "H.L. Bedford Memoirs," University of Tennessee, Knoxville, Special Collections, Manuscript 2176, 9.

17. Van L. Riggins, "A History of Fort Donelson National Military Park Tennessee," *Park Histories* (1958), https://www.nps.gov/parkhistory/online_books/fodo/fodo_history.pdf (January 3, 2019), 21.

18. Benjamin F. Cooling, *Fort Donelson's Legacy: War and Society in Kentucky and Tennessee, 1862–1863* (Knoxvlle, TN: University of Tennessee Press, 1997), 101.

19. Riggins, "A History of Fort Donelson National Military Park Tennessee," 54.

20. *National Cemetery Records, Series 1: War Department*, National Park Service, Fort Donelson National Battlefield Park.

21. Today, one of the 32-pounders original to the Battle of Fort Donelson remains as the centerpiece in the National Cemetery. According to former Fort Donelson Park Historian, Jimmy Jobe, the other two 32-pounders original to the fort have been remounted in the Lower Battery (gun positions 6 and 8). The remaining two guns are mounted in the fort proper. These guns have been the focus of much speculation and debate. Some believe they are 9-pounders. Because of their crude casting, others question whether they are actually authentic. The bore diameter of the two guns measure 4.6" which identifies them as 12-pounders. One gun is so pitted, no markings can be seen. However, the other gun bears the following inscription: Memphis & Charleston R R 392 Memphis, Tenn. According to records, the Memphis & Charleston Railroad produced a number of guns in varying sizes (from six-pounders, to three-inch rifles, to 12-pounders) and varying sizes of artillery ammunition. In September 1861, "two 12-pound guns on carriages complete" at a cost of $741.93 were supplied to the Confederate Ordnance Department in Memphis by the Memphis and Charleston Railroad. These are the only 12-pounders found in their records. It is believed these could be the two Memphis and Charleston 12-pounders at Fort Donelson. War Department. The Adjutant General's Office. War Records Office., "Confederate Papers Relating to Citizens or Business Firms, 1861–65," M346 R677, General Services Administration National Archives and Record Service (Washington, D.C.).

22. Lee H. Hanson, Jr., *Archaeological Excavations in the Water Batteries At Fort Donelson National Military Park* (N.P.: National Park Service; U.S. Department of the Interior, 1968), 15.

23. Wilbur F. Creighton, *The Life of Major Wilbur Fisk Foster* (Nashville, TN: Ambrose Printing, 1961), 20.

24. Riggins, "A History of Fort Donelson National Military Park Tennessee," 31.

25. *Ibid.*, 38.

26. *Ibid.*

27. *Ibid.*, 46.

28. Hanson, *Archaeological Excavations*, 1.

29. *Ibid.*, 71.

30. David Nolin, Interview by M. Todd Cathey, November 14, 2019.

31. Edwin Olmstead, Wayne E. Stark, and Spencer C. Tucker, *The Big Guns: Civil War Siege, Seacoast, and Naval* Cannon (Alexandria Bay, NY: Museum Restoration Service, 1997), 210.

32. *Ibid.*

33. Cwt stands for hundredweight.

34. Olmstead, *The Big Guns: Civil War Siege, Seacoast, and Naval Cannon*, 210.

35. *Ibid.*

36. *Ibid.*, 210.

37. *Ibid.*, 250.

38. James Jobe, Interview by M. Todd Cathey and Ricky W. Robnett, October 7, 2019. Further research revealed the contents of the note recovered in the tube of the columbiad. The note is in possession of the Vicksburg National Military Park. The note reads: "This cannon was buried August 18, 1900 in the Lum tract of ground. It was the Confederate cannon which sunk the U. S gunboat *Cincinnati* while trying to run past Vicksburg during the siege. After the Yankees came into Vicksburg it was placed in a Fort built on the site where it was buried. The Lum property was owned by Mrs. Ann Lum and was occupied by Genl. U.S. Grant as headquarters after Vicksburg fell. After Genl. Grant's removal from the city the house was torn down and a fort built by the U.S. government on this site. During the siege the gun was located at the corner of Washington and Jackson Streets. It was in that locality when it fired the fatal shot that sank the *Cincinnati*. The gun was buried by the levee contractor, H.F. Garbish, who had the contract for grading the Lum property, was superintended by Mr. E. Bussey. Written by Leila A. Lum. Witnessed by W.L. Nicholson, Mary L. Nicholson, Orla Griffin." The *Cincinnati* was sunk on May 27, 1863. National Park Service, Vicksburg National Military Park Archives (Vicksburg, MS).

39. There is only one 6.4-inch rifle known to still exist. It is on display in Mobile, Alabama. It was cast on October 17, 1861 by Tredegar and bears the foundry number 1285. Olmstead, Stark, and Tucker, *The Big Guns*, 219.

Appendix 1

1. W.C. Allen, "Population Schedules of the Eighth Census of the United States, 1860, Tennessee: Montgomery and Morgan Counties," M653 R1266, General Services Administration National Archives and Record Service (Washington, D.C.: National Archives Records Administration, 1965).

2. "Compiled Service Records of Confederate Soldiers Who Served in Organizations from the State of Tennessee, 50th Tennessee Infantry," M268 R319, General Services Administration National Archives and Record Service (Washington, D.C.: National Archives Records Administration, 1960).

3. *Ibid.*

4. *Ibid.*

5. W.C. Allen, "Tennessee Marriage Records, 1780–2002," https://www.ancestry.com/interactive/1169/VRMUSATN1780_040295-02157?pid

=598411&treeid=&personid=&usePUB=true&_phsrc=gfh5894&_phstart=successSource (October 26, 2019).

6. W.C. Allen, Population Schedules of the Twelfth Census of the United States, 1900, Tennessee: Montgomery and Morgan Counties," T623 R1590, General Services Administration National Archives and Record Service (Washington, D.C.: National Archives Records Administration, 1965).

7. W.C. Allen, "Find a Grave, Allen Cemetery, Montgomery County, TN," https://www.findagrave.com/memorial/167977139 (October 26, 2019).

8. "Adna Anderson, M. Am. Soc. C.E. ," *Procedings of the American Society of Engineers* 14, January to December (1888): 166.

9. Juliet C. Van Wyck, "District of Columbia, Marriage Records, 1810–1953, Ancestry.com., https://search.ancestry.com/cgi-bin/sse.dll?dbid=61404&h=900262073&indiv=try&o_vc=Record:OtherRecord&rhSource=60525 (November 29, 2019).

10. Adna Anderson, "Population Schedules of the Eighth Census of the United States, 1860, Tennessee: Nashville, Ward 5," M653 R1246, General Services Administration National Archives and Record Service (Washington, D.C.: National Archives Records Administration, 1965), 183.

11. Wilbur F. Creighton, Jr., "Wilbur Fisk Foster: Soldier and Engineer," *Tennessee Historical Quarterly* 31/3 (Fall 1972): 262.

12. *Ibid.*, 263.

13. J.L. Nichols, *Confederate Engineers* (Tuscaloosa, AL: The Confederate Publishing Company, 1957), 42.

14. Military and Financial Board, "Military and Financial Board Nashville, Tenn., Records, 1861—addition," M623 R1, Tennessee State Library and Archives (Nashville, TN).

15. Bushrod Johnson to Isham Harris, June 11, 1861, *Governor Isham G. Harris Papers 1857 to 1862*, GP 19, Box 3, No. 2, War Correspondence May 1861—February 19, 1863 (Tennessee State Library and Archives).

16. *War of the Rebellion: Official Records of the Union and Confederate Armies.*, Series I vol. 21 (Harrisburg, PA: National Historical Society, 1971), 866.

17. *Ibid.*, 25, Pt. 2: 160.

18. "Adna Anderson, M. Am. Soc. C.E. ," 166.

19. *Ibid.*, 167.

20. "Shot Himself in a Hotel," *Evening Star* (Washington, D.C.), May 15, 1889.

21. "General Anderson Temporarily Insane," *Tribune* (New York, NY), May 17, 1889.

22. Adna Anderson, "Find a Grave, Oak Hill Cemetery, Washington, D.C.," https://www.findagrave.com/memorial/94316435/adna-anderson (November 28, 2019).

23. Thomas Beaumont, *Population Schedules of the Seventh Census of the United States, 1850, Tennessee: Montgomery and Morgan Counties*" M432 R891, National Archives Microfilm Publications, Washington, D.C..

24. Ursula S. Beech, *Along the Warioto; or, A History of Montgomery County, Tennessee. In Cooperation with the Clarksville Kiwanis Club and the Tennessee Historical Commission* (Clarksville, TN: Tennessee Historical Commission, 1964), 138–39.

25. "Beaumont Withdraws," *Clarksville Chronicle* (Clarksville, TN), March 23, 1860, 3.

26. "Public Speaking in Montgomery County," *Clarksville Chronicle* (Clarksville, TN), May 31, 1861, 3.

27. Tennessee Civil War Centennial Commission, *Tennesseans in the Civil War: A Military History of Confederate and Union Units with Available Rosters of Personnel*, 2 vols., vol. 1 (Nashville, TN: Civil War Centennial Commission, 1964), 285.

28. Thomas W. Beaumont, "Compiled Service Records of Confederate Soldiers Who Served in Organizations from the State of Tennessee, 50th Tennessee Infantry," M268 R319, General Services Administration National Archives and Records Service (Washington, D.C.: National Archives Records Administration, 1960).

29. Lindsley, *Annals*, 560.

30. *Ibid.*, 561.

31. "Confederate Dead at Chickamauga," *Union and American* (Nashville, TN), July 24, 1867, 2.

32. *Catalogue of the Officers and Students of the Law Department of Cumberland University at Lebanon, TN for the Academic Year 1857-8* (Lebanon, TN: Neal & Spillers, 1858), 7.

33. J. Harvey Mathes, *The Old Guard in Gray* (Memphis, TN: S.C. Toof, 1897), 39.

34. Hugh L. Bedford, "H.L. Bedford Memoirs," University of Tennessee, Knoxville, Special Collections, Manuscript 2176, 2.

35. *Ibid.*, 12.

36. *War of the Rebellion: Official Records of the Union and Confederate Armies*, Series I vol. 7 (Harrisburg, PA: National Historical Society, 1985), 411, 393.

37. Hugh L. Bedford, "Compiled Service Records of Confederate General and Staff Officers and Non-regimental Enlisted Men," M331 R20, General Services Administration National Archives and Record Service (Washington, D.C.: National Archives Records Administration, 1960).

38. *Ibid.*

39. Mathes, *The Old Guard in Gray*, 41.

40. H.L. Bedford, *Population Schedules of the Ninth Census of the United States, 1870, Tennessee: Shelby County*, M593 R1561, National Archives Microfilm Publications, Washington, D.C.., 63.

41. H.L. Bedford, *Population Schedules of the Twelfth Census of the United States, 1900, Tennessee: Shelby County*, T623 R1596, National Archives Microfilm Publications, Washington, D.C.., 5.

42. Hugh Lawson Bedford, "Tennessee Death Records, 1908-1958.," R12, Tennessee State Library and Archives (Nashville, TN).

43. Charles Bidwell, "Index to Compiled Service Records of Volunteer Soldiers Who Served During the War of 1812," M602 R24, General Services Administration National Archives and Record Service (Washington, D.C.).

44. *Catalogue of the Officers and Students of Cumberland University at Lebanon, Tenn., for the Academic Year 1859-60* (Lebanon, TN: Neal & Spillers, 1860), 9.

45. Tennessee Civil War Centennial Commission, *Tennesseans in the Civil War*, 1, 237–38.

46. *O.R.* I, 7, 394–96.

47. Bell G. Bidwell, "Compiled Service Records of Confederate Soldiers Who Served in Organizations from the State of Tennessee, 30th Tennessee Infantry," M268 R242, General Services Administration National Archives and Record Service (Washington, D.C.: National Archives Records Administration, 1960).

48. B.G. Bidwell, *Population Schedules of the Ninth Census of the United States, 1870, Kentucky: McCracken, McLean, and Meade Counties* M593 R487, National Archives Microfilm Publications, Washington, D.C.. (Washington, D.C.: National Archives Records Administration, 1965), 25.

49. B.G. Bidwell, "Kentucky Marriage Records, 1783–1965," Ancestry.com https://search.ancestry.com/cgi-bin/sse.dll?indiv=1&dbid=4428&h=100179&tid=&pid=&usePUB=true&_phsrc=ZpM52&_phstart=successSource (17 January 2020).

50. M.V. Ingram, "Maj. Bell G. Bidwell," *Confederate Veteran* 16/8 (1908): 410.

51. Bell G. Bidwell, "Find a Grave, City Greenwood Cemetery, Weatherford, TX," https://www.findagrave.com/memorial/20186372 (October 12, 2019).

52. Jacob Culbertson, "U.S. Military Academy Cadet Application Papers, 1805–1866," M688 R1, General Services Administration National Archives and Record Service (Washington, D.C.: National Archives Records Administration).

53. Jacob Culbertson, "Find a Grave, Farm Burial, Hinds County, Mississippi," https://www.findagrave.com/memorial/110570243 (October 12, 2019).

54. Jacob Culbertson, "U.S. Military Academy Cadet Application Papers, 1805–1866," M688 R1, General Services Administration National Archives and Record Service (Washington, D.C.: National Archives Records Administration).

55. Jacob Culbertson, "Compiled Service Records of Confederate General and Staff Officers, and Non-Regimental Enlisted Men." M331 R68, General Services Administration National Archives and Record Service (Washington, D.C.: National Archives Records Administration, 1960).

56. "Returns from U.S. Military Posts, 1800–1916." Ancestry.com https://search.ancestry.com/cgi-bin/sse.dll?indiv=1&dbid=1571&h=1810662&tid=&pid=&usePUB=true&_phsrc=ZpM53&_phstart=successSource (January 17, 2020).

57. S. Worrel, "Northern Kentucky Marriages, 1795–1850" Ancestry.com, 1998, https://search.ancestry.com/cgi-bin/sse.dll?dbid=3455&h=1644&indiv=try&o_vc=Record:OtherRecord&rhSource=60525 (September 9, 2019).

58. Jacob Culbertson, "1860 United States Federal Census, Kenton County, Kentucky," M653 R379,

General Services Administration National Archives and Record Service (Washington, D.C.: National Archives Records Administration, 1860), 8.

59. Culbertson, "Compiled Service Records of Confederate General and Staff Officers, and Non-Regimental Enlisted Men."

60. *Ibid.*

61. Jacob Culbertson, "Compiled Service Records of Confederate Soldiers Who Served in Organizations from the State of Mississippi, Byrne's Battery, Artillery, Capt. Cook's Company, Horse Artillery. Culbertson's Battery, Light Artillery. Capt. Darden's Co. Light Artillery (Jefferson Artillery)," M269 R94, General Services Administration National Archives and Record Service (Washington, D.C.: Natonal Archives Records Administration, 1960).

62. Culbertson, "Compiled Service Records of Confederate General and Staff Officers, and Non-Regimental Enlisted Men."

63. *War of the Rebellion: Official Records of the Union and Confederate Armies.*, Series I vol. 37 (Harrisburg, PA: National Historical Society, 1971), 80–81.

64. Culbertson, "Compiled Service Records of Confederate General and Staff Officers, and Non-Regimental Enlisted Men."

65. Jacob Calbertras, *Population Schedules of the Ninth Census of the United States, 1870, Mississippi: Rankin County.* M593 R748 (Washington, D.C.: National Archives Records Administration, 1965), 1. In this census record, Culbertson's name is misspelled (Calbertras).

66. Jacob Culbertson, "Find a Grave, Farm Burial, Hinds County, Mississippi," https://www.findagrave.com/memorial/110570243 (September 9, 2019).

67. Joseph Dixon, *Population Schedules of the Seventh Census of the United States, 1850, Tennessee: McMinn County,"* M432 R887, General Services Administration National Archives and Record Service (Washington, D.C.: National Archives Records Administration), 366.

68. Joseph Dixon, "U.S. Military Academy Cadet Application Papers, 1805–1866," M688 R1, *Records of the Adjutant General's Office, 1780s-1917, Record Group 94*, General Services Administration National Archives and Record Service (Washington, D.C.: National Archives Records Administration).

69. Francis B. Heitman, *Historical Register and Dictionary of the United States Army, From Its Organization, September 29, 1789 to March 2, 1903*, 2 vols., vol. 1 (Washington, D.C.: Government Printing Office, 1903), 375.

70. Dixon, Joseph, "Population Schedules of the Eigth Census of the United States, 1860, Washington Territory: Clarke County, M653 R1398, National Archives and Record Service, General Services Administration National Archives and Record Service (Washington, D.C.: National Archives Records Administration), 108.

71. Heitman, *Historical Register*, 1, 375.

72. "Accessions from U.S. Army," *Athens Post* (Athens, TN) August 30, 1861; "General Johnston's Staff" *Athens Post* (Athens, TN) October 25, 1861.

73. *O.R.*, I, 4, 440

74. "Captain Jo. Dixon" *Athens Post* (Athens, TN) February 21, 1862.

75. *Ibid.*

76. *O.R.* I, 7, 280.

77. "Capt. Jo. Dixon."

78. P.L. Fitzgerald, "Population Schedules of the Eighth Census of the United States, 1860, Tennessee: Maury County," M653 R1264, General Services Administration National Archives and Record Service (Washington, D.C.: National Archives Records Administration, 1965), 103.

79. *Ibid.*, 131.

80. P.L. Fitzgerald, "Compiled Service Records of Confederate Soldiers Who Served in Organizations from the State of Tennessee, Capt. Sparkman's Co., Light Artillery (Maury Artillery)," M268 R98, General Services Administration National Archives and Record Service (Washington, D.C.: National Archives Records Administration, 1960).

81. Garrett, *Civil War in Maury County*, 52.

82. Fitzgerald, "Compiled Service Records."

83. Reuben R. Ross, "Reuben R. Ross Journal," *Ross Family Journals 1851–1871* (Tennessee State Library and Archives, 1862), 2.

84. *Ibid.*, 24.

85. Frank H. Smith, *Frank H. Smith's History of Maury County, TN* (Columbia, TN: The Society, 1969), 193.

86. Fitzgerald, "Compiled Service Records Sparkman's Light Artillery."

87. P.L. Fitzgerald, "Compiled Service Records of Confederate Soldiers Who Served in Organizations from the State of Tennessee, 19th Tennessee Cavalry," M268 R67, General Services Administration National Archives and Record Service (Washington, D.C.: National Archives Records Administration, 1960).

88. *Ibid.*

89. P.L. Fitzgerald, *Population Schedules of the Ninth Census of the United States, 1870, Tennessee: Maury County*, M593 R1538, General Services Administration National Archives and Record Service (Washington, D.C.: National Archives Records Administration, 1965), 17.

90. Patrick L. Fitzgearld, *Population Schedules of the Tenth Census of the United States, 1880, Texas: Montague County*, T9 R1320, General Services Administration National Archives and Record Service (Washington, D.C.: National Archives Records Administration), 30.

91. P.L. Fitzgerald, *Population Schedules of the Twelfth Census of the United States, 1900, Texas: Hunt, Irion, Jack. Jackson, Jasper and Jeff Davis Counties* T623 R1648, General Services Administration National Archives and Record Service (Washington, D.C.: National Archives Records Administration), 13.

92. "Texas, Wills and Probate Records, 1833–1974," ancestry.com, https://www.ancestry.com/inte

ractive/2115/007574071_00040?pid=1974790&treeid=&personid=&usePUB=true&_phsrc=gfh6050&_phstart=successSource (September 25, 2019).

93. Maggie Elizabeth Belschner, "Find a Grave, Memory Gardens of Edna Cemetery, Jackson County, TX," https://www.findagrave.com/memorial/50562166/maggie-elizabeth-belschner (25 September 2019).

94. Wilbur F. Creighton, *The Life of Major Wilbur Fisk Foster* (Nashville, TN: Ambrose Printing, 1961), 6–7.

95. *Ibid.*, 7.

96. *Ibid.*, 8–10.

97. *Ibid.*, 13.

98. W.F. Foster, *Compiled Service Records of Confederate Soldiers Who Served in Organizations from the State of Tennessee, 1st (Feild's) Tennessee Infantry*, M268 R102, Washington, D.C.: National Archives Records Administration, 1960.

99. Wilbur F. Creighton, Jr., "Wilbur Fisk Foster: Soldier and Engineer," *Tennessee Historical Quarterly* 31/3 (Fall 1972): 261–62.

100. Bromfield Lewis Ridley, *Battles and Sketches of the Army of Tennessee* (Mexico, MO: Missouri Print. & Pub. Co., 1906), 65.

101. Van L. Riggins, "A History of Fort Donelson National Military Park Tennessee," *Park Histories* (1958), https://www.nps.gov/parkhistory/online_books/fodo/fodo_history.pdf (January 3, 2019), 1; "Letter from Donelson" *Union and American* (Nashville, TN) January 1, 1862.

102. Creighton, *The Life of Major Wilbur Fisk Foster*, 14.

103. Wilbur F. Foster, "Compiled Service Records of Confederate General and Staff Officers and Nonregimental Enlisted Men," M331 R97, General Services Administration National Archives and Record Service (Washington, D.C.: National Archives Records Administration, 1960).

104. Creighton, *The Life of Major Wilbur Fisk Foster*, 23.

105. Wilbur Fisk Foster, "Find a Grave, Mount Olivet Cemetery, Nashville, Tennessee," https://www.findagrave.com/memorial/35340312/wilbur-fisk-foster. (September 25, 2019).

106. James Grant and John Fiske Wilson, eds., *Appletons' Cyclopedia of American Biography, 1600–1889, Vol II: Crane—Grimshaw* (New York, NY: D. Appleton and Company, 1887), 657.

107. *Fourth Annual Reunion of the Association of Graduates of the United States Military Academy Annual Reunion June 12th, 1873* (New York, NY: D. Van Nostrand, 1873), 75.

108. Clement A. Evans, ed., *Confederate Military History*, 12 vols., vol. 4 (Atlanta, GA: Confederate Publishing Company, 1899), 309.

109. *Ibid.*, 310.

110. *Ibid.*

111. Jeremy F. Gilmar, "Georgia Marriages 1699–1944," ancestry.com, https://search.ancestry.com/cgi-bin/sse.dll?indiv=1&dbid=7839&h=71694&tid=&pid=&usePUB=true&_phsrc=igT479&_phstart=successSource (October 2, 2019).

112. Jeremy F. Gilmer, "Find a Grave, Laurel Grove Cemetery, Savannah, Georgia" https://search.ancestry.com/cgi-bin/sse.dll?indiv=1&dbid=60525&h=1427011&tid=&pid=&usePUB=true&_phsrc=igT197&_phstart=successSource (September 3, 2019).

113. *Ibid.*

114. Milton A. Haynes, "Find a Grave, Elmwood Cemetery, Memphis, Tennessee," https://www.findagrave.com/memorial/89161652/milton-andrews-haynes (October 2, 2019).

115. Army Service Schools, *Fort Henry and Fort Donelson Campaigns, February 1862. Sourcebook* (Fort Levenworth, KS: The General Service Schools Press, 1923), 1398.

116. Heitman, *Historical Register*, 1, 516.

117. Army Service Schools, *Source Book*, 1398.

118. Heitman, *Historical Register*, 1, 516.

119. Milton A. Haynes, "Compiled Service Records of Volunteer Soldiers Who Served During the Mexican War in Organizations from the State of Tennessee," M638 R4, General Services Administration National Archives and Record Service (Washington, D.C.: National Archives Records Administration).

120. Army Service Schools, *Source Book*, 1398.

121. Haynes, "Find a Grave, Elmwood Cemetery, Memphis, Tennessee," https://www.findagrave.com/memorial/89161652/milton-andrews-haynes (August 29, 2019).

122. "Proclamation by Governor," *Union and American* (Nashville, TN) May 19, 1861.

123. "Instructions in Field Artillery, Horse, and Foot," *Republican Banner* (Nashville, TN) December 1, 1861, 3.

124. *O.R.* I, 7, 388.

125. *Ibid.*

126. *Ibid.*, 145–47.

127. *Ibid.*, 389, 410–11.

128. Milton A. Haynes, "Compiled Service Records of Confederate Soldiers Who Served in Organizations from the State of Tennessee, Capt Winson's Co, Light Artillery (Belmont Battery), D-Y AND First Zouaves AND First Light Artillery (First Battalion, Light Artillery) AND Artillery (McCown's) Corps," M268 R100, General Services Administration National Archives and Record Service (Washington, D.C.: National Archives Records Administration, 1960).

129. Haynes, "Find a Grave, Elmwood Cemetery, Memphis, Tennessee."

130. George S. Martin, "Find a Grave, St. John's Church Cemetery, Ashwood, TN," https://www.findagrave.com/memorial/9337007 (August 22, 2019).

131. *University of Nashville, Collegiate Department, Western Military Institute, Regiser of Cadets for the Collegiate Year 1856-7* (Nashville, TN: Cameron & Fall, 1857), 11.

132. George S. Martin, *Population Schedules of the Eighth Census of the United States, 1860, Tennessee: Maury County* M653 R1264, General Services Administration National Archives and Record

Service (Washington, D.C.: National Archives Records Administration, 1965).

133. George S. Martin, "Compiled Service Records of Confederate Soldiers Who Served in Organizations from the State of Tennessee, Capt. Sparkman's Co., Light Artillery (Maury Artillery); Capt. Sterling's Co., Heavy Artillery; Capt. Stewart's Co., Artillery; Capt. Tobin's Co., Light Artillery (Memphis Light Battery)," M268 R99, General Services Administration National Archives and Record Service (Washington, D.C.: National Archives Records Administration, 1960).

134. *O.R.* I, 7, 409.

135. *Ibid.*, 397.

136. *Ibid.*, 281.

137. *Ibid.*, 297.

138. Martin, "Compiled Service Records of Confederate Soldiers Who Served in Organizations from the State of Tennessee, Capt. Sparkman's Co., Light Artillery (Maury Artillery); Capt. Sterling's Co., Heavy Artillery; Capt. Stewart's Co., Artillery; Capt. Tobin's Co., Light Artillery (Memphis Light Battery)."

139. "Tennessee Marriage Records 1780–2002," (Lehi, UT: Ancestry.com, 2008).

140. George S. Martin, "Tennessee Wills and Probate Records, 1779–2008," (Ancestry.com).

141. Garrett, *Civil War in Maury County*, 771.

142. "Death of a Veteran Printer," *Republican Banner* (Nashville, TN), October 14, 1871.

143. McDaniel, "Compiled Service Records of Volunteer Soldiers Who Served During the Mexican War in Organizations From the State of Tennessee."

144. James J. McDaniel, "Tennessee Marriage Records."

145. *O.R.* I, 7, 388.

146. "Death of a Veteran Printer."

147. J.J. McDaniel, "Find a Grave, Mount Olivet Cemetery, Nashville, TN," (2019); "Death of a Veteran Printer," 4.

148. James K. Ramey, "Population Schedules of the Eighth Census of the United States, 1860, Tennessee: Montgomery and Morgan Counties," M653 R1266, General Services Administration National Archives and Record Service (Washington, D.C.: National Archives Records Administration, 1965), 5.

149. Raimey, "Tennessee Confederate Pension Applications, Soldiers, 1891–1965." Captain Abraham Lot, Company D, 4th Iowa Cavalry.

150. *Ibid.*

151. J.K. Raimey, "Compiled Service Records of Confederate Soldiers Who Served in Organizations from the State of Tennessee, 50th Tennessee Infantry," M268 R321, General Services Administration National Archives and Records Service (Washington, D.C.: National Archives Records Administration, 1960).

152. Ishom Jones, "Tennessee Confederate Pension Applications, Soldiers, 1891–1965," in *Record Group 3, Tennessee Board of Pension Examiners*, ed. Tennessee State Library and Archives (Nashville, TN: 1910).

153. Raimey, "Tennessee Confederate Pension Applications, Soldiers, 1891–1965."

154. James K. Ramey, *Population Schedules of the Twelfth Census of the United States, 1900, Tennessee: Montgomery, Moore, and Morgan Counties* T623 R1590 General Services Administration National Archives and Record Service (Washington, D.C.: National Archives Records Administration), 19.

155. Raimey, "Tennessee Confederate Pension Applications, Soldiers, 1891–1965."

156. James K. Ramey, "Tennessee Death Records, 1908–1958," R87, Tennessee State Library and Archives (Nashville, TN).

157. *Catalogue of the Officers and Students of Cumberland University, at Lebanon, Tenn. for the Academic Year 1858–59*, 4.

158. C.W. Robertson, "Compiled Service Records of Confederate Soldiers Who Served in Organizations from the State of Tennessee, 50th Tennessee Infantry," M268 R321, General Services Administration National Archives and Records Service (Washington, D.C.: National Archives Records Administration, 1960).

159. Tennessee Civil War Centennial Commission, *Tennesseans in the Civil War*, 1, 285.

160. *O.R.* I, 7, 397.

161. Robertson, "Service Record."

162. Tennessee Civil War Centennial Commission, *Tennesseans in the Civil War*, 1, 286.

163. *Ibid.*, 287.

164. Robertson, "Service Record."

165. Lindsley, *Annals*, 561–62.

166. Eleanora Willauer, "The Diary of Eleanora Willauer," in *Special Collections Online*, The University of Tennessee (Knoxville, TN: Special Collections Library, 1862), Sunday May 1, 1864.

167. Ross, "River Batteries at Fort Donelson," 393.

168. Heitman, *Historical Register*, 1, 847.

169. Dodd, "Kentucky, Compiled Marriages, 1851–1900."

170. Reuben Ross, *Population Schedules of the Eighth Census of the United States, 1860, Tennessee: Montgomery and Morgan Counties*, M653 R1266, General Services Administration National Archives and Record Service (Washington, D.C.: National Archives Records Administration, 1965), 168; Reuben Ross, *Population Schedules of the Ninth Census of the United States, 1870, Tennessee: Montgomery and Morgan Counties*, M593 R1551, General Services Administration National Archives and Record Service (Washington, D.C.: National Archives Records Administration, 1965), 8.

171. "Proclamation by Governor."

172. Ross, "Reuben R. Ross Journal," 54–55.

173. Ross, "Compiled Service Records of Confederate General and Staff Officers and Nonregimental Enlisted Men."

174. Ross, "Reuben R. Ross Journal," 15–16.

175. Ross, "River Batteries at Fort Donelson," 398.

176. *War of the Rebellion: Official Records of the Union and Confederate Armies.*, Series I vol. 117

(Harrisburg, PA: National Historical Society, 1971), 392–93.

177. Ross, "Compiled Service Records of Confederate General and Staff Officers and Nonregimental Enlisted Men."

178. *Ibid.*

179. *Ibid.*

180. *Ibid.*

181. *Ibid.*

182. Ross, "River Batteries at Fort Donelson," 398.

183. Willauer, "The Diary of Eleanora Willauer," December 1864.

184. *War of the Rebellion: Official Records of the Union and Confederate Armies.*, Series I vol. 93 (Harrisburg, VA: National Historical Society, 1971), 792.

185. Reuben R. Ross, "Find a Grave, Meriweather Cemetery, Guthrie, Kentucky," https://www.findagrave.com/memorial/62126866/reuben-reddick-ross.

186. Jacob P. Shuster, *Seventh Census of the United States, 1850, Virginia: Norfolk City,* M432 R964, General Services Administration National Archives and Record Service (Washington, D.C.: National Archives Records Administration), 147.

187. *O.R.* I, 7, 388.

188. *Ibid.*, 410.

189. *Ibid.*, 391.

190. *Ibid.*

191. *Ibid.*, 396.

192. J.P. Shuster, "Compiled Service Records of Confederate General and Staff Officers and Nonregimental Enlisted Men," M331 R225, General Services Administration National Archives and Record Service (Washington, D.C.: National Archives Records Administration, 1960), 393.

193. *Ibid.*

194. *Ibid.*

195. *Ibid.*

196. *Ibid.*

197. *Sholes' Directory of the City of Augusta* (Augusta, GA: A.E. Sholes, 1877), 292.

198. James M. Sparkman, *Population Schedules of the Seventh Census of the United States, 1850, Tennessee: Maury County,"* M432 R890, General Services Administration National Archives and Record Service (Washington, D.C.: National Archives Records Administration, 1965), 356.

199. "Tennessee, Marriage Records, 1780–2002," ancestry.com, https://search.ancestry.com/cgi-bin/sse.dll?_phsrc=igT204&_phstart=success Source&usePUBJs=true&indiv=1&dbid=1169&gsfn=James%20A.&gsln=Sparkman&gsfn_x=NN&gsln_x=1&msgpn__ftp=maury,%20tennessee,%20usa&msgpn=1939&new=1&rank=1&uidh=qs4&redir=false&msT=1&gss=angs-d&pcat=34&fh=1&h=1143743&recoff=&ml_rpos=2 (September 10, 2019).

200. James M. Sparkman, *Population Schedules of the Eighth Census of the United States, 1860, Tennessee: Maury County,* M653 R1264, General Services Administration National Archives and Record

Service (Washington, D.C.: National Archives Records Administration, 1965), 132.

201. Garrett, *Civil War in Maury County,* 52.

202. "Camp Weakley," *Daily Patriot* (Nashville, TN) October 29, 1861.

203. Garrett, *Civil War in Maury County,* 53.

204. Ross, "Reuben R. Ross Journal," 55.

205. Sparkman, "Compiled Service Records of Confederate Soldiers Who Served in Organizations from the State of Tennessee, Capt. Sparkman's Co., Light Artillery (Maury Artillery); Capt. Sterling's Co., Heavy Artillery; Capt. Stewart's Co., Artillery; Capt. Tobin's Co., Light Artillery (Memphis Light Battery)."

206. *War of the Rebellion: Official Records of the Union and Confederate Armies.*, Series I vol. 15 (Harrisburg, PA: National Historical Society, 1971), 1033.

207. *Ibid.*, 1027.

208. Garrett, *Civil War in Maury County,* 62.

209. *War of the Rebellion: Official Records of the Union and Confederate Navies,* Series I vol. 19 (Washington, D.C.: Government Printing Office, 1908), 680.

210. Garrett, *Civil War in Maury County,* 63.

211. Elijah Thompson, *Population Schedules of the Seventh Census of the United States, 1850, Tennessee: Maury County,* M432 R890, General Services Administration National Archives and Record Service (Washington, D.C.: National Archives Records Administration), 493.

212. *Catalogue of the Officers and Students of Cumberland University, at Lebanon, Tenn. for the Academic Year 1858–59,* 8.

213. E.B. Thompson, "Compiled Service Records of Confederate Soldiers Who Served in Organizations from the State of Tennessee, Capt. Sparkman's Co., Light Artillery (Maury Artillery); Capt. Sterling's Co., Heavy Artillery; Capt. Stewart's Co., Artillery; Capt. Tobin's Co., Light Artillery (Memphis Light Battery)," M268 R98, General Services Administration National Archives and Record Service (Washington, D.C.: National Archives Records Administration, 1960).

214. Smith, *Frank H. Smith's History of Maury County, TN,* 184.

215. "Camp Weakley," *Daily Patriot* (Nashville, TN), October 29, 1861.

216. Ross, "Reuben R. Ross Journal," 19.

217. Thompson, "Compiled Service Records of Confederate Soldiers Who Served in Organizations from the State of Tennessee, Capt. Sparkman's Co., Light Artillery (Maury Artillery); Capt. Sterling's Co., Heavy Artillery; Capt. Stewart's Co., Artillery; Capt. Tobin's Co., Light Artillery (Memphis Light Battery)."

218. *Ibid.*

219. Smith, *Frank H. Smith's History of Maury County, TN,* 184.

220. "Maury County Historical Society, Historic Homes," http://historicmaury.com/mchs-history/historic-homes/ (September 30, 2019).

221. Jamie Gillum, *Twenty-five Hours to Tragedy:*

the Battle of Spring Hill and Operations on November 29, 1864: Precursor to the Battle of Franklin (Spring Hill, TN: James F. Gillum, 2014), 314–15.

222. Elijah B. Thompson, *Population Schedules of the Ninth Census of the United States, 1870, Tennessee: Maury County*, M593 R62, General Services Administration National Archives and Record Service (Washington, D.C.: National Archives Records Administration, 1965), 56.

223. "Maury County Historical Society, Historic Homes."

224. Absalom Thompson, "Find a Grave, Old Brick Church Cemetery, Maury County, Tenessee," https://www.findagrave.com/memorial/13198822 (November 21, 2019).

225. Amelia Lewis Thomson, "Ohio, County Marriage Records, 1774–1993," ancestry.com, https://www.ancestry.com/interactive/61378/TH-1-18059-97783-44?pid=900005298&backurl=http://search.ancestry.com/cgi-bin/sse.dll?dbid%3D61378%26h%3D900005298%26indiv%3Dtry%26o_vc%3DRecord:OtherRecord%26rhSource%3D60525%26requr%3D2550866976735232%26ur%3D0%26lang%3Den-U.S.&usePUB=true&usePUBJs=true&_ga=2.109532224.49564304.1575130822-1789622900.1552615280&_gac=1.155346633.1572102139.CjwKCAjw3c_tBRA4EiwAICs8CurqyPbpcEDfyhvuOiCN7bg-tdG7lNrDNaVEbMGKHJ5RJt0cubbxNBoCOwcQAvD_BwE. (November 21, 2019).

226. Amelia Watts, *Population Schedules of the Seventh Census of the United States, 1850, Ohio: Hamilton County*, M432 R691, General Services Administration National Archives and Record Service (Washington, D.C.: National Archives Records Administration, 1964), 522.

227. William Watts, *Population Schedules of the Eighth Census of the United States, 1860, Tennessee: Nashville* M653 R1246, General Services Administration National Archives and Record Service (Washington, D.C.: National Archives Records Administration, 1965), 180.

228. *O.R.* I, 7, 144.

229. W. Ormsby Watts, "Compiled Service Records of Confederate Soldiers Who Served in Organizations from the State of Tennessee, Capt. Weller's Co., Light Artillery," M268 R99, General Services Administration National Archives and Record Service (Washington, D.C.: National Archives Records Administration, 1960).

230. "Compiled Service Records of Confederate General and Staff Officers, and Nonregimental Enlisted Men," M331 R261, General Services Administration National Archives and Record Service (Washington, D.C.: National Archives and Record Service Administration, 1960).

231. William Ormsby Watts, "Find a Grave, Girod Cemetery, New Orleans, Louisiana," https://www.findagrave.com/memorial/128667318 (November 20, 2019).

232. Amelia Watts, *Population Schedules of the Seventh Census of the United States, 1850, Ohio: Hamilton County*, M593 R1207, General Services Administration National Archives and Record Service (Washington, D.C.: National Archives Records Administration, 1965), 32; Amelia Lewis Thompson Watts, "Find a Grave, Spring Grove Cemetery, Cincinnati, Ohio," https://www.findagrave.com/memorial/79065997/amelia-lewis-watts (November 20, 2019).

Appendix 3

1. *Ordnance Department—Record of Ordnance and Ordnance Stores Received and Issued, Arsenals at Nashville, Tennessee and Atlanta, Georgia, 1861–1862*, Record Group 109, Chapter IV, Volume 104, National Archives Records Administration, Washington, D.C.; *Ordnance Department—Invoices of Supplies Sent to Various Stations, December 1861—August 1862*, Record Group 109, Chapter IV, Volume 108, National Archives Records Administration, Washington, D.C..

Bibliography

Primary Sources

Letters, Diaries
and Manuscript Materials

Army Service Schools. *Fort Henry and Fort Donelson Campaigns, February 1862. Sourcebook.* Fort Leavenworth, KS: The General Service Schools Press, 1923.

Bedford, H.L. "H.L. Bedford Memoirs." Special Collections. University of Tennessee, Knoxville, TN.

Cook, James Calvin. "Diary of James Calvin Cook." 50th Tennessee Infantry File. Fort Donelson National Battlefield, Dover, TN.

Dickenson, Russell, Joseph Bryan, and Ahnna Reyes, ed. *Diary of First Sergeant William E. Maurey, 49th Tennessee Infantry.* Forty-ninth Tennessee Infantry File. Battle of Franklin Trust.

Gilmer, Jeremy Francis. "Letters to Loulie Gilmer." September—December 1861. Jeremy Francis Gilmer Papers, 1839–1894, Series 3, Civil War Papers 1861–1865. Southern Historical Collection. University of North Carolina, Chapel Hill.

Harris, Isham G. "Letters to Beriah Magoffin." August 30 and September 4, 1861. Governor Isham G. Harris Papers 1857–1862. Tennessee State Library and Archives, Nashville, TN.

_____. "Letter to Bushrod Johnson. June 14, 1861. Governor Isham G. Harris Papers 1857–1862. Tennessee State Library and Archives, Nashville, TN.

_____. "Letter to General Leonidas Polk." September 4, 1861. Governor Isham G. Harris Papers 1857–1862. Tennessee State Library and Archives, Nashville, TN.

_____. "Letter to Jefferson Davis." September 4, 1861. Governor Isham G. Harris Papers 1857–1862. Tennessee State Library and Archives, Nashville, TN.

Heiman, Adolphus. "Letter to Governor Isham G. Harris." October 18, 1861. Governor Isham G. Harris Papers 1857–1862. Tennessee State Library and Archives, Nashville, TN.

Hinkle, Joseph A. Unpublished Reminiscences. Southern Historical Collection. University of North Carolina Chapel Hill.

Johnson, Bushrod R. "Letter to Isham Harris." June 11, 1861. Governor Isham G. Harris Papers 1857–1862. Tennessee State Library and Archives, Nashville, TN.

MacGavock, Randal W. Unpublished Diary October 5, 1860—February 5, 1862. Randall W. MacGavock Papers 1848–1898. Tennessee State Library and Archives, Nashville, TN.

Ordnance Department—*Invoices of Supplies Sent to Various Stations, December 1861—August 1862.* Record Group 109, Chapter IV, Volume 108, National Archives Records Administration, Washington, D.C.

Ordnance Department—*Record of Ordnance and Ordnance Stores Received and Issued, Arsenals at Nashville, Tennessee, and Atlanta, Georgia, 1861-1862.* National Archives Records Administration. Record Group 109, Chapter IV, Volume 104, Washington, D.C.

Ordnance Department—*Record of Stores Purchased, Received and Issued, Nashville, Tennessee, and Atlanta Arsenal, Georgia, 1861-1862.* Record Group 109, Chapter IV, Volume 19, National Archives Records Administration, Washington, D.C.

Robison, J.W. "Letter to Father." December 10, 1861. John Wesley Robison Papers, 1861–1863. Tennessee State Library and Archives, Nashville, TN.

_____. "Letter to Father, Mother, and Sisters." November 22, 1861. John Wesley Robison Papers, 1861–1863. Tennessee State Library and Archives, Nashville, TN.

_____. "Letter to Josephine Robison." November 13, 1861. John Wesley Robison Papers, 1861–1863. Tennessee State Library and Archives, Nashville, TN.

_____. "Letter to Josephine Robison." January 23, 1862. John Wesley Robison Papers, 1861–1863. Tennessee State Library and Archives, Nashville, TN.

Ross, Reuben Reddick. Unpublished Journal. Ross Family Journals 1851–1871. Tennessee State Library and Archives, Nashville, TN.

Tennessee Civil War Correspondence, vol. 3 Middle Tennessee. Tennessee Historical Records Survey. Edited by Mrs. John Trotwood Moore. Nashville, TN: N.P., 1939.

Terrell, Spot F. "Spot F. Terrell Diary." In *Civil War Collection: Confederate and Federal 1861-1865,*

Confederate Collection: Tennessee State Library and Archives.

Williams, G.T. "Letter to Cousin." January 18, 1862. 30th Tennessee Infantry File. National Park Service, Fort Donelson National Battlefield, Dover, TN.

Newspapers

Athens Post (Athens, TN)
Clarksville Chronicle (Clarksville, TN)
Daily Patriot (Nashville, TN)
Evening Star (Philadelphia, PA)
Republican Banner (Nashville, TN)
Tribune (New York, NY)
Union and American (Nashville, TN)
Weekly Messenger (St. Albans, VT)
Weekly News Democrat (Emporia, KS)

Microfilm, War Papers and Periodicals

"Adna Anderson, M. Am. Soc. C.E." *Proceedings of the American Society of Engineers* 14, January to December (1888): 166–68.

Bedford, H.L. "Fight Between the Batteries and Gunboats at Fort Donelson." *Southern Historical Society Papers* 13, January—December (1885): 165–73.

Compiled Service Records of Confederate General and Staff Officers and Nonregimental Enlisted Men. National Archives Microfilm Publications, Washington, D.C. M331.

Compiled Service Records of Confederate Soldiers Who Served in Organizations from the State of Mississippi. National Archives Microfilm Publications, Washington, D.C. M269.

Compiled Service Records of Confederate Soldiers Who Served in Organizations from the State of Tennessee. National Archives Microfilm Publications, Washington, D.C. M268.

Compiled Service Records of Confederate Soldiers Who Served in Organizations Raised Directly by the Confederate Government, Engineers. National Archives Microfilm Publications, Washington, D.C. M258.

Compiled Service Records of Volunteer Soldiers Who Served During the Mexican War in Organizations from the State of Tennessee. National Archives Microfilm Publications, Washington, D.C. M638.

Confederate Papers Relating to Citizens or Business Firms, compiled 1874-1899, documenting the period 1861-1865. National Archives Microfilm Publications, Washington, D.C. M346.

Hinkle, J.A. "J.A. Hinkle." *Confederate Veteran* vol. 5 no. 12 (December 1897), 624.

Index to Compiled Service Records of Volunteer Soldiers Who Served During the War of 1812. National Archives Microfilm Publications, Washington, D.C. M602.

Ingram, M.V. "Maj. Bell G. Bidwell." *Confederate Veteran* vol. 16 no. 8 (August 1908): 409–10.

Military and Financial Board Nashville, Tenn.,

Records, 1861--addition. Tennessee State Library and Archives, Nashville, TN M623.

M'Neilly, J.H. "A Queer Order." *Confederate Veteran* vol. 1 no. 10 (October 1893): 308.

National Cemetery Records, Series 1: War Department. Cemetery Inspection Reports 1867 Box 2, Folder 1. National Park Service. Fort Donelson National Battlefield Park, Dover, TN.

Population Schedules of the Eighth Census of the United States, 1860, Kentucky: Kenton County. National Archives Microfilm Publications, Washington, D.C. M653 R1246.

Population Schedules of the Eighth Census of the United States, 1860, Tennessee: Maury County. National Archives Microfilm Publications, Washington, D.C. M653 R1264.

Population Schedules of the Eighth Census of the United States, 1860, Tennessee: Montgomery and Morgan Counties. National Archives Microfilm Publications, Washington, D.C. M653 R1266.

Population Schedules of the Eighth Census of the United States, 1860, Tennessee: Nashville. National Archives Microfilm Publications, Washington, D.C. M653 R1246.

Population Schedules of the Eighth Census of the United States, 1860, Washington Territory: Clarke County. National Archives Microfilm Publications, Washington, D.C. M653 R1398.

Population Schedules of the Ninth Census of the United States, 1870, Kentucky: McCracken, McLean, and Meade Counties. National Archives Microfilm Publications, Washington, D.C. M593 R487.

Population Schedules of the Ninth Census of the United States, 1870, Mississippi: Rankin County. National Archives Microfilm Publications, Washington, D.C. M593 R748.

Population Schedules of the Ninth Census of the United States, 1870, Ohio: Hamilton County. National Archives Microfilm Publications, Washington, D.C. M593 R1207.

Population Schedules of the Ninth Census of the United States, 1870, Tennessee: Hickman County. National Archives Microfilm Publications, Washington, D.C. M593 R1538.

Population Schedules of the Ninth Census of the United States, 1870, Tennessee: Maury County. National Archives Microfilm Publications, Washington, D.C. M593 R1547.

Population Schedules of the Ninth Census of the United States, 1870, Tennessee: Montgomery and Morgan Counties. National Archives Microfilm Publications, Washington, D.C. M593 R1551.

Population Schedules of the Ninth Census of the United States, 1870, Tennessee: Shelby County. National Archives Microfilm Publications, Washington, D.C. M593 R1561.

Population Schedules of the Seventh Census of the United States, 1850, Ohio: Hamilton County. National Archives Microfilm Publications, Washington, D.C. M432 R691.

Population Schedules of the Seventh Census of the United States, 1850, Tennessee: Maury County."

National Archives Microfilm Publications, Washington, D.C. M432 R890.

Population Schedules of the Seventh Census of the United States, 1850, Tennessee: McMinn County." National Archives Microfilm Publications, Washington, D.C. M432 R887.

Population Schedules of the Seventh Census of the United States, 1850, Tennessee: Montgomery and Morgan Counties." National Archives Microfilm Publications, Washington, D.C. M432 R891.

Population Schedules of the Seventh Census of the United States, 1850, Virginia: Norfolk City." National Archives Microfilm Publications, Washington, D.C. M432 R964.

Population Schedules of the Tenth Census of the United States, 1880, Texas: Montague County. National Archives Microfilm Publications, Washington, D.C. T9 R1320.

Population Schedules of the Twelfth Census of the United States, 1900, Tennessee: Montgomery, Moore, and Morgan Counties. National Archives Microfilm Publications, Washington, D.C. T623 M1590.

Population Schedules of the Twelfth Census of the United States, 1900, Tennessee: Shelby County. National Archives Microfilm Publications, Washington, D.C. T623 R1596.

Population Schedules of the Twelfth Census of the United States, 1900, Texas: Hunt, Irion, Jack. Jackson, Jasper and Jeff Davis Counties. National Archives Microfilm Publications, Washington, D.C. T623 R1648.

Returns from U.S. Military Posts, 1800–1916. National Archives Microfilm Publications, Washington, D.C. M617.

Ross, Edward B. "River Batteries at Fort Donelson." *Confederate Veteran* vol. 4 no. 11 (November 1896): 393–98.

Tennessee Confederate Pension Applications, Soldiers, 1891–1965. Tennessee State Library and Archives, Nashville, TN.

Tennessee Death Records, 1908–1958. Tennessee State Library and Archives. Nashville, TN.

U.S. Military Academy Cadet Application Papers, 1805–1866. National Archives Microfilm Publications, Washington, D.C. M688.

United States War Department. *Confederate Papers Relating to Citizens or Business Firms, 1861–65.* National Archives Microfilm Publications, Washington, D.C. M346 R677.

Books

Catalogue of the Officers and Students of Cumberland University, at Lebanon, Tenn. for the Academic Year 1858–59. Lebanon, TN: Neal & Spillers, Printers, 1859.

Catalogue of the Officers and Students of Cumberland University at Lebanon, Tenn., for the Academic Year 1859–60. Lebanon, TN: Neal & Spillers, 1860.

Catalogue of the Officers and Students of the Law Department of Cumberland University at Lebanon, TN for the Academic Year 1857–8. Lebanon, TN: Neal & Spillers, Printers, 1858.

Evans, Clement A., ed. *Confederate Military History.* 12 vols. Vol. 4, Atlanta, GA: Confederate Publishing Company, 1899.

Foster, Wilbur F. "The Building of Forts Henry and Donelson." In *Battles and Sketches of the Army of Tennessee,* edited by Bromfield L. Ridley, Mexico, MO: Missouri Printing and Publishing, 1906.

Fourth Annual Reunion of the Association of Graduates of the United States Military Academy Annual Reunion June 12th, 1873. New York, NY: D. Van Nostrand, 1873.

Gower, Herschel, and Jack Allen. *Pen and Sword: The Life and Journals of Randal W. McGavock.* Nashville, TN: Tennessee Historical Commission, 1959.

Grant, U.S. *Personal Memoirs of U.S. Grant.* New York, NY: Charles L. Webster, 1885. Project Gutenberg EBook.

Heitman, Francis B. *Historical Register and Dictionary of the United States Army, From Its Organization September 29, 1789 to March 2, 1903.* 2 vols. Washington, D.C.: Government Printing Office, 1903.

Johnston, William Preston. *The Life of Gen. Albert Sidney Johnston: Embracing His Services in the Armies of the United States, the Republic of Texas, and the Confederate States.* New York, NY: Da Capo Press, 1997.

Lindsley, John Berrien. *Military Annals of Tennessee: Confederate.* Nashville, TN: J.M. Lindsley & Co., 1886. Facsimile of the first edition, Wilmington NC: Broadfoot Publishing, 1995.

Mathes, J. Harvey. *The Old Guard in Gray.* Memphis, TN: S.C. Toof, 1897.

Ridley, Bromfield Lewis. *Battles and Sketches of the Army of Tennessee.* Mexico, MO: Missouri Print. & Pub. Co., 1906.

Sholes' Directory of the City of Augusta. Augusta, GA: A.E. Sholes, 1877.

Taylor, Jesse. "The Defense of Fort Henry." In *Battles and Leaders of the Civil War,* 368–72. Edison, NJ: Castle, n.d.

United States War Department. *Instruction for Heavy Artillery.* Washington, D.C.: Gideon and Co., 1851.

———. *Official Records of the Union and Confederate Navies in the War of the Rebellion.* Washington, D.C.: Reprint, Gettysburg, PA: National Historical Society, 1987.

———. *The War of the Rebellion: A Compilation of the Official Records of the Union and Confederate Armies.* Washington, D.C.: Reprint, Gettysburg, PA: National Historical Society, 1972.

University of Nashville, Collegiate Department, Western Military Institute, Register of Cadets for the Collegiate Year 1856–7. Nashville, TN: Cameron & Fall, 1857.

Walke, H. *Naval Scenes and Reminiscences of the Civil War in the United States, on the Southern and Western Waters During the Years 1861, 1862 and 1863.* New York, NY: F.R. Reed & Company, 1877.

———. "The Western Flotilla at Fort Donelson, Island Number Ten, Fort Pillow, and Memphis."

In *Battles and Leaders of the Civil War,* 430–52. NP: Castle, 1887.

Wilson, James Grant and John Fiske, eds. *Appletons' Cyclopedia of American Biography, 1600–1889, Vol II: Crane—Grimshaw.* New York, NY: D. Appleton and Company, 1887.

Electronic Information

Dorris, Wesley Smith. "Wesley Smith Dorris Diary." *Special Collections Online.* The University of Tennessee. https://dlc.lib.utk.edu/spc/view?docId=tei/0012_003114_000201_0000/0012_003114_000201_0000.xml;brand=default;;query=Dorris.

Willauer, Eleanora. "The Diary of Eleanora Willauer." *Special Collections Online.* The University of Tennessee. https://dlc.lib.utk.edu/spc/view?docId=ead/0012_001496_000000_0000/0012_001496_000000_0000.xml;query=Willauer;brand=default.

Secondary Sources

Manuscript Materials and Interviews

Hanson, Lee H., Jr. *Archaeological Excavations in the Water Batteries At Fort Donelson National Military Park.* N.P.: National Park Service; U.S. Department of the Interior, 1968.

Hawkins, Susan. "Forts Henry, Heiman, and Donelson: The African American Experience." Master's Thesis, Murray State University, 2003.

Jobe, James. "Interview Regarding the History of the Water Batteries." M. Todd Cathey and Ricky W. Robnett. Fort Donelson National Park, Dover, TN. October 7, 2019.

Nolin, David. "Interview Regarding the Restoration of the Water Batteries." Phone Interview by M. Todd Cathey. November 14, 2019.

Newspapers

Tennessean (Nashville, TN)

Microfilm, War Papers, and Periodicals

Bearss, Edwin C. "The Fort Donelson Water Batteries, Fort Donelson National Military Park, Historic Structures Report Part 2." National Park Service. Fort Donelson National Battlefield Archives.

———. "Full Speed Ahead: Yankee Ironclads Unleashed into the Volunteer State." *Tennessee Historical Quarterly* 69, no. 1 (Spring 2010): 18–39.

Creighton, Wilbur F., Jr. "Wilbur Fisk Foster: Soldier and Engineer." *Tennessee Historical Quarterly* 31, No. 3 (Fall 1972): 261–75.

Jobe, James. "The Battles for Forts Henry and Donelson." *Blue & Gray* vol. 28, no. 4 (2011): 6–27, 43–50.

Books

Beech, Ursula S. *Along the Warioto; or, A History of Montgomery County, Tennessee.* In cooperation with the Clarksville Kiwanis Club and the Tennessee Historical Commission. Clarksville, TN: Tennessee Historical Commission, 1964.

Bell, Jack. *Civil War Heavy Explosive Ordnance: A Guide to Large Artillery Projectiles, Torpedoes, and Mines.* Denton, TX: University of North Texas Press, 2003.

Bishop, Randy. *Civil War Generals of Tennessee.* Gretna, LA: Pelican, 2013.

Connelly, Thomas Lawrence. *Army of the Heartland: The Army of Tennessee, 1861–1862.* Baton Rouge, LA: Louisiana State University Press, 1967.

Cooling, Benjamin F. *Fort Donelson's Legacy: War and Society in Kentucky and Tennessee, 1862–1863.* Knoxville, TN: University of Tennessee Press, 1997.

Cooling, Benjamin Franklin. *Forts Henry and Donelson—The Key to the Confederate Heartland.* Knoxville, TN: University of Tennessee Press, 1987.

Creighton, Wilbur F. *The Life of Major Wilbur Fisk Foster.* Nashville, TN: Ambrose Printing, 1961.

Daniel, Larry J., and Lynn N Bock. Island No. 10 Struggle for the Mississippi Valley. Tuscaloosa, AL University of Alabama Press.

———, and Riley W. Gunter. *Confederate Cannon Foundries.* Union City, TN: Pioneer Press, 1977.

Dew, Charles B. *Ironmaker to the Confederacy: Joseph R. Anderson and the Tredegar Iron Works.* Richmond, VA: Virginia State Library, 1999.

Ferrell, Carolyn Stier. *Occupied: The Story of Clarksville, Tennessee During the Civil War.* Nashville, TN: Westview, Inc., 2012.

Garrett, Jill Knight. *A History of Humphreys County, Tennessee.* Columbia, TN: Jill Knight Garrett, 1963.

———, and Marise Parrish Lightfoot. *The Civil War in Maury County, Tennessee.* Columbia, TN: Maury County Public Library, 2014.

Gillum, Jamie. *Twenty-five Hours to Tragedy: the Battle of Spring Hill and Operations on November 29, 1864: Precursor to the Battle of Franklin.* Spring Hill, TN: James F. Gillum, 2014.

Gosnell, H. Allen. *Guns on the Western Waters: The Story of River Gunboats in the Civil War.* Baton Rouge, LA: Louisiana State University Press, 1949.

Horn, Stanley F. *The Army of Tennessee.* Wilmington, NC: Broadfoot, 1987.

Hughes, Nathaniel Cheairs. *The Battle of Belmont: Grant Strikes South.* Chapel Hill, NC: University of North Carolina, 1991.

———, and Roy P. Stonesifer. *The Life and Wars of Gideon J. Pillow.* Chapel Hill, NC: University of North Carolina Press, 1993.

Joiner, Gary D. *Mr. Lincoln's Brown Water Navy.* Plymouth, UK: Rowman & Littlefield Publishers, 2007.

Milligan, John. *From the Fresh Water Navy: 1861–1865; The Letters of Acting Master's Mate Henry*

R. Browne and Acting Ensign Symmes E. Browne. Annapolis, MD: Naval Institute Press, 1971.

Nichols, J.L. *Confederate Engineers.* Tuscaloosa, AL: The Confederate Publishing Company, 1957.

Olmstead, Edwin, Wayne E. Stark, and Spencer C. Tucker. *The Big Guns: Civil War Siege, Seacoast, and Naval Cannon.* Alexandria Bay, NY: Museum Restoration Service, 1997.

Page, Dave. *Ships Versus Shore: Civil War Engagements along Southern Shores and Rivers.* Nashville, TN: Rutledge Hill Press, 1994.

Parks, Joseph Howard. *General Leonidas Polk, C.S.A.: The Fighting Bishop.* Baton Rouge, LA: Louisiana State University Press, 1990.

Sifakis, Stewart *Who was Who in the Confederacy: A Comprehensive, Illustrated Biographical Reference to more than 1,000 of the Principal Confederacy Participants in the Civil War.* New York, NY: Facts on File, 1988.

Silverstone, Paul H. *Warships of the Civil War Navies.* Annapolis, MD: Naval Institute Press, 1989.

Smith, Frank H. *Frank H. Smith's History of Maury County, TN.* Columbia, TN: The Society, 1969.

_____. "Maury Light Artillery." In *The Civil War in Maury County,* edited by Jill K. Garrett and Marise P. Lightfoot. Columbia, TN: Maury County Public Library, 2014.

Smith, Myron J. *The USS Carondelet: A Civil War Ironclad on the Western Waters.* Jefferson, NC: McFarland, 2010.

Smith, Samuel D., Charles P. Stripling, and James M. Brannon. *A Cultural Resource Survey of Tennessee's Western Highland Rim Iron Industry, 1790s-1930s.* Nashville, TN: Tennessee Department of Conservation, Division of Archaeology, 1988.

Smith, Timothy B. *Grant Invades Tennessee: The 1862 Battles for Forts Henry and Donelson.* Lawrence, KS: University Press of Kansas, 2016.

Tennessee Civil War Centennial Commission. *Tennesseans in the Civil War: A Military History of Confederate and Union Units with Available Rosters of Personnel.* 2 vols. Vol. 1, Nashville, TN: Civil War Centennial Commission, 1964.

Tomblin, Barbara Brooks. *The Civil War on the Mississippi: Union Sailors, Gunboat Captains, and the Campaign to Control the River.* Lexington, KY: University Press of Kentucky, 2016.

Warner, Ezra J. *Generals in Blue: Lives of the Union Commanders.* Baton Rouge, LA: Louisiana State University Press, 1964.

_____. *Generals in Gray: Lives of the Confederate Commanders.* Baton Rouge, LA: Louisiana State University, 1987.

Woodworth, Steven E. *Jefferson Davis and His Generals: The Failure of Confederate Command in the West.* Lawrence, KS: University Press of Kansas, 1990.

Wyeth, John A. *That Devil Forrest: Life of General Nathan Bedford.* Baton Rouge, LA: Louisiana State University Press, 1989.

Electronic Information

Arther, Matthew. "Medal of Honor, Civil War." https://www.army.mil/medalofhonor/crandall/medal/citations1.htm.

"District of Columbia, Marriage Records, 1810–1953." Ancestry.com. https://www.ancestry.com/search/collections/61404/.

Find a Grave. https://www.findagrave.com/.

"Georgia Marriages 1699–1944." ancestry.com. https://www.ancestry.com/search/collections/7839/.

"Kentucky Marriage Records, 1783–1965. https://www.ancestry.com/search/collections/61372/.

"Maury County Historical Society, Historic Homes." http://historicmaury.com/mchs-history/historic-homes/.

"Ohio, County Marriage Records, 1774–1993." ancestry.com. https://www.ancestry.com/search/collections/61378/.

Riggins, Van L. "A History of Fort Donelson National Military Park Tennessee." *Park Histories* (1958). https://www.nps.gov/parkhistory/online_books/fodo/fodo_history.pdf.

"Tennessee Marriage Records, 1780–2002." https://www.ancestry.com/search/collections/1169/.

"Tennessee Wills and Probate Records, 1779–2008." https://www.ancestry.com/search/collections/9176/.

"Texas, Wills and Probate Records, 1833–1974." Ancestry.com. https://www.ancestry.com/search/collections/2115/.

Whiteaker, Larry H. "Tennessee Encyclopedia, "Civil War." https://tennesseeencyclopedia.net/entries/civil-war/.

Index

Numbers in **_bold italics_** indicate pages with illustrations